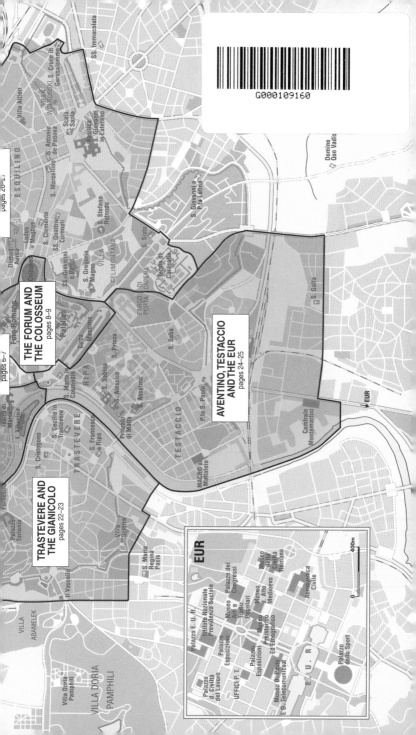

THE FORUM AND
THE COLOSSEUM
pages 8-9

TRASTEVERE AND
THE GIANICOLO
pages 22-23

AVENTINO, TESTACCIO
AND THE EUR
pages 24-25

EUR

Palazzo E. U. R.

Istituto Nazionale
Previdenza Sociale

Palazzo dei
Congressi

Museo
della
Civiltà
Romana

Museo Arti e
Tradiz.
Popolari

Museo
d. Alto
Medioevo

Palazzo
Esposizioni

Palazzo
d. Civiltà
del Lavoro

Palazzo
Esposizioni

Museo
Preistorico
Ed Etnografico

Accademia
Civile

UFFICI P. T.

Museo D. Poste
Ed. Telecomunicaz.

Palazzo
dello Sport

E. U. R.

0   400m

SS. Immacolata

VILLA
VOLKONSKI

S. Croce in
Gerusalemme

Villa Altieri

ESQUILINO

S. Antonio
da Padova

Scala
Santa

Basilica
S. Giovanni
in Laterano

S. Marcellino

S. Stefano
Rotondo

Domine
Quo Vadis

Domus
Aurea

Ludus
Magnus

S. Clemente

SS. Quattro
Coronati

S. Giovanni
a P.ta Latina

S. Giovanni
e Paolo

S. Gregorio
Magno

VILLA
CELIMONTANA

S. Sisto

S. Galla

Colosseo

Foro-Romano

Palatino

DI
CARENA

PARCO
DI
PORTA

Terme di
Caracalla

Circo
Massimo

S. Maria in
Cosmedin

S. Prisca

S. Saba

S. Sabina

RIPA

S. Alessio

S. Anselmo

S. Sabina

TESTACCIO

P.ta S. Paolo

Centrale
Montemartini

Teatro di
Marcello

I. Tiburina

S. Cristoforo

S. Cecilia in
Trastevere

TRASTEVERE

S. Francesco
a Ripa

Priorato
di Malta

MACRO al
Mattatoio

Farnesina

Palazzo
Torlonia

Il Vascello

Villa
Sciarra

S. Maria
Regina
Pacis

VILLA
ABAMELEK

Villa Doria
Pamphili

VILLA
DORIA
PAMPHILI

INSIGHT GUIDES

ROME
smart guide

Part of the Langenscheidt Publishing Group

Contents

Areas

A–Z

Below: A detail from the remarkably well-preserved Pantheon.

Left: Rome's rooftops, as seen from the Aventino (Aventine Hill).

Atlas

Below: A statue at the Terme di Diocleziano (Baths of Diocletian).

3

Rome

Once the heart of an empire, Rome has attracted poets, artists, writers and travellers for thousands of years. With its soft, ochre-coloured *palazzi*, classical colonnades, atmospheric squares and dramatic centrepieces, such as the Colosseum and Pantheon, it is a city that inspires the mind, appeals to the senses and captures the heart.

Destination Facts and Figures

Population: 2.7 million
Population density: 2,105.5 per sq km
City area: 1,285sq km
Founded: 21 April 753 BC
Visitors to the Vatican: the Vatican museums receive an average of 15,000 visitors a day
Elevation: 20m
Green spaces: 3 percent of the area of the municipality of Rome is parks and gardens
Number of Hills: 7 (Capitoline, Palatine, Aventine, Quirinal, Viminal, Esquiline, Caelian)
Number of palaces in the city centre: more than 200
Patron saints: Saint Peter and Saint Paul

Contemporary Rome

Since its millennial revamp for Holy Year in 2000, Rome has rarely looked lovelier. The Eternal City has shaken off its dusty toga and slipped into contemporary clothes. The facelift to its ancient sites has been matched by subtle plastic surgery to its arts scene. Revamped galleries, new contemporary art museums, a cinema festival and the creation of a superb music complex have helped turn the city's face towards the future. While not a new *dolce vita*, there is a cinematic gloss to the emerging city: eclectic festivals, a funky club scene, sleek cafés, boutique hotels and a more cosmopolitan air.

Orientation

The Eternal City remains chaotic but compact, bewildering but walkable, beguiling yet exhausting. Unfortunately, the public transport system, from the pointless metro to the overcrowded buses, is woefully inadequate. Work on a new metro line, running north-west to south-east, will daringly slice through the heart of the Imperial city. Fear of damaging ancient sites and becoming ensnared in modern bureaucracy is why radical measures have never been contemplated before now. When the new metro line is complete, in 2013 at the earliest, all Romans can be assured of is that the 24km of track and the 30 new stations will become mired in controversy connected to the hundreds of archaeological sites that will be unearthed in the process.

In the meantime, the demented locals will continue to fume in traffic jams, flit by on flimsy Vespas, or rattle around in speed-crazed buses. For visitors, the good news is that, with stoicism, sturdy shoes and enough caffeine-fuelled café stops, Rome is still a heavenly walking city.

Neighbourhoods

Few Romans live in the historic centre any more. In the 1960s the tradesmen moved to the suburbs in search of comfortable apartments while the *centro storico* succumbed to

Below: Ancient Rome-inspired mosaics at Mussolini's Foro Italico stadium.

gentrification; once-crumbling *palazzi* were snapped up by astute investors, from bankers to politicians. Yet individuals remain attached to their *rione* or neighbourhood: the original 14 date from the time of the Emperor Augustus, but have grown to 22, each with its own civic crest. Romans also harbour attachments to mythologised quarters in the *centro storico*, such as the Ghetto, the former Jewish district, or Campo de' Fiori, once peopled by fruit-sellers and furniture-restorers but now full of funky bars and fashion victims.

Local neighbourhoods can be both cosmopolitan and homely, ranging from the formalised domesticity of Parioli, framed by embassies, to mellow Trastevere, dotted with arty bars and galleries. Looming above Trastevere is the leafy *fin de siècle* Gianicolo district, home to retiring residents and ex-patriate newcomers.

Rome can be rough around the edges, but its lack of manicured perfection is part of its charm. The Esquilino area, around the Fascist-Modernist Termini Station, nick-named 'the dinosaur', is a case in point, as is Testaccio, the former meat-packing district that is, with Ostiense, the pulsating heart of clubland. Once dilapidated, these districts are being gentrified but retain their edginess, youthful spirit and multi-ethnic flavour. Rome today is more cosmopolitan than at any time since the Empire.

Highlights

▲ **The Musei Capitolini** The Capitoline Museums' collections of ancient art and Roman statuary are a must. ▶ **The Galleria Borghese** One of the finest collections of paintings and statuary in Rome, the legacy of an art-loving cardinal.

▶ **The Colosseum** Iconic symbol of Rome and an evocative reminder of the brutality of the *Imperiali*.

▲ **The Spanish Steps** Tourists and Romans alike congregate to people-watch at the heart of Rome's main shopping district.

▲ **The Forum** The majestic ruins of the civic centre of ancient Rome. ▶ **The Vatican Museums** This extraordinary collection merits more than one visit. Don't miss the Sistine Chapel.

The Capitoline Hill

The Capitoline Hill, the lowest of the city's seven hills, started life as a fortified stronghold and later became the political and religious power centre of the ancient world. During the Renaissance it was glorified with a harmonious square designed by Michelangelo. The neighbouring Vittoriano monument is undeniably impressive, but bombastic compared to the elegance and majesty of the grand master's Piazza del Campidoglio. The world's oldest public collection of sculpture can be found here at the Musei Capitolini. Overlooking the Forum on one side, and the traffic-clogged Piazza Venezia on the other, the Capitoline Hill links the ancient world with our own.

See Atlas Page 137

Piazza del Campidoglio

There's no better place to start exploring ancient Rome than the **Piazza del Campidoglio** (Capitol Square) ①, which sits between the Capitoline Hill's two peaks. Built on the site of an ancient sanctuary, the square, the staircase that leads to it, and the buildings that flank it were designed by Michelangelo. Pope Paul III commissioned him to create a majestic setting for the reception of the Holy Roman Emperor, Charles V, on his visit to Rome in 1536. As it turned out, the square wasn't completed until the 17th century. Two imposing statues of Castor and Pollux stand guard at the top of the **Cordonata**, as the elegant staircase is known. The piazza's centrepiece is a first-rate copy of an immense equestrian **statue of Emperor Marcus Aurelius**. The original is kept inside the Capitoline Museums. The building straight ahead is the **Palazzo Senatorio** ②, where the city council still convenes. At the bottom of its double staircase is a fountain of Minerva flanked by two giant reclining statues, representing the Nile and the Tiber.

The flight of steps adjacent to Michelangelo's Cordonata leads to the church of **Santa Maria in Aracoeli** (St Mary of the Altar in the Sky), which stands at the

Above: hand fragment from colossal statue of Constantine.

highest point of the Capitoline Hill. It occupies the site of a temple dedicated to Juno where Augustus later built an altar.

The two grand *palazzi* facing each other across the square – the Palazzo Nuovo and Palazzo dei Conservatori – together house the **Musei Capitolini** ③, one of the world's oldest public museums, containing a rich collection of ancient sculpture and late Renaissance and Baroque art.

The road to the right of the Palazzo Senatorio leads to the **Tarpeian Rock** at the southern tip of the Capitoline

In ancient times the hill looked quite different, with steep cliffs of porous tufa rock falling steeply on all sides of its twin crowns. On the southern crown, known as the Campidoglio, stood the Temple of Jupiter, which was the religious hub of the state. The other crown of the hill housed the temple to the goddess Juno Moneta. The Roman mint also stood here, hence the word *moneta*, meaning money.

Left: Castor (left) and Pollux watch over the Campidoglio.

Dominating the square, next to the Campidoglio stands **Il Vittoriano** ⑤, an overblown monument erected in honour of Victor Emmanuel II, the first king of a newly unified Italy. The monument houses a military museum of limited interest, but entrance is free, and views from the top terrace are wonderful.

Although the Vittoriano is the most dominant, the **Palazzo Venezia** ⑥ is the most interesting building on this square. The 15th-century palace now houses a fascinating museum.

Behind the palace is the **church of San Marco**, one of the oldest basilicas in Rome, with a lovely mosaic in its 9th-century apse. Outside the church stands the buxom **statue of Madama Lucrezia**, one of Rome's so-called 'Talking Statues' *(see box, p.43)*.
SEE ALSO MONUMENTS, P.82; MUSEUMS AND GALLERIES, P.91

Hill. In ancient times, anyone found guilty of treason was thrown from this precipice.

The road to the left of the Palazzo Senatorio winds its way down to the church of **San Giuseppe dei Felagnami** and the **Carcere Mamertino** ④. Defeated kings and generals, having been paraded through the streets in their victor's triumphal march, were imprisoned here before being executed. A small chapel next to a spring commemorates St Peter, who is said to have been incarcerated here, and to have baptised his guards with water from a spring he miraculously created. From the prison, the road leads down to the Forum.
SEE ALSO CHURCHES, P.42; MUSEUMS AND GALLERIES, P.90

Piazza Venezia

If all roads lead to Rome, then all roads in Rome lead to the Piazza Venezia, the hub of the city's road network since 1881. Some 800,000 Romans squeeze their cars through here every day, and it's not the best place to be during rush hour.

Below: the statue of Marcus Aurelius in the Piazze del Campidoglio is a copy, the original is in the Musei Capitolini.

The Forum and the Colosseum

Here, in the heart of the city, lie the monumental remains of ancient Rome, where the Empire thrived, declined and eventually fell. The Via dei Fori Imperiali, a Mussolini-built boulevard, slices through the scattered ruins of temples, government buildings and markets. Rising above the Forum, the more pastoral Palatine Hill was former home to the nobility and Rome's mythical founder, Romulus. At the end of all this ruined splendour stands the Colosseum, the city's most stirring sight.

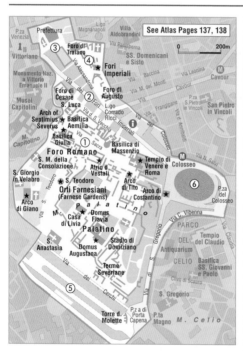

Above: the Arch of Septimius Severus at the Forum.

sculptors and architects, the Forum remains Rome's most majestic and evocative sight. Between the triumphal **Arch of Septimius Severus** (Arco di Settimio Severo) at one end and the **Arch of Titus** (Arco di Tito) at the other, the columns and stones of great temples and government buildings lie scattered along the length of the **Via Sacra** (the Sacred Way) ①, the route taken by victorious generals as they rode in procession to the foot of the Capitoline Hill.

The best place to begin a tour of the Forum is at the main entrance on Via dei Fori Imperiali. Use the map and the descriptions on pages 83–5, to help you make sense of the ruins and orientate yourself.

SEE ALSO MONUMENTS, P.83–5

The Foro Romano

Originally a marshy valley between the Capitoline and Palatine hills, the area became a marketplace that developed into the religious, political and commercial centre of Republican Rome. Under the emperors the Forum attained unprecedented splendour,

with marble, golden-roofed temples and law courts.

By the time excavations began in the 18th century, most of the Forum was buried under rubble, and the site was used for grazing cattle. But despite centuries of neglect and the plundering of monuments by generations of

Left: the Colosseum is perhaps the defining image of Rome.

of the best-preserved ancient Roman streets.
SEE ALSO MONUMENTS, P.82–3

The Palatine Hill

Rising above the Forum, the Palatine Hill is Rome's legendary birthplace. The story goes that Romulus defeated his twin brother Remus on this hill, and became the city's first ruler in 753 BC. At the height of Roman opulence, the area offered a beautiful panorama of the city, and expansive villas occupied by Rome's rich and famous packed the area. Today the Palatine Hill is a romantic spot with palace ruins, a well-tended ornamental garden, an archaeological museum and views over the **Circus Maximus** ⑤, one of Rome's oldest arenas.
SEE ALSO MONUMENTS, P.85–6; MUSEUMS AND GALLERIES, P.91

The Colosseum

At the far end of the Roman Forum lie the remains of the majestic **Colosseum** ⑥, the most enduring symbol of ancient Rome. Its monumental grandeur and violent history have enthralled and appalled visitors for over 2,000 years. It was begun by Vespasian, inaugurated by his son Titus in AD 80, and completed by Domitian (AD 81–96). It could seat over 50,000 bloodthirsty spectators who revelled in the gladiatorial battles. With the fall of the Empire, the Colosseum fell into disuse. During the Renaissance, the ruins were plundered of their travertine to build churches and palaces all over Rome.

Quarrying was only halted by Pope Benedict XIV in the 18th century, and the site dedicated to Christian martyrs.
SEE ALSO MONUMENTS, P.86–7

Before working your way around the Forum, it's a good idea to get an overview of the site. The best vantage point for this is the Tabularium, accessible from inside the Capitoline Museums *(see p. 90)* or the terrace behind the Vittoriano monument *(see p. 82).* The Forum is a particularly dramatic sight when it is floodlit at night.

The Imperial Fora

As Rome became more powerful, its population grew and the original Roman Forum was no longer big enough to serve the city's needs. The Imperial Fora were built by a succession of statesmen and emperors from Caesar to Trajan.

The **Via dei Fori Imperiali** ② which slices through the heart of Rome's ancient sites was commissioned by Mussolini for the greater glory of his Fascist empire. Bulldozers flattened one of the city's oldest medieval quarters to make way for the route, destroying ancient walls, imperial palaces, temples and arches.

The remains of the **Fori Imperiali** (Imperial Fora) lie on either side of the wide boulevard and buried beneath it. Look out for the intricately carved **Trajan's Column** ③, erected in AD 113, and **Trajan's Markets** ④, where you can see some

Below: the Via dei Fori Imperiali.

The Trevi Fountain and Quirinale

The Quirinal Hill is the highest of Rome's seven classical hills. On its summit stands the official residence of the Italian president. Behind the imposing palace lies a cluster of Baroque masterpieces in the shape of a church by Bernini, one by his arch-rival Borromini, four Baroque fountains and the Barberini Palace which houses a fine collection of art. At the foot of the hill, hidden in the maze of narrow streets, is one of Rome's most flamboyant Baroque monuments – the iconic Trevi Fountain.

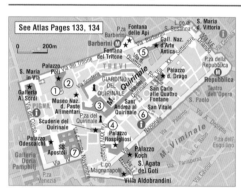

Above: stamp featuring Bernini's *Ecstacy of St Theresa*.

Trevi Fountain

A good place to begin a tour of the area is the **Fontana di Trevi** (Trevi Fountain) ①, which rose to fame in Fellini's 1960 classic *La Dolce Vita* when blonde bombshell Anita Ekberg plunged provocatively into it for a midnight bathe. Nowadays, if you try to put a foot in the water, a whistle blast from the city police will stop you in your tracks. That, and a €500 fine. However, no one will stop you from throwing a coin in the fountain (over your shoulder with your back to the fountain), an old custom said to ensure your return to the Eternal City. The steps around the fountain are always packed with tourists tossing coins, eating ice creams and taking endless photos.

It's a five-minute walk from the fountain to the **Galleria dell'Accademia di San Luca** ②, Rome's school of art named after St Luke, the patron saint of painters.

Between the Trevi Fountain and Piazza del Quirinale, look out for the **Museo Nazionale delle Paste Alimentari** (Pasta Museum), which explores the history of Italy's favourite food. SEE ALSO MONUMENTS, P.87; MUSEUMS AND GALLERIES, P.91–2

The Quirinal

Follow Via San Vincenzo uphill from the Fontana di Trevi, then turn left into Via Dataria and take the steps up to **Piazza del Quirinale**. In the centre of the square are colossal statues of the twins, Castor and Pollux, with their horses. They

came from Constantine's baths and were arranged around the obelisk (taken from Augustus' mausoleum) in the 18th century. The square is dominated by the **Palazzo del Quirinale** ③, which was the summer palace of the popes until 1870, when it became the palace of the kings of the newly unified Italy. Today it is the official residence of the President of the Republic.

Across the square from the Quirinale Palace, the sugary-white **Palazzo della Consulta** ④ houses Italy's Supreme Court. The structure was built atop the ruins of Constantine's baths. The former palace stables, or **Scuderie**, opposite, have been converted into an elegant art gallery for temporary exhibitions.

Left: the Trevi Fountain.

Fountain, 1641), on the north side of the square, features the ubiquitous bee, symbol of the powerful Barberini family.

From here Via Barberini leads to Largo Santa Susanna and the church of **Santa Maria della Vittoria**, home to Bernini's *Ecstasy of St Teresa*, another masterpiece of Baroque sculpture *(see p.187)*.

SEE ALSO CHURCHES, P.42; MUSEUMS AND GALLERIES, P.92; PALAZZI, P.104

Via Nazionale

Running parallel to Via del Quirinale is Via Nazionale (laid in 1870 when Rome gained its new status as capital), which links Piazza della Repubblica with the Imperial Fora. Towards the southern end are **San Vitale**, built in the 5th century and restored in the 15th century, and the **Palazzo delle Esposizioni** ⑥, a grandiose building housing a vibrant cultural centre. Across the road are the impressive **Palazzo Koch**, headquarters of the Banca d'Italia, and the **Villa Aldobrandini**, behind which is a small public park (entrance on Via Mazzarino).

Via Nazionale curves around into Via IV Novembre (leading to Piazza Venezia), passing Trajan's Markets and the **Palazzo Colonna** ⑦, which has housed over 23 generations of the Colonna family, and represents a fascinating, if often juxtaposing, architectural panorama spanning four centuries (1300–1700). Its **Galleria Colonna** houses fine works by Veronese and Tintoretto.

From the palace, Via della Pilotta leads back to the Trevi Fountain.

SEE ALSO MUSEUMS AND GALLERIES, P.92–3

> WIth arguably the finest ice cream in town, the Gelateria San Crispino near the Trevi Fountain serves up original flavours made with all-natural ingredients. The signature flavour, *Il Gelato di San Crispino*, is a basic *crema* made with wild Sardinian honey.

Via del Quirinale runs along the south-east flank of the palace and, on the opposite side, passes two pretty parks (dotted with shaded benches if you need a rest), and two exquisite Baroque churches: Bernini's small but perfectly formed **Sant' Andrea al Quirinale** and Borromini's curvaceous **San Carlo alle Quattro Fontane**.

From the Quirinal, Via delle Quattro Fontane leads to **Palazzo Barberini** ⑤, the family palace of Pope Urban VIII (1623–44), built by three of Rome's most prominent 17th-century architects, Bernini, Borromini and Maderno. It houses the **Galleria Nazionale d'Arte Antica**, a fine collection of paintings from the 13th–17th centuries.

In the **Piazza Barberini** are two Bernini fountains. The **Fontana del Tritone** (1632–7) features four dolphins supporting a shell on which the water-spouting Triton sits. The **Fontana delle Api** (Bee

Below: the Trevi Fountain is very popular with tourists.

Piazza di Spagna and Tridente

One of the liveliest and most picturesque neighbourhoods of Rome, the Tridente draws droves of eager shoppers ready to heat up their credit cards. The streets in the area flanking the landmark Spanish Steps are packed with shops filled with haute couture and *prêt-à-porter* designs by luminaries of the Italian fashion world. Piazza di Spagna was for centuries the centre of artistic and literary life. Today, crowded as it is, it remains one of Rome's most welcoming urban spaces.

SEE ALSO BARS AND CAFÉS, P.33; CHURCHES, P.42–3

The Corso

The most important of the trio of streets that fan out from the Piazza del Popolo is Via del Corso, a long thoroughfare that links the square with the Piazza Venezia *(see page 7)*. The name 'Corso' dates from the 15th century, when Pope Paul II introduced horse racing *(corsi)* along its length. These days, the only people racing along the Corso are politicians being whisked at high speed to **Palazzo Chigi** ②, the prime minister's official residence, and the neighbouring **Palazzo di Montecitorio** ③, the Chamber of Deputies, both on Piazza Colonna. This square marks the halfway point of the Via del Corso.

The southern half of the Corso between Piazza Colonna, dominated by the **Column of Marcus Aurelius**, and Piazza Venezia is lined with stately palaces, most of which are banks, while the northern half, between Piazza Colonna and Piazza del Popolo, is a much more pedestrian-friendly shopping area. In the early evening and on Saturdays, Romans swarm into town for a stroll and to window-shop on this

Above: Via dei Condotti is packed with designer stores.

stretch of the Corso and the surrounding streets.

The palace on the right at the end of the Corso houses the **Galleria Doria Pamphilj** ④, a collection of masterpieces from the 15th–17th centuries, including works by Raphael, Titian, Tintoretto, Velázquez and Caravaggio. SEE ALSO MONUMENTS, P.87; MUSEUMS AND GALLERIES, P.93; PALAZZI, P.104

The Spanish Steps

The sweeping Spanish Steps combine with the twin towers of the church of **Trinità dei Monti** on top and the harmonious square below to form one of the most distinctive of Roman scenes. The **Piazza di Spagna** ⑤ (named after the nearby residence of the Spanish Ambassador to the

Piazza del Popolo

Piazza del Popolo is one of the most impressive squares in Rome. Its most striking feature is the obelisk at its centre. Stolen from Egypt by Emperor Augustus, it once decorated the Circus Maximus, where it was used as a turning point during chariot races. The square takes its name from the Renaissance church of **Santa Maria del Popolo** ① at the northern gateway to the piazza. According to legend it was built on the site of Nero's tomb, to rid the area of evil spirits. It is filled with art treasures, including two Caravaggio masterpieces. Two of Rome's most historic cafés, **Canova** and **Rosati**, face each other across the square.

Left: Richard Meier's modern complex for the Ara Pacis.

Elegant **Via dei Condotti** is designer-label heaven. This street, plus the parallel **Via Borgognona** and **Via Frattina**, which are linked by the equally sumptuous **Via Bocca di Leone**, are home to all the top fashion outlets. **Via del Babuino** is lined with interesting design and antique shops. Parallel to this is **Via Margutta**, a pretty, narrow street (once home to Federico Fellini), with artists' studios, galleries and workshops. Matching the expensive shops in this area are some of the best hotels in Rome.

Towards the end of Via dei Condotti is the world-famous tourist trap **Antico Caffè Greco**. The great and the good down the centuries have frequented this café, including Baudelaire, Wagner, Taine, Liszt, Stendhal, Goethe, Byron, Keats and Shelley.

The third road in the trident of streets, **Via di Ripetta**, leads from the Piazza del Popolo towards the Vatican, via the **Mausoleum of Augustus** ⑥ and the **Ara Pacis** ⑦, two ancient monuments dating from the time of Augustus.

SEE ALSO BARS AND CAFÉS, P.33; FASHION, P.52–7; MONUMENTS, P.87–8; SHOPPING, P.122–5

The Grand Tourists of the 18th century, most of whom were English aristocrats, stayed in this area on their visits to Rome (it came to be known as the English Ghetto). In the 19th century many illustrious artists, writers and musicians followed in their footsteps: Keats, Tennyson, Stendhal, Balzac, Wagner and Liszt among them.

Vatican) and the cascading Spanish Steps are perennially crowded with visitors. The poet John Keats died of consumption in 1821, aged just 25, in a small room overlooking the steps. His residence has since been preserved as the **Keats-Shelley House**. On the other side of the Steps, at No. 23, the quintessentially English **Babington's Tea Rooms** has been serving tea and scones since the 1890s. The centrepiece of the square is the **Fontana della Barcaccia**, a marble fountain in the shape of a half-sunken boat fed by water from the ancient aqueduct Aqua Virgo. It was designed by Pietro Bernini, with the help of his more famous son, Gian Lorenzo.

SEE ALSO BARS AND CAFÉS, P.34; MUSEUMS AND GALLERIES, P.93

Shopping Streets

The area between Piazza di Spagna and Via del Corso is for dedicated fashionistas.

Below: locals and tourists congregate on the Spanish Steps to chat, relax and watch the world go by.

The Vatican and Prati

The fabulous wealth and extravagance of the Catholic Church through the ages is celebrated without restraint in the Vatican State. Covering a total area of a little more than 40 hectares, Vatican City is by far the world's smallest sovereign entity, and yet its treasures are unmatched. The immense basilica of St Peter's, with its dome by Michelangelo and an interior sumptuously bedecked with Bernini's glistening creations, is impressive enough. Then there are the Vatican Museums, mile upon mile of rooms and corridors containing historic treasures, and, of course, the unmissable Sistine Chapel.

Above: the glorious interior of the Basilica di San Pietro.

Piazza San Pietro

St Peter's Square was laid out by Bernini in 1656–67 for Pope Alexander VII. Its double-colonnaded wings symbolise the outstretched arms of Mother Church, embracing and protecting the congregation. The piazza itself is keyhole-shaped, echoing St Peter's role as holder of the keys to heaven. In the centre are fountains by Maderno and della Fontana, and an Egyptian obelisk, brought to Rome by Emperor Caligula in AD 37. Between the obelisk and each fountain is a round marble slab, from where the spectator obtains

the illusion that each colonnade has only a single row of columns. At the end of the square, above a triple flight of steps, stands the **Basilica di San Pietro** ①, the world's largest Catholic church. An undeniably impressive structure, its dimensions are vast: 212m long on the outside, 187m inside and 132m to the tip of the dome. Among the many treasures within is Michelangelo's sublime *Pietà*.
SEE ALSO CHURCHES, P.43–4

The Vatican Museums

The **Vatican Museums** ② are a good 15-minute walk from

St Peter's Square; just follow the walls north until you reach the entrance. Expect a long queue, especially at weekends and on the last Sunday of the month, when the place gets mobbed as admission is free. There are 10 collections in all, plus the papal apartments, but the undisputed highlights are the **Sistine Chapel** ③ and the **Raphael Rooms**. To help visitors out, the museum authorities have devised four routes lasting from 1½ to 5 hours. All, including the shortest, take in the Sistine Chapel. You'll find plenty of detailed information at the entrance.
SEE ALSO MUSEUMS AND GALLERIES, P.93–4

Left: Giuseppe Momo's magnificent helicoidal staircase.

today. The relaxed charm of this atmospheric neighbourhood will soothe your tired feet as you meander along its medieval lanes and admire its ancient, ivy-clad *palazzi*. Unfortunately, a large part of the Borgo was destroyed when Mussolini decided that St Peter's needed a more grandiose approach and tore the area in two with the **Via della Conciliazione** ⑥, which ruins the effect of Bernini's piazza, but allows for a full view of St Peter's.

South of the boulevard is Borgo Santo Spirito. The church of **Santo Spirito in Sassia**, built for the Saxons in 689, was rebuilt in the 16th century. Next door, the **Ospedale Santo Spirito** was set up by Pope Innocent III in the 13th century as an orphanage. Within the hospital is the fascinating little **National Historical Museum of Medicine**.

SEE ALSO MUSEUMS AND GALLERIES, P.94

Prati

North of the Vatican lies the elegant residential area of Prati. Its strategic position just outside the Vatican walls makes this district a convenient base for sightseeing and shopping. Prati is easily reached on metro line A (get off at Lepanto, Ottaviano-San Pietro or Cipro-Musei Vaticani), or one of the many bus routes that terminate at Piazza del Risorgimento. Most of the shops and markets are concentrated around the **Via Cola di Rienzo** and **Via Ottaviano**, around **Piazza Mazzini**, which is laid out in a large star-shaped plan, and on palm-lined **Piazza Cavour**.

SEE ALSO SHOPPING, P.122

> St Peter's is the longest basilica in the world. The nave is the size of two football fields, and the *baldacchino* is as high as a nine-storey building. The church has 21 altars, 14 chapels, 9 domes and capacity for a 60,000 congregation.

Castel Sant'Angelo

Castel Sant'Angelo ④ is approached from across the Tiber by means of the delightful **Ponte Sant' Angelo** ⑤, a pedestrian bridge adorned with statues of Saints Peter and Paul and 10 angels sculpted by Bernini and his students. The castle was conceived by Hadrian as his family mausoleum and became part of the defensive Aurelian Wall a century later. For centuries it was Rome's mightiest military bastion and a refuge for popes in times of trouble. Today, it houses artefacts from all periods of Roman history. If you're travelling with children, the ramparts, trap doors, prison chambers and drawbridge will keep them amused.

SEE ALSO MONUMENTS, P.88

The Borgo

If you've energy left after visiting St Peter's and the Vatican Museums, wander the warren of pedestrian streets just east of the Vatican. The first pilgrims to St Peter's were housed in hostels here, and the area is still a colony of international pilgrims

Below: the rather flamboyant Vatican Guard.

Piazza Navona and the Pantheon

The area loosely referred to as the *centro storico* (the historic centre) is contained between the great bend of the Tiber to the west and the Via del Corso to the east. At its heart, the Pantheon has stood for almost 2,000 years, while Piazza Navona is built on the foundations of a Roman stadium. Today, the tangle of streets and alleys in this compact area is filled with Baroque palaces and churches, small shops and picturesque alfresco cafés.

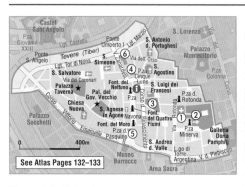

See Atlas Pages 132–133

Above: bars and restaurants line the Piazza Navona.

Piazza della Rotonda

In the heart of the *centro storico*, the Piazza della Rotonda is one of the busiest squares in the city. Lined with cafés and with an obelisk at its centre, this quaint but small square can barely accommodate the throngs of tourists that pour into it to see the **Pantheon** ①, one of the most memorable and impressive of Rome's many architectural marvels, and the best-preserved ancient building in Rome. It's worth trying to beat the crowds by getting here as early as you can.

South-east of the Pantheon, the Gothic church of **Santa Maria sopra Minerva** ② contains the relics of St Catherine of Siena, Italy's patron saint. Outside, the jovial little **elephant statue**

carrying an ancient Egyptian obelisk on its back was designed by Bernini in 1667.

Between Piazza della Rotonda and Piazza Navona, the elegant **Palazzo Madama** ③, originally built for the Medici family, is now the seat of the Italian Senate. Opposite is the Baroque church of **San Luigi dei Francesi**, worth a visit to see the dramatic paintings by Caravaggio in the Contarelli Chapel. These were the artist's first great religious works.

SEE ALSO CHURCHES, P.44; MONUMENTS, P.88–9; PALAZZI, P.104

Piazza Navona

Piazza Navona is one of the most animated squares in Rome, invariably full of

Romans and foreign visitors wandering among stalls set up by hopeful artists, relaxing with a coffee in one of the many bars, or stopping for a chat by its gushing fountains.

Piazza Navona was built over the remains of the Emperor Domitian's ancient athletics stadium: the stand forms part of the foundations of the flanking houses, and you can see one of the original entrances just behind the north end of the square.

Piazza Navona owes much of its Baroque appearance to the Pamphilj Pope Innocent X (1644–55), who enlarged his family palace and commissioned Bernini's magnificent **Fontana dei Quattro Fiumi** (Fountain of

Left: the porticos at the Pantheon tell of its origins.

Pasquino. The mutilated marble torso leaning against the wall is thought to date from the 3rd century BC. It was found in Piazza Navona and brought here in the 15th century when it became one of Rome's 'talking statues' *(see box, p. 43)*. The statue leans against a wall of the **Palazzo Braschi** ⑤, one of the last papal palaces built in Rome, in the 18th century. The *palazzo* is home to the newly renovated **Museo di Roma**. SEE ALSO CHURCHES, P.44–5; MUSEUMS AND GALLERIES, P.94–5

The Embankment

North of Palazzo Altemps, Via dei Soldati leads to the River Tiber and the **Museo Napoleonico** ⑥ at **Ponte Umberto I**. The nearby **Via dell'Orso** used to be lined with inns and was a favourite haunt of courtesans. Today, the area is better-known for its antique shops, interspersed with classy boutiques selling modern designer furniture. The **Via dei Coronari** is packed with some of the best antiques and arts shops in Rome, including Marmi Line. SEE ALSO MUSEUMS AND GALLERIES, P.95; SHOPPING, P.122

From December until early January, Piazza Navona hosts a colourful Christmas fair at which all sorts of decorations, toys, sweets and Baroque-style nativity scenes are sold, culminating in a carnival on the night before the Epiphany (6 January)

were added in the 19th century to create symmetry.

Pope Innocent also commissioned Borromini's **Church of Sant'Agnese in Agone**. Just north of Piazza Navona, **Palazzo Altemps** ④ is one of the four sites of the **Museo Nazionale Romano**, which holds the state collection of ancient treasures.

Off the southern end of Piazza Navona is **Piazza di**

the Four Rivers). The rivers in question – the Danube, the Ganges, the Nile and the Plate – are represented by four huge allegorical figures which in turn represent the four continents Europe, Asia, Africa and America. The Nile is blindfolded because the source of the river was then still a mystery. To the south of the square is the **Fontana del Moro** (Fountain of the Moor). Its central figure was also designed by Bernini. The **Fontana del Nettuno** (Fountain of Neptune) at the northern end was originally just a large basin. The sculptures

Below: the Via dei Cestari (connecting the Pantheon and Largo Argentina) is lined with shops selling religious raiments.

Campo de' Fiori and the Ghetto

The southern part of Rome's *centro storico* is a triangle of tightly packed streets between Corso Vittorio Emanuele II, Via del Teatro Marcello and the river, with the lively market square of Campo de' Fiori at its hub, and its eastern corner occupied by the medieval streets of Europe's longest-surviving Jewish community. Here, one of Rome's oldest bridges links the left bank to the tiny, tranquil Tiber Island, which has long been associated with healing and is still home to a hospital founded in the 16th century.

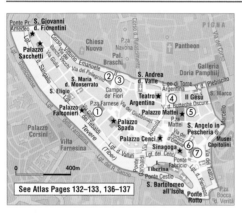

See Atlas Pages 132–133, 136–137

Above: artichokes are much-used in Roman-Jewish cuisine.

Campo de' Fiori

The **Campo de' Fiori** has been the site of a **produce market** for centuries, and was one of the liveliest areas of medieval and Renaissance Rome, when cardinals and pilgrims would rub shoulders with fishmongers, vegetable-sellers and prostitutes. Today, the Campo flourishes, thanks to a perfectly balanced infra-structure. It has everything from butcher's and baker's shops to clothes boutiques, a cinema and a bustling morn-ing food market. At night, the Campo plays host to hun-dreds of Romans and visitors who frequent the bars and restaurants or simply hang out under the **statue of Gior-**dano Bruno, sipping beers until late into the night.

The streets around Campo de' Fiori still retain the names of trades originally practised in them. **Via dei Giubbonari**, named after the sellers and makers of *gipponi* or bodices, is still lined with clothes shops, which are among some of the cheapest in town. Via dei Baullari, the luggage-makers, leads to the **Piazza Farnese**, a picturesque square flanked by the magnifi-cent **Palazzo Farnese** ①, now the French Embassy.

North of the Campo, **Via del Pellegrino** is lined with artisans' workshops, book-shops and antique dealers. Backing on to this street is the impressive **Palazzo della Cancelleria** ②, former seat of the papal government. Another elegant palace in the vicinity is the **Piccola Far-nesina** ③ in Piazza San Pan-taleo, home to the **Museo Barracco**, a prestigious col-lection of ancient sculpture. Further along Corso Vittorio is the church of **Sant' Andrea della Valle**, which boasts the city's second-tallest dome.

SEE ALSO CHURCHES, P.45; FASHION, P.53, 55; FOOD AND DRINK, P.64; MONUMENTS, P.89; MUSEUMS AND GALLERIES, P.95; PALAZZI, P.105; SHOPPING, P.122

Largo di Torre Argentina

Largo di Torre Argentina on Corso Vittorio is one of the busiest crossroads in the city

18

Left: the Ancient Ponte Fabricio leads to Isola Tibernina.

trendy boutiques and one of Rome's most delightful fountains, the 16th-century **Fontana delle Tartarughe** (Tortoise Fountain).
SEE ALSO CHURCHES, P.45; MUSEUMS AND GALLERIES, P.95

Jewish Ghetto

A small but vibrant Jewish community still lives in and around the **Via del Portico d'Ottavia**.The streets are dotted with kosher shops and restaurants serving the city's distinctive Roman/Jewish cuisine. The church of **Sant'Angelo in Pescheria**, where Jews were once forced to attend penitential services, was built on the ruins of the **Portico d'Ottavia** ⑥, a crumbling arched façade more than 2,000 years old. Beyond it extends the **Teatro di Marcello** (Theatre of Marcellus) ⑦, said to be the architectural model for the Colosseum. The main **synagogue** down by the river bank houses the small Museo Ebraico dedicated to local Jewish history.
SEE ALSO MONUMENTS, P.89; MUSEUMS AND GALLERIES, P.95–6

Tiber Island

The **Ponte Fabricio**, one of Rome's oldest bridges (62 BC), links the left bank to the leafy Isola Tiberina, a tiny island in the middle of the Tiber. In Roman times it was the sacred domain of Aesculapius, god of healing, to whom a temple and hospital were dedicated. The island is now the site of the Fatebenefratelli (the 'do-good-brothers') hospital founded in 1548. A second bridge, the **Ponte Cestio**, built in 42 BC but remodelled in the 19th century, connects the island to the neighbourhood of Trastevere (see p.22).

In the Middle Ages Rome's Jewish population enjoyed relative freedom, but in 1555, Pope Paul IV's zero-tolerance policy ordered the confinement of the Jewish population into an enclosed area around the Portico d'Ottavia, which became known from then on as the Ghetto. The area was surrounded by high walls which weren't torn down until 1848.

and a major bus interchange. Its architecture – *palazzi*, banks and insurance companies – isn't very exciting. Only **Teatro Argentina**, a state-funded theatre and official home of the Teatro di Roma, radiates any atmosphere. The real attraction are the excavated temples in the middle of the square. Known as the **Area Sacra** ④, the site dates from around the 3rd and 4th centuries BC. Some of the remains can be seen from above.

East of the square is **Il Gesù**, mother church of the Jesuits and a prime example of Counter-Reformation Baroque. The nearby **Crypta Balbi** ⑤, one of the four homes of the Museo Nazionale Romano collection, occupies the site of an ancient Roman theatre and housing block.

Just south of here is the cosy little **Piazza del Mattei**, with a funky bar, a couple of

Below: a backstreet in the Campo de' Fiori.

Via Veneto and Villa Borghese

I n the 1950s and '60s, when the Cinecittà film studios were thriving and
Rome was the Hollywood of Europe, the Via Veneto became the hang-
out for the rich and famous – the focal point of the so-called *dolce vita*.
Those heady days may be long gone, but glimpses of the avenue's glamorous past can be seen in some of the landmark cafés and de luxe hotels.
At its northern end is the lovely Villa Borghese park, a popular Sunday
strolling ground for Romans containing some of the city's finest museums.

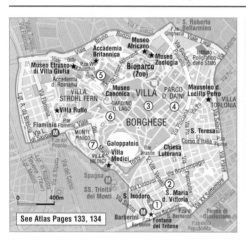

See Atlas Pages 133, 134

Above: locals out and about in the park.

Via Veneto

The southern end of Via
Veneto begins in **Piazza Barberini**, a busy square with a
cinema and fast-food joints.
In its centre sits, rather for-
lornly, Bernini's **Fontana del
Tritone** (Triton Fountain). Via
Veneto itself, lined with plane
trees and pavement cafés,
was once the symbol of
Roman fashion and style.
However, the glorious days of
the *dolce vita*, immortalised
on screen by Fellini, are long
gone. The long, twisting
avenue is now filled for the
most part with luxury hotels,
embassies and offices. Only a
few historic cafés – Harry's

Bar at No. 150, Café de Paris
at No. 90 and the Art Deco
Doney at No. 145 – still bear
witness to the street's heyday
as the place to be seen in
Rome. At the southern end of
the Via Veneto, the Baroque
church of **Santa Maria della
Concezione** ① is best known
for its gruesome collection of
bones kept in the crypt.
About halfway up, where the
street bends, is the **Palazzo
Margherita** ②, completed in
1890 and now home to the
American Embassy. To the
south of the *palazzo*, on the
corner of Piazza San
Bernardo and Via XX Settembre, the church of **Santa**

Maria della Vittoria is known
for Bernini's famously sensual
statue of Teresa of Avila.
SEE ALSO CAFÉS AND BARS, P.36;
CHURCHES, P.45; PALAZZI, P.105

Villa Borghese

At the northern end of Via
Veneto, outside the Porta Pinciana, is the the main
entrance to the **Villa Borghese park** ③, once the
estate of Cardinal Scipione
Borghese, the nephew of
Pope Paul V. The gardens are
laid out over rolling hills, with
winding paths, little lakes,
statues and pretty flower
beds hidden here and there.
On Sunday, the people of
Rome take over the park.
Every corner is full of picnick-

Left: Sunday activity at the Villa Borghese.

large neoclassical building houses the **Galleria Nazionale d'Arte Moderna** ⑤, a collection of predominantly Italian art from the 19th and 20th centuries. Next door, in the Piazza Winston Churchill, is the **Accademia Britannica**, designed by Lutyens and home to visiting scholars. Italy's finest Etruscan art collection is housed in the nearby **Villa Giulia**, a splendid late Renaissance palace built as a summer villa for Julius III between 1551 and 1553.

Near the **Galoppatoio** (horse-racing track), the newly renovated orangery houses the **Museo Carlo Bilotti** ⑥, a small museum of modern and contemporary art with numerous works by Giorgio de Chirico.
SEE ALSO MUSEUMS AND GALLERIES, P.96–7

PINCIO GARDENS
These formal gardens at the southwest corner of the park were designed by Valadier in the 19th century. Of particular interest are the **water clock** and the **Casina Valadier** ⑦, once a favourite meeting spot among the bigwigs of the Roman *belle époque*, now an expensive restaurant with a fabulous view.

The park's terrace also provides great views across the city and is a particularly nice spot for an evening stroll.

A wide *viale* leads from the Pincio Gardens back towards the middle of the park and the pretty **Giardino del Lago**, with a tiny lake in the middle of which stands a reproduction of a Greek temple of Aesculapius.
SEE ALSO PARKS, GARDENS AND BEACHES, P.109–10

Add some romance to your jaunt in the park: pick up a gourmet picnic-to-go from nearby Piazza di Spagna-area restaurant GiNa. Luxury packs come complete with chequered cloth, plates, flatware, wineglasses, a bottle of your wine of choice, a thermos of espresso and, of course, a sumptuous meal. GiNa: 7a Via San Sebastionello; tel: 06-678 0251; www.ginaroma.com.

---

home for the worldly, pleasure-loving Cardinal Scipione Borghese between 1613 and 1615. The cardinal was a great patron of the arts, and the paintings and sculptures he acquired form the core of this precious art collection.

The Villa Borghese's two other main museums are across the park to the west, on Viale delle Belle Arti. A

Below: Canova's sculpture of Pauline Borghese.

ing families, strolling lovers, cyclists, joggers and squealing children at play.
SEE ALSO PARKS, GARDENS AND BEACHES, P.109

THE MUSEUMS
The extensive park (6.5km in perimeter) contains several museums. In the eastern corner is the **Galleria Borghese** ④, one of the world's great private art collections, housed in the Casino Borghese, built as a summer

Trastevere and the Gianicolo

Across the river *(trans Tiberim)* from the *centro storico* lies Trastevere, Rome's former working-class district, now a gentrified haven for expats and middle-class Romans. During the day, it is left to its sleepy self: residents exercise dogs and do their daily shopping, while children play and the elderly sit outside their houses. In the evening, the streets and squares are packed with locals and tourists, who flock here to eat, drink or stroll among the craft stalls and street performers.

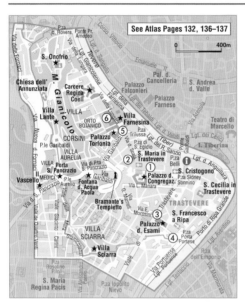

See Atlas Pages 132, 136–137

0   400m

Above: the Fontana del Aqua Paola.

Piazza Santa Maria in Trastevere ①

This cobbled square is the heart of the neighbourhood and one of the most charming *piazzas* in Rome. There's a steady ebb and flow of tourists and locals whiling away their time in the cafés or sitting on the steps of the **fountain** (1692) around which musicians perform in summer. The *piazza* is named after the **basilica** on its eastern side,

thought to be the oldest Christian church in Rome. North-west of the square on Piazza Sant'Egidio is the **Museo di Roma in Trastevere** ②, housed in a beautifully restored Carmelite convent, dedicated to Roman folklore. SEE ALSO CHURCHES, P.46; MUSEUMS AND GALLERIES, P.98

Viale di Trastevere ③

Like every old quarter of Rome, Trastevere had to make

sacrifices when the capital started expanding after 1870. Many historic buildings and streets were destroyed in order to make way for the Viale di Trastevere, a broad boulevard that cuts through Trastevere's little streets. At its northern end, on the banks of the Tiber, is **Piazza Belli**, named after the 19th-century Roman dialect poet, Giuseppe Gioacchino Belli (1791–1863), whose statue stands here. Behind Piazza Belli is **Piazza Sidney Sonnino**. The **Torre degli Anguillara**, the last of many towers that once guarded Trastevere, displays a plaque commemorating Dante's stay here in 1300. The nearby church of **San Crisogono** was built over one of the oldest sites of Christian

Left: one of many busts of Italian patriots on the Gianicolo.

Garibaldi climbs to the Gianicolo. This route was used in the Middle Ages by pilgrims going to the Vatican, before the building of the 'retifili' – the long, straight roads built by the Renaissance popes. The longest of these is **Via della Lungara**, laid out in the early 16th century to connect Trastevere with the Borgo. It's a short walk along Via della Lungara to the **Villa Farnesina**, a Trastevere gem. Built in 1508 for the wealthy banker Agostino Chigi, the highlight is Raphael's classic *Triumph of Galatea*. Opposite, the 15th-century **Palazzo Corsini** ⑥ houses a fine collection of 16th- to 18th-century art. The palace gardens are now Rome's **Botanical Gardens** (Orto Botanico), planted with species from all over the world.
SEE ALSO MUSEUMS AND GALLERIES, P.98–9; PARKS, GARDENS AND BEACHES, P.108

The Gianicolo hill was the site of one of Italy's decisive battles for independence, when in 1849 Garibaldi and his army defeated French troops sent to restore papal rule. At noon, a cannon blast sounds in commemoration of the struggle.

worship in Rome, dating from the 3rd century.

On the south side of the Viale di Trastevere lie two noteworthy churches. **Santa Cecilia in Trastevere**, with its leaning Romanesque tower, is dedicated to the patron saint of music. The church of **San Francesco a Ripa** contains a powerful late work by Bernini, the statue of *The Blessed Ludovica Albertoni*.
SEE ALSO CHURCHES, P.46

Porta Portese

The church is not far from **Porta Portese** ④, a gateway built by Urban VIII on the site of the ancient Porta Portuen-

sis. Rome's **flea market** is held here on Sunday mornings. Go early if you want to avoid the crowds.
SEE ALSO SHOPPING, P.125

Via della Lungara

Via della Scala leads from Piazza Santa Maria in Trastevere to the **Porta Settimiana** ⑤, a gate erected by Emperor Septimius Severus and replaced by Pope Alexander VI in 1498. From here Via

Below: graffiti is particularly prolific in Trastevere.

The Gianicolo

If you don't fancy the long walk up the Gianicolo (Janiculum Hill) on the **Via Garibaldi**, you can hop on a bus (115 or 870) to **Piazzale Garibaldi**. The broad square is dominated by a monument to the freedom-fighter, while further north is another for his wife Anita, represented as an Amazon. Views from the terrace are magnificent. If you're catching the bus up, it's worth jumping off to see **Bramante's Tempietto**, one of the gems of the Renaissance. A little further uphill stands the **Fontana dell'Acqua Paola**, a fountain commissioned in 1612 by Pope Paul V to grace the end of an ancient aqueduct built by Trajan.
SEE ALSO MONUMENTS, P.89

23

Aventino, Testaccio and the EUR

The most southerly of Rome's seven hills, the Aventine is a tranquil, well-heeled oasis and the site of some of the city's earliest Christian churches. Neighbouring Testaccio, on the other hand, is still one of the city's most down-to-earth and genuinely Roman districts, though it, too, is slowly succumbing to the effects of gentrification. The stark EUR district was Mussolini's attempt to make his mark on Rome and to create a city fit for Fascists. Today it is another sought-after residential neighbourhood.

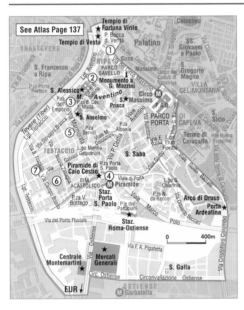

Above: the ornate ceiling of the church of Sant' Alessio.

Cavalieri di Malta and the residence of the Grand Master of the Order of the Knights of St John. The square and the monumental gates of the **Priorato di Malta** ③ were designed by Piranesi. Peep through the keyhole of the gates for a perfectly framed view of the dome of the distant St Peter's.
SEE ALSO CHURCHES, P.47; MONUMENTS, P.89

Piramide

Originally called the Porta Ostiense, because it marked the beginning of the road to Ostia, **Porta San Paolo** ④ is one of the best-preserved of the ancient city gates. It was renamed after St Paul, who entered Rome through it. Impressive though the gateway is, it is overshadowed by the **Piramide di Caio Cestio**,

The Aventine Hill

At the bottom of the Aventine Hill is **Piazza della Bocca della Verità**, once the site of the Forum Boarium, the cattle market of ancient Rome. The square is named after the legendary Bocca della Verità, the 'Mouth of Truth' (see p. 47), which is in the portico of the church of **Santa Maria in Cosmedin** ①. Also on the square stand the **Tempio di Vesta** (Temple of Hercules)

and the **Tempio di Fortuna Virile** (Temple of Portunus), Rome's best-preserved Republican temples.

High on the hill is the **Parco Savello**, a peaceful destination for walks or picnics, overlooking the river towards the Vatican. The gardens flank the early Christian basilica of **Santa Sabina** ②, skilfully restored in 1936.

From here, Via Santa Sabina leads into **Piazza dei**

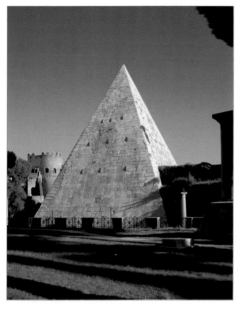

Left: the strangely un-Roman Piramide de Caio Cestio.

home to some trendy restaurants and leads to **Monte Testaccio** ⑥, which is bounded by Via di Monte Testaccio, an uninhabited, quasi-rural lane that is best visited at night when its clubs, bars and restaurants really get going. Between Monte Testaccio and the river lies the **Mattatoio** ⑦, a former slaughterhouse, converted into an arts complex (MACRO al Mattatoio).

South of Testaccio, in the scruffy old industrial district of Ostiense, the **Centrale Montemartini** is an unusual sculpture museum worth seeking out if you're in the area.
SEE ALSO BARS AND CAFÉS, P.36–7; MUSEUMS AND GALLERIES, P.99; NIGHTLIFE, P.102–3; RESTAURANTS, P.119–120

The Piazza dei Cavalieri di Malta is named after the ancient chivalric order founded in 1080 as the Hospitallers of St John to run a hospital for pilgrims in Jerusalem. The Hospitallers became a powerful military order, based in Malta until they were expelled by Napoleon in 1798. The Knights of Malta have been based in Rome ever since.

the tomb of a vainglorious Roman officer, Gaius Cestius, buried here in 12 BC. Adjoining the pyramid is Rome's Cimitero Acattolico, known in English as the **Protestant Cemetery** (Mon–Sat 9am–5pm). Romantic poets Shelley and Keats are buried here. A number of prominent Italians are also buried here, including Antonio Gramsci, founder of the Italian Communist Party.

Testaccio

Testaccio, the area west of Porta San Paolo, doesn't fea-

ture on most tourist itineraries, but it's worth a visit if you want to experience a genuine Roman working-class district, before trendification changes its character for good. It is now one of the most culturally active areas in Rome, with theatres, a cinema, a music school and some of the liveliest nightlife in town.

The boisterous daily produce market in **Piazza Testaccio** ⑤ is a testimony to the area's working-class roots. To the south, **Via Galvani** is

Below: street art in Ostiense.

EUR

This stark district was Mussolini's attempt to build a city fit for Fascists. The complex of white marble buildings, wide avenues and open spaces grouped around an artificial lake was designed for the World Fair in 1942 – hence the name EUR (Esposizione Universale di Roma). The war interrupted construction, however, and the fair never took place. In recent years, EUR has developed into a thriving township of government ministries, offices and fashionable apartments. Several buildings from Mussolini's time remain, most notably the **Palazzo della Civiltà del Lavoro**, known as the 'Square Colosseum'. The huge, domed **Palazzo dello Sport** was designed for the 1960 Olympics. For visitors, there are several museums, an amusement park, Luneur, and open-air swimming pool.
SEE ALSO CHILDREN, P.40

Celio, Monti and Esquilino

These neighbourhoods east of the Colosseum are more off the beaten track, but worth exploring. The area around the Caelian Hill (Celio), once the seat of the Catholic Church and one of the seven classical hills of Rome, is packed with striking ancient monuments and churches steeped in history. Beyond the busy thoroughfare of Via Nazionale, the hilly back-streets of bohemian Monti and multicultural Esquilino are also peppered with fine churches and an increasing number of trendy bars and boutiques.

Above: the Parco Celio.

III and once stood in the Circus Maximus.

Across the street from the Lateran Palace is the entrance to the **Scala Santa** ② (Apr–Sept daily 6.30am–noon, 3–6.15pm) said to be the stairs that Christ ascended when he was tried by Pontius Pilate. Brought to Rome by Constantine's mother, Helena, they have a protective layer of wood, but you still have to mount them on your knees, and the devout (who arrive in bus loads) do so slowly, stopping on each of the 28 steps to pray.

The Piazza di San Giovanni is linked to the Colosseum by the Via di San Giovanni in Laterano. Two important churches lie off this straight road: the 11th-century **Santi Quattro Coronati**, featuring beautiful cloisters, and the 12th-century basilica of **San**

The Lateran

At the heart of the Lateran district is **Piazza di San Giovanni**, flanked by the Baroque **Palazzo Lateranense** (Lateran Palace) ①. Next to the palace stands

San Giovanni in Laterano, the first Christian basilica in Rome.

Standing 30m high, **the obelisk** on the square is the tallest and oldest in Rome; it honours the Pharaoh Tutmes

Left: the façade of the Scala Santa.

SEE ALSO CHURCHES, P.48–9; MONUMENTS, P.89

Monti

Traffic thunders along Via Nazionale and Via Cavour, two characterless thoroughfares intersecting the area north of the Colosseum, but between the lower end of them is a cluster of pretty, narrow, cobbled streets lined with bars, restaurants and boutiques, which make up the heart of the trendy bohemian district known as Rione Monti, or simply called Monti. Notable churches include **Santa Maria Maggiore**, **Santa Prassede** and **San Pietro in Vincoli**.

SEE ALSO CHURCHES, P.49

Esquilino

Northeast of Monti, centred around the faded splendour of Piazza Vittorio, lies the slightly shabby Esquilino quarter, now Rome's prime multicultural district, with many shops and restaurants owned by North Africans, Indians and Chinese.

There is plenty to see in the area, including the **Baths of Diocletian** ⑥ on Piazza della Repubblica, one of the four sites of the Museo Nazionale Romano. On Piazza dei Cinquecento is the imposing **Palazzo Massimo alle Terme** ⑦, the main site of the museum quartet.

On the other side of the piazza is the graceful ticket hall of **Stazione Termini**, designed by Angiolo Mazzoni. The remains of the Servian Walls are visible through long glass windows. Uncovered during the building of the first station in 1867, they are believed to date from the 6th century BC.

SEE ALSO MUSEUMS AND GALLERIES, P.99

Rome's main train station offers a vast selection of services to keep you occupied while waiting for your train, including a shopping centre, an excellent art gallery (by platform 24), a gym, restaurants, a post office, a church and a medical centre.

Clemente ③, built over an ancient **Temple of Mithras**.

SEE ALSO CHURCHES, P.47–8; PALAZZI, P.105

The Celio

The Celio is home to Villa Celimontana, set in the pleasant **Parco del Celio**. On the southeastern edge of the park is the 5th-century church of **Santo Stefano Rotondo**, one of the few remaining circular churches in the city. There are three other noteworthy churches in this area: **Santa Maria in Domnica**, which boasts a fabulous mosaic, **Santi Giovanni e Paolo** and **San Gregorio Magno**.

Via di San Paolo della Croce is straddled by the 1st-century AD **Arco di Dolabella** ④, part of Nero's great aqueduct, built to supply water for the fountains and baths of the emperor's Golden Palace.

South of the Caelian Hill are the remains of **The Baths of Caracalla** ⑤, which at one time could accommodate 1,600 people. They are beautifully lit after dark.

Below: enjoying a drink in one of Monti's bars.

A–Z

In the following section Rome's attractions and services are organized by theme, under alphabetical headings. Items that link to another theme are cross-referenced. All sights that are plotted on the atlas section at the end of the book are given a page number and grid reference.

Architecture

R ome is a city standing on the shoulders of its predecessors, where layers of history run into each other. Materials have been taken from older buildings to make new ones, and buildings adapted to suit changing needs. Medieval churches rise from the remains of ancient houses; a Renaissance palace balances on top of the Theatre of Marcellus, next to 20th-century apartments. Even if buildings disappear, their shapes remain. Three great eras – the ancient city, the Renaissance and the Baroque – have largely defined Rome's visual identity, blending in an astonishingly harmonious mix, studded with masterpieces.

Ancient Rome

Rome's first permanent civic buildings were erected in the **Forum**, in Republican times, but Julius Caesar was the first to set out on a programme to improve and glorify the city. Caesar's nephew the Emperor Augustus (27 BC–AD 14) liked to boast that he had found Rome made of brick and left it of marble, but while the wealthy lived in elegant houses, the masses lived in insanitary *insulae* or apartment blocks of mud-bricks and timber. The city centre was destroyed by fire in AD 64 – legend has it that Nero started it himself, to clear space for his vast palace. Most of Nero's constructions were destroyed by his successors Vespasian (69–79) and his sons, Titus and Domitian, who erected the **Colosseum** on land originally covered by Nero's private lake. One of Rome's greatest architects was Apollodorus of Damascus, master builder of Emperor Trajan (98–117), responsible for the Forum and the semicircular market behind it, and a massive bath complex. Few civic buildings survive from the centuries between the fall of the Empire and the Renaissance, but this was the time when Rome's major churches were founded, often incorporating parts of pagan temples.
SEE ALSO MONUMENTS, P.82–7

The Renaissance

The Renaissance stemmed from a rediscovery of the ancient art and culture that had been abandoned after the fall of the Roman Empire in the 5th century. Most great artists of the era came to Rome at some point, to study the ancient relics or carry out commissions for the popes. In 1506, Pope Julius II commissioned the building of **St Peter's**, which took 120 years to complete and incorporated contributions from the masters of Renaissance painting, sculpture and architecture. These same masters left their mark elsewhere in Rome, most notably Bramante (the **Tempietto**) Raphael (**Vatican** frescoes) and Michelangelo (**St Peter's** dome, the **Sistine Chapel**, the *Pietà*). Artists continued to flock to Rome in

Above: Bramante's Tempietto was completed in 1502.

the 16th century to work for the popes and noble families like the Barberini, Borghese, Farnese and Pamphili. Churches including **Santa Maria del Popolo** and **Santa Maria della Pace**, and the Via Giulia *palazzi* date from this time.
SEE ALSO CHURCHES, P.42–4; MONUMENTS, P.89

City of the Baroque

The ornate Roman Baroque of the 17th century was provoked by the fear of Protestantism. By the 1620s, extravagantly decorated churches with *trompe l'œil*

Left: Michelangelo's Piazza del Campidoglio.

SEE ALSO PIAZZA DI SPAGNA AND TRIDENTE, P.12–3; MONUMENTS, P.87

Mussolini's Legacy

We might not consider it when we think of Roman architecture, but Mussolini's Fascist regime of the 1920s and 1930s left a powerful imprint on the city. Whole areas of Rome are dominated by massive, conspicuous buildings with façades of white columns against a plain white or reddish-brown background, adorned with statues. The EUR district is the best place to see Mussolini's vision.
SEE ALSO AVENTINO, TESTACCIO AND THE EUR, P.25

Modern Architecture

Modern architecture was a rarely seen phenomenon in Rome until a few years ago, when the state-of-the-art **Auditorium** by Genoese architect Renzo Piano spawned a wave of major architectural projects by big-name architects. These include Richard Meier's uplifting **Jubilee Church** in the eastern suburbs, his more controversial new pavilion housing the **Ara Pacis**, and Zaha Hadid's ambitious new contemporary art centre, **MAXXI**, slated to open in 2008. Across the city, disused industrial buildings have been transformed: an old abattoir in Testaccio (**al Mattatoio**) and a converted Peroni brewery now house Rome's contemporary art museum (**MACRO**). An old power station in Ostiense, **Centrale Montemartini**, is home to part of the Capitoline collection. Rome, it seems, is on the up.
SEE ALSO MUSEUMS AND GALLERIES, P.97–8; MUSIC, THEATRE AND DANCE, P.100

A huge proportion of Rome's architectural gems date from the years between 1454 and 1670, when Rome was again one of Europe's great power centres, and at the heart of Renaissance and Baroque art and architecture.

ceiling paintings and gold-encrusted altars were thought more likely to keep people in the Catholic fold than portrayals of suffering. The Baroque was eagerly taken up by Rome's great families, keen to demonstrate their wealth by building massive city palaces and villas. The **Villa Borghese** dates from this time, as do parts of **Palazzo Doria Pamphilj**, **Villa Doria Pamphilj** and the **Palazzo Barberini**. This was the age of Bernini and Borromini, whose façades, fountains and sculptures grace streets, palaces and piazzas. Once again, artists like Velázquez and Rubens travelled to Rome to study and find patrons among its great families. After about 1660, funding dried up, and the papacy and aristocracy had to moderate their designs. No era since has marked the city so deeply.
SEE ALSO MUSEUMS AND GALLERIES, P.92, 93, 96

The 18th Century

The Church continued to commission buildings and improvements in the 18th century, but on a far smaller scale. Stylistically, rococo flourishes were added to the Baroque, but most of the city's architects lived on the legacy of the past. Nevertheless, two of Rome's most famous sights date from this time: the **Spanish Steps** and the **Trevi Fountain**.

Below: the Jubilee Church.

Bars and Cafés

R omans often stop at the local bar or café a
few times a day, first for a breakfast of
espresso or cappuccino and a *cornetto* (the Italian
version of a croissant), then another espresso and
a savoury snack or light lunch later in the day,
and maybe for an early evening *aperitivo* before
going home or out for dinner. Many Roman bars
and cafés also sell ice cream, but for the real
thing you must be selective. The city's favourite
gelaterie are listed here with a selection of trendy,
traditional, cosy or characterful bars and cafés.
For a list of Roman bars with a literary slant, *see
Literature, p.81.*

Capitoline Hill

Caffè Capitolino
Palazzo dei Conservatori, adjacent to Piazza Campidoglio; tel:
06-6710 2475; Tue–Sun 9am–
8pm; bus: Piazza Venezia; map
p.137 D4
This café at the top of the
Palazzo dei Conservatori has
one of the best panoramic
views in Rome. Outdoor
seating under elegant sunshades is expensive but
delightful if it's not too hot.
Inside, cafeteria-style service
is cheaper.

Caffetteria Italia
Above the Vittoriano, entrance
from the museum in Via San
Pietro in Carcere or from the
Campidoglio; tel: 06-6780 905;
daily 9.30am–5.45pm; bus:
Piazza Venezia; map p.137 E4
Another great, if touristy, spot
for a drink that affords fine
views of the Forum and the
Roman skyline.

Il Centrale Ristotheatre
6 Via Celsa; tel: 06-6780 501;
www.centraleristotheatre.com;
daily 6.30pm–1am; bus: Largo
Argentina; map p.137 D4
Just off Piazza Venezia to the
east is a former theatre that
attracts a thirty-something

Roman crowd looking for a
quirky night out. It has a bar
with a lounge area and
restaurant with live music,
theatre or cabaret. From
7.30pm–midnight on Sundays you can have one drink
and all you can eat from the
buffet for a set price.

The Forum and Colosseum

Oppio Caffè
72 Via delle Terme di Tito;
tel: 06-4745 262; www.oppio
caffe.it; daily 7pm–2am; metro
and bus: Colosseum; map p.138
A4
Hi-tech meets classical
Rome: plexiglass and video
screens contrast with ancient
brickwork. Outside seating
provides stunning views of
the Colosseum. Live music
some nights.

The Trevi Fountain and the Quirinale

Dagnino
75 Via V. E. Orlando; tel: 06-4818
660; www.pasticceriadagnino.it;
daily 7am–11pm; metro and
bus: Repubblica; map p.134 B2
In an anonymous gallery off
the street is the vast olde-

Above: deep in conversation
between drinks.

worlde Sicilian pastry shop
(try their speciality, the
ricotta-stuffed *cannoli*) and
tavola calda (snack bar) serving all-day sweet and
savoury specialities.

Il Gelato di San Crispino
42 Via della Panetteria, Fontana
di Trevi; tel: 06-6793 924;
www.ilgelatodisancrispino.com;
Mon, Wed–Sun 11am–12.30am;
bus: 52, 80 express, 116, 119;
map p.133 E2
The *cognoscenti* consider
this the cream of Rome's ice
creamers. The serious whitecoat-clad staff serve ice
cream from stainless steel
vats to avoid mixing

Left: live music and a relaxing drink.

crammed with bottles of wine and regional specialities.

Café Canova-Tadolini
150a Via del Babuino; tel: 06-3211 0702; Mon–Sat 8am–8.30pm; metro: Spagna; map p.133 E3

What was once the atelier of sculptor Canova, and later handed down to the Tadolini family, is now a unique café, where you can sip or sup in an elegant space, complete with chandeliers, parquet floors, antique furniture and marble sculptures.

Canova and Rosati
16 Piazza del Popolo; tel: 06-3612 231; Mon–Fri 7.30am–midnight, Sat, Sun 8am–midnight/5 Piazza del Popolo; tel: 06-3225 859; daily 7.30am–midnight; metro: Flaminio, bus: Piazza del Popolo; map p.133 D3

These long-time rivals face each other across the grand expanse of Piazza del Popolo. Both are good, but Rosati wins hands down for ambience. Furthermore, its cakes are mouth-watering, and the cocktails are a cut above the usual.

Ciampini al Café du Jardin
Viale Trinità dei Monti; tel: 06-6785 678; Thur–Tue 8am–1am;

For Romans, *gelato* (ice cream) is not so much a dessert as an afternoon or after-dinner snack to accompany a stroll around town. Accordingly, *gelaterie* are never far away and stay open late. .

---

flavours, and no cones are allowed, only cups, as cones would interfere with the taste. Unusual flavours vary by season.

The News Café
72 Via della Stamperia; tel: 06-6992 3473; daily 8am–1am; bus: Piazza San Silvestro; map p.133 E2

Takes its name from the racks of newspapers available for customers to read. A good all-day option for salads, soups and pastas.

Piazza di Spagna and Tridente

Antico Caffè Greco
86 Via dei Condotti; tel: 06-6791 700; Sun 10.30am–7pm, Mon–Sat 9am–7.30pm; metro: Spagna; map p.133 E2

A beautiful café with marble tables and red-velvet chairs, frequented mostly by

tourists, but the bar out the front makes the most delicious coffee. Drink it standing at the bar, as it's much cheaper than when you are sitting at a table.

Buccone
19 Via di Ripetta; tel: 06-3612 154; Mon–Thur 9am–8.30pm, Fri, Sat 9am–11.30pm; bus: 698, 926; map p.133 D2

Buccone existed long before wine bars became fashionable, and it is a joy just to take in the sheer authenticity of this high-ceilinged, old-fashioned emporium

---

Below: the outside tables at Canova are particularly pleasant on a sunny day, but its rival Rosati has the edge food-wise.

B

metro: Spagna; map p.133 E3
For the ultimate view of Rome, head for this café at the top of the Spanish Steps, where you can have light meals and cocktails as the sun sets on the Eternal City.

Enoteca Antica Via della Croce
76b Via della Croce; tel: 06-6790 896; daily noon–midnight; metro: Spagna; map p.133 E3
Dimly lit and generally crowded, this is one of the area's favourite wine bars. Grab a table or squeeze in at the bar and order from their lengthy wine list and savoury bruschetta.

'Gusto
9 Piazza Augusto Imperatore; tel: 06-3226 273; wine bar: daily 11.30am–2am; bus: Piazza Augusto Imperatore; map p.133 D2
A buzzing complex where you can eat a full meal or just go to the wine bar for a drink and snack.
SEE ALSO RESTAURANTS, P.113

The Vatican and Prati
Antonini
19–20 Via G. Sabotino; tel: 06-

For a taste of old-fashioned English style in the heart of the capital, try **Babington's Tea Rooms**. The creaky wood floors, serious black-skirted staff and all-round austere feel are like a trip back in time. The teapots for €11 a person will bring you right back to the present day, and one of the world's most pricey piazzas: 23 Piazza di Spagna; tel: 06-678 6027; map p.133 E3.

3725 052; daily 7am–9pm; bus: 30, 32, 495; map p.132 B4
A luxurious bakery, coffee bar and café, this is the place for melt-in-the-mouth croissants, fancy tarts and sandwiches, or an early evening Prosecco, accompanied by miniature delicacies.

Centro Vini Arcioni
11–13 Via della Giuliana; tel: 06-3973 3205; Mon–Sat 9.30–2am, 4–9pm; bus: 23, 70, 492; map p.132 B3
While technically a well-stocked wine shop, Arcioni tops its bar with snacks for the *aperitivo* in late afternoon, as customers sample wines while considering a

purchase or simply pay by the glass.

Pellacchia
103 Via Cola di Rienzo; tel: 06-3210 807; daily 6am–midnight; metro: Lepanto, bus: 23, 30, 81; map p.133 C3
Popular with the nearby RAI production stars and staff, this café and homemade ice-cream parlour has tables flooding the pavement of this shopping boulevard. Hot chocolate and lemon *gelato* are divine.

Piazza Navona and the Pantheon
Le Coppelle
52 Piazza delle Coppelle; tel: 06-3497 404620; daily 6.30pm–2am; bus: Corso Rinascimento; map p.132 D2
Centrally located, with a great line in cocktails. Outdoor seating in summer and a cosmopolitan vibe.

Enoteca Capranica
99–100 Piazza Capranica; tel: 06-6994 0992; Mon–Fri 12.30–3.30pm, 7.30–10.30pm (kitchen closes), Sat 7.30–10.30pm; bus: Piazza San Silvestro, Largo Argentina; map p.133 D1
The wine list is triple the delicious, and while dishes are delicious, wine is the real deal at this historic wine bar and restaurant. Ask the expert sommelier staff for the perfect pairing with your meal, or simply to suggest a good bottle.

Giolitti
40 Via Uffici del Vicario, Pantheon; tel: 06-6991 243; daily 7am–1am; bus: Largo Argentina; map p.133 D2
Grandma Bernardina established the Giolitti brand in 1890 by seating her eight *bambini* outside while they ate ice creams, and when passers-by asked her how she managed to raise such beautiful children, she told them it was her milk products

Below: while pasta is most commonly served at dinner, some cafés and *enotecas* serve heartier lunchtime fare.

that did the magic. The old-fashioned ice-cream parlour is a joy to nostalgics, and the countless flavours present a delicious challenge.

Mimi e Coco
72 Via del Governo Vecchio; tel: 06-6821 0845; daily 9.30am–2am; bus: Chiesa Nuova; map p.133 D1

The sounds of jazz, world music and laughter characterise this little café, with tables spilling out onto the narrow street. It is open for all meals of the day, with a good selection of hot and cold plates, coffee service, cocktails and wine.

Cafè Novecento
12 Via del Governo Vecchio; tel: 06-6865 242; Tue–Sat 9am–8pm, Sun 3pm–8pm; bus: Chiesa Nuova, Corso Rinascimento; map p.133 C1

Escape for a delicate lunch or afternoon tea in this prim little teahouse and café. Tasteful artwork, fresh flowers and antique furniture, along with a cool, bohemian staff, make this place one of a kind.

Bar Sant'Eustachio
82 Piazza Sant'Eustachio; tel: 06-6861 309; daily 8.30am–1am; bus: Largo Argentina, Corso Rinascimento; map p.133 D1

Widely regarded as the city's best espresso, the *gran caffè*, made from beans roasted on the spot, comes with a sugary foam you can eat with a spoon. For those who like it black, be sure to specify when ordering at the bar.

Tazza D'Oro
84 Via degli Orfani; tel: 06-6792 768; Mon–Sat 7am–8pm; bus: Largo Argentina; map p.133 D1

Serves some of the tastiest coffee in town. Standing room only.

Also at: Casina dei Tre Laghi (EUR).

I Tre Scalini
28–32 Piazza Navona; tel: 06-6868 986; daily: noon–2am; bus: Chiesa Nuova, Corso

Above: the futuristic bar at Supperclub, where you can dine, relax and then party to the small hours *(see Nightlife, p.103 for details).*

Rinascente; map p.133 D1

The home of *tartufo* ice cream sits on Piazza Navona beckoning passers-by to try its famed chocolate truffle. Each of these deep chocolate ice cream bombs is rolled, dipped and infused by hand.

Campo de' Fiori and the Ghetto

Alberto Pica
12 Via della Seggiola; tel: 06-6875 990; Apr–Sept Mon–Sat 8.30am–2am, Sun 4.30pm–2am, Jan–Mar, Oct, Nov Mon–Sat 8.30am–2am; tram: 8; map p.137 D4

The award-winning ice-cream maker has been making *gelato* all his life and is rather better at it than most. People travel from all over Rome to enjoy his superlative ice creams.

Il Goccetto
14 Via dei Banchi Vecchi; tel: 06-6864 268; Mon–Sat 11.30am–2pm, 6.30pm–midnight; bus: San Andrea delle Valle, Corso Vittorio; map p.133 C1

This *enoteca* has been serving good wines and even better cheeses for over two

decades in this medieval bishop's palace with frescoed ceilings. Some 800 different labels are available for sale, of which about 40 can be tasted by the glass.

Lot 87
87 Via del Pellegrino; tel: 06-9761 8344; www.lot87.it; Mon–Sat 7am–midnight; bus: 40, 62, 64; map p.133 C1

For a hot or cold drink, or an innovative cocktail any time of the day or night, head to this modern bar just off Campo de' Fiori. Nurse a drink for as long as you like, and browse the papers and magazines kept in the racks by the door.

Sciam
56 Via del Pellegrino; tel: 06-6830 8957; daily 3.30pm–2am; bus: 40, 62, 64; map p.133 C1

A laid-back Middle Eastern tearoom with a tempting selection of sweet and savoury dishes. You may even be tempted to take a puff of the aromatic hookah pipes.

Via Veneto and Villa Borghese

Caffè delle Arti
73 Via Gramsci; tel: 06-3265 1236; Mon 8am–6pm, Tue–Sat

35

8am–9pm; tram: 2, 19; map p.133 E4

This café in the Villa Borghese's Galleria Nazionale d'Arte Moderna is touted as the finest museum café in Italy. It has a beautiful terrace and a fine interior. Open in the evenings, and also serves Sunday brunch.

SEE ALSO MUSEUMS AND GALLERIES, P.97

Doney

145 Via Veneto; tel: 06-4708 2783; daily 8.30am–2am; metro: Barberini, bus: 80 express; map p.134 A2

The recently revamped Doney harks back to Dolce Vita glamour. A good bet for everything from breakfast to dinner, cocktails and *aperitivi*.

Above: a barman mixes up an *aperitivo*, the Roman way to start an evening.

Trastevere and the Gianicolo

Freni e Frizioni

4–6 Via del Politeama; tel: 06-5833 4210; www.frenifrizioni.com; daily 10am–2am; bus: 23, 280; map p.137 C3

A buzzy bar open for breakfast, lunch and dinner, but most popular for *aperitivi* in the early evening, when the crowds spill out onto the piazza outside.

Friends Art Café

34 Piazza Trilussa; tel: 06-5816 111; Mon–Sat 7.30am–2am, Sun 6.30pm–2am; bus: 23, 280, tram: 8; map p.137 C4

The ever-popular café stays open until late at night. A good place for a quick bite or an expertly mixed cocktail.

Caffè del Gianicolo

5 Piazzale Aurelio; tel: 06-5806 275; Tue–Sat 6am–1am, Sun 6am–9pm; map p.136 B3

A simple bar on the scenic Gianicolo Hill, where light snacks and fruit-shakes can be consumed indoors and out.

Caffè di Marzio

15 Piazza Santa Maria in Trastevere; tel: 06-5816 095; daily

7am–2am; bus: H, tram: 8; map p.137 C3

The best-priced café in this lovely square. Friendly staff and excellent opportunities for people-watching.

Ombre Rosse

12 Piazza San Egidio; tel: 06-5884 155; Mon–Sat 8am–2am, Sun 6pm–2am; tram: 8; map p.136 C3

The perfect place for a pre-dinner cocktail or a post-dinner drink is this bar in a scenic piazza. It has a lively atmosphere and is open all

The Milan-born tradition of an early evening *aperitivo* accompanied by buffets of savoury edibles has exploded to epic scale in Rome. Gone are the days of humble olives and nuts; opulent spreads now top the counters of even the tiniest bars from around 6 to 8pm each evening. The classic Roman *aperitivo* is bubbly Prosecco; Campari and soda is another best-seller. Otherwise opt for a glass of red or white wine, or the cocktail of your choice.

day from Monday to Saturday and Sunday afternoon.

Bar San Calisto

Piazza San Calisto; no phone; Mon–Sat 5.30am–2am; bus: 780, tram: 8; map p.137 C3

This casual, if a little rough bar and café pulls in a very local crowd during the day and a raucous, young crowd in the late hours.

Stardust

4 Vicolo de Renzi; tel: 06-5832 0875; daily noon–2am; bus: 23, 280, tram: 8; map p.137 C3

Open late, and attracts an arty, trendy crowd.

Trasté

76 Via della Lungaretta; tel: 06-5894 430; daily 5pm–2am; bus: 23, 280, tram: 19; map p.137 C3

Bedecked with low seats and tables and lots of cushions, Trasté serves all kinds of teas, fruit- and milk-shakes as well as alcoholic beverages.

Aventino and Testaccio

Doppio Zero

68 Via Ostiense; tel: 06-5730 1961; Tue–Sat 7.30am–12.30am, Sun dinner only, Mon lunch only; metro: Garbatella,

bus: 23, 271

A chic new café which offers light meals and snacks, as well as a selection of delicious cakes at teatime.

Fata Morgana

36e Via Ostiense; no phone; daily noon–midnight; metro: Piramide

The wildest and healthiest ice cream in town, here you'll find gluten-free ice cream, as well as lactose-free options made with organic ingredients. There's no need for anything artificial with flavours like cream of lavender with wild rice, tobacco-scented dark chocolate, or fennel, liquorice and honey.

Oasi della Birra

41 Piazza Testaccio; tel: 06-5746 122; daily 7pm–12.30am; bus: 23, 30 express, metro: Piramide; map p.137 D1

A popular meeting spot for young Romans, with a choice of more than 500 beers from all over the world.

Il Seme e la Foglia

18 Via Galvani; tel: 06-5743 008; Mon–Sat 8–1.30am, Sun 6.30pm–1.30am; bus: 23, 30 express, metro: Piramide; map

Above: at the weekend, Testaccio's bars are full of preclubbers.

p.137 D1

Trendy spot for an espresso, cappuccino or light lunch.

Celio, Monti and Esquilino

The Fiddler's Elbow

43 Via del Olmata; tel: 06-4872 110; daily 10.30am–2.30pm, 5pm–1am; metro: Cavour; map p.138 B4

A lively Irish pub offering Guinness on tap and reasonable pub food.

Hotel Gladiatori

125 Via Labicana; tel: 06-7759 1380; daily noon–2pm, 4pm–midnight; metro: Colosseo; map p.138 B3

The rooftop bar of this hotel gives you an unparalleled

view of the Colosseum; a charming place for an atmospheric *aperitivo*.

Il Palazzo del Freddo di Giovanni Fassi

65–7 Via Principe Eugenio; tel: 06-4464 740; summer Tue–Sun noon–midnight, winter noon–9pm; metro: Vittorio Emanuele; map p.139 C4

The jazzy interior belies a tradition that dates back to 1890. Fun fruit and chocolate flavours can be specially packaged to take away.

Radisson ES Hotel

171 Via Filippo Turati; tel: 06-444 841; www.rome.radissonsas.com; daily 10am–1am; metro and bus: Termini; map p.134 C1

Here at the rooftop chill-out bar of this luxury hotel, you can sip a cocktail as you lounge on leather sofas and look out onto the streamlined spectacle of Termini Station below.

SEE ALSO HOTELS, P.77

Vineria Monti doc

93 Via Giovanni Lanza; tel: 06-4872 696; Mon–Sat 10–1am; metro: Cavour; map p.138 B4

A great local *enoteca* which serves hot and cold meals.

Below: relax with a typical Roman *aperitivo* of Campari served with a slice of orange, with olives to snack...

Below: or refuel on *espresso* before hitting the streets again.

Catacombs

A ncient Romans have always paid great attention to hygiene, and their strict sanitary laws
provided that no one be buried inside a sacred city
boundary known as the *pomerium*. The designated
areas for burial – tombs, vaults and mausoleums –
were situated outside the city walls, along the
military roads *(vie consolari)* connecting Rome to
the rest of Italy. Later these roads became the site
of the first catacombs built by Christians; from
the 2nd to the 4th century, 40 catacombs were
created by excavating over 300km of tufa rock.
The most important surviving catacombs can be
found on the Via Salaria and on the Via Appia.

A Multi-Level Cemetery

The high cost of land along
the *vie consolari* meant that
the early Roman Christians
were forced to create an
underground network of their
own cemetery tunnels, the
catacombs. The Jews had
their own catacombs, and,
like the Christians, they
interred the bodies without
cremation.

In the 8th century, following the barbarian sackings,
the bodies and reliquaries of
many Christian martyrs previ-
ously buried in the catacombs
were moved to the safer
Roman churches.

The Appian Way

Also known as the 'Queen of
Roads', the Appian Way was
the main route to the Eastern Empire. A walk along
this picturesque road
reveals ancient mausoleums
and vaults, but below lie
miles of subterranean
labyrinthine burial tunnels.
Centuries of looting have left
some of the monuments in a
pretty sorry state, but the
weather-worn tombs con-
tinue to impress.

Catacombs of San Sebastiano

136 Via Appia Antica; tel: 06-
7850 350; Mon–Sat 8.30am–
noon, 2.30–5pm, closed mid-
Nov–mid Dec; entrance charge;
bus: 118, 218, 660; map above
The first of the underground
burial sites to be called a 'catacomb' due to its proximity to
a cave (from the Greek *kata*,
near, and *kymbas*, cave).
There are three exquisitely
preserved mausoleums, and
miles of subterranean galleries
over four levels.

Catacombs of San Callisto

78, 110 and 126 Via Appia
Antica; tel: 06-5130 151;

www.catacombe.roma.it; Mon,
Tue, Thur–Sun 9am–noon,
2–5pm, closed Feb; entrance
charge; bus: 118, 218, 660; map
left
These important catacombs
spread out for over 17km and
are stacked as high as five
levels at some points throughout the structure. The tunnels
house thousands of Christian
bodies, including dozens of
martyrs and 16 popes. The
most ancient crypts, namely
the **Papal Crypt** and the
Crypt of Saint Cecilia, date
back to the 2nd century and

Below: exquisite frescoes in the
Jewish Catacombs.

Left: the eery tunnels of the Catacombe de Priscilla.

Jewish Community to make an appointment, tel: 06-6840 061; bus: 118, 218, 660; map left
The Vigna Randanini Jewish catacomb, discovered in 1859, is only visible with the permission of Rome's Jewish Community. The frescoed walls depict traditional Jewish symbols, such as peacocks, menorahs, fish and leaves. Sadly, many tombstones have been misplaced over the years or stolen by tomb robbers.

Via Salaria

Via Salaria was an important road leading to the Adriatic coast, named after the salt (*sale*) that was transported from the sea to the hills. In the early years of Christianity, many churches and catacombs were built here.

Catacombs of Priscilla
430 Via Salaria; tel: 06-8620 6272; Feb–Dec Tue–Sun 8.30am–noon, 2.30–5pm; entrance charge; bus: 86, 92, 63
Entered through the cloister of a Benedictine monastery, the 13km network of catacombs houses the tombs of seven early popes and numerous martyrs, hence the high-quality frescoes and stucco decorations. The catacombs extend under the park of Villa Ada, which is open to the public.
SEE ALSO PARKS, GARDENS AND BEACHES, P.108

Catacombs of Sant' Agnese
349 Via Nomentana; tel: 06-8610 840; www.santagnese.org; Mon 9am–noon, Tue–Sat 9am–noon, 4–6pm, Sun and religious holidays 4–6pm; entrance charge; bus: 36, 60
Linked to the martyrdom of St Agnes, these catacombs feature miles of decorated tunnels.

An entrance in the park of Villa Torlonia leads to a Jewish catacomb, discovered in 1918 and only recently opened to the public. Ironically, this catacomb lies just underneath the Villa, which was Benito Mussolini's residence during the Fascist period. Jewish Catacombs of Villa Torlonia; 192 Viale Regina Margherita; appointment required, tel: 06-8530 1758; bus: 90; map p.134 C4.

house the remains of at least five martyred popes who reigned between 230 and 283. The elegant decorations were added by Pope Damasus I in the 4th century.

Catacombs of Santa Domitilla

282 Via delle Sette Chiese; tel: 06-5110 342; Mon, Wed–Sun 9am–noon, 2–5pm, closed Jan; entrance charge; bus: 118, 218, 660; map left
These larger, less crowded catacombs owe their name to the fact that they stand in what was once the property of martyred Saint Domitilla, a member of the distinguished Flavian family. The guided

visit is highly recommended as it will prevent you from finding yourself alone in the maze; it starts at the Basilica of Saints Narius and Achilleus. A particularly beautiful tomb bears 4th-century frescoes of Saint Peter and Paul on either side of the dead woman's ghostly black square icon. Under the arch of the tomb, visible only if you kneel, is a Last Supper painted a millennium before Leonardo da Vinci's.

The Jewish Catacombs
119a Via Appia Antica; call the

Below: a detail from a marble sarcophagus at San Sebastiano.

Children

V isiting Rome with children requires good organisational skills: the city is big, and attractions are scattered all over its surface. With careful planning, the city's numerous attractions and events, however, will help to ensure their, and your, happy stay. The city's parks and almost year-round sunny weather allow for picnics and pleasant walks, while child-friendly museums will entertain the whole family. Italians adore children, and they'll go out of their way to see them smile. And do not forget to remind your kids that Rome itself was founded by two children – Romulus and Remus – just like them!

Outdoor Activities

Rome's parks are home to myriad attractions for adults and children alike. **Villa Borghese** is the place to go to combine an open-air day with indoor sightseeing, with galleries, a playhouse, a cinema and Rome's zoo. At **Parco della Caffarella** you'll encounter sheep and horses, whereas **Villa Pamphilj**, **Villa Ada** and **Villa Glori** have pony rentals.

SEE ALSO PARKS, GARDENS AND BEACHES, P.108–10

Bioparco

Villa Borghese; 1 Piazzale del Giardino Zoologico; tel: 06-3608 211; www.bioparco.it; autumn–winter: daily 9.30am–5.30pm, spring–summer and weekends/holidays: 9.30am–7pm; entrance charge; bus: 910, tram: 3, 19

This fairly large zoo is home to all the usual suspects. A farmyard area hosts piglets, sheep, goats and chickens. There's also a picnic area, and a restaurant at the entrance.

Luneur

Via delle Tre Fontane, EUR; tel: 06-5925 933; www.luneur.it; summer: Wed–Thur 3–7pm, Sat

Above: not so much fun for the people waiting in line...

3pm–midnight, Sun 11am–9pm, winter: Wed–Sun 11am–9pm; no entrance charge, prices of rides vary; metro: EUR Magliana or Palasport

Rome's amusement park is not central, but worth knowing about. The 130+ rides and attractions will entertain all ages, and include rollercoaster rides and magic shows.

Pony rides

Flaminia, Villa Glori; Piazzale del Parco della Rimembranza; tel:

> Children who are under 3 feet 3 inches tall travel free on public transportation.

06-85 41 461; Mon–Sun 7am–7pm; bus: 910

Green Villa Glori is the most popular spot for pony rentals.

Parco dei Mostri in Bomarzo

Bomarzo; tel: 07-6192 4029; daily from dawn to dusk; nearest railway statons are Orte and Attigliano

About a half-hour drive from Rome, this 16th-century park was commissioned by a Roman nobleman and owes its fame to large grotesque statues inspired by mythology and fantasy, including dragons and ogres.

Museums and Attractions

Ancient Weapon Museum
50 Lungotevere Castello, Vatican and Prati; tel: 06-6875 036; www.castelsantangelo.com; Tue–Sun 9am–7pm; no entrance charge for children; guided tours in English, Sun from 9.30am, tel: 06-3996 7600; bus 40; map p.132 C2

An authentic arsenal containing weapons from prehistory to the 1800s.

Auditorium
17 Viale de Coubertin, Flaminia; tel: 06-8024 1281; www.

Left: the Colosseum should fire the imagination.

p.134 B2

During performances, the theatre offers babysitting services for children 6–11, who take part in a creative workshop on theatre, music and games, while their parents enjoy the show.
SEE ALSO MUSIC, THEATRE AND DANCE, P.101

Technotown
Villa Torlonia, 1 Via Spallanzani; tel: 06-8205 9127; www.techno town.it; Mon 7pm–midnight, Tue–Sun 10am–midnight; no entrance charge; bus: 90; map p.134 D4

A multimedia playhouse for older kids, including fun exhibits about robotics and 3D photography.

Time Elevator
20 Via SS Apostoli; tel: 06-9774 6243; www.time-elevator.it; daily screenings 11am–7.30pm; entrance fee; metro: Spagna; map p.133 E1

A cinematic roller-coaster ride through history with famous protagonists (such as Nero and Michelangelo) playing major parts. A cheesy but fun introduction to the city.

Wax Museum
67 Piazza SS Apostoli; tel: 06-6796 482; daily 9am–8pm; entrance charge; metro: Spagna; map p.133 E1

Over 250 wax statues, including actors, history characters and football stars.

Zoology Museum
18 Via Aldrovandi, north of Villa Borghese; tel: 06-6710 9279; www.museodizoologia.it; Tue–Sun 9am–5pm; entrance charge; bus: 910, tram: 3, 19

Some children find it scary, others just love it; the show-cases in this museum display animal skeletons, embalmed and stuffed animals, and there's an area dedicated to animal habitats.

Most restaurants do not have special menus for kids, but don't be shy to ask any restaurant to prepare a simple plate of spaghetti with tomato sauce or cheese. Restaurant staff members often work extra hard to please their little customers.

auditorium.com; metro: Flaminio, bus: M from Termini, tram: 2

In winter, this important arts complex features musical shows for children and families. The Auditorium also offers babysitting services during performances.
SEE ALSO MUSIC, THEATRE AND DANCE, P.100

Casina di Raffaello
Viale della Casina di Raffaello (Piazza di Siena), Villa Borghese; tel: 06-3996 7800; www.casina diraffaello.it; daily 9am–7pm; entrance charge; metro: Flaminio

A playhouse for 3–10-year-olds, featuring a fake forest, and an elegant 1700s room.

Explora-Il Museo dei Bambini
82 Via Flaminia; tel: 06-3613 776; www.mdbr.it; Tue–Sun 9.30am–7pm; visits by prior booking on weekends, four slots daily; entrance fee; metro: Flaminio, bus: 88, 495, tram: 2, 19

Rome's only children's museum. With four sections dedicated to humans, the environment, communications and society, there are plenty of signs and materials in English. Kids can star in their own TV show and have fun with the interactive displays.

Teatro dell'Opera
1 Piazza Beniamino Gigli, Esquilino; tel 06-481 601; www.operaroma.it; metro: Repubblica, bus: 40, 60, 70; map

Below: Villa Borghese has plenty to entertain the family.

41

Churches

Rome is a city of churches; over 400 are crammed inside its boundaries. Often built on the site of, or incorporating the remains of ancient Roman temples and buildings, few churches can be said to date from one single period. As the Roman Church gained power and status, so its churches became more opulent with sculptures, frescoes, plasterwork and marble adornments to rival the most distinguished museum. There are too many churches to list here in full, so we have provided a list of those we think most historically important or architecturally noteworthy.

The Capitoline Hill

Santa Maria in Aracoeli
Scala dell'Arca Capitolina; daily 9am–12.30pm, 3–6.30pm; bus: Piazza Venezia; map p.137 E4
Built on the site of the ancient Temple of Juno Moneta, there are records of a church here as early as AD 574. The present building was constructed by Franciscans around 1250, although the columns date from much earlier. Highlights include a striking Cosmatesque floor and an ornate coffered ceiling dating from 1572–5. Renaissance frescoes by Pinturicchio from the life of St Bernard can be found in the first chapel on the right. The recent restoration of the Chapel of San Pasquale Baylon brought to light some beautiful 13th-century frescoes concealed behind lesser 16th-century works.

The Quirinale

Sant'Andrea al Quirinale
29 Via del Quirinale; daily 8.30am–noon, 3.30–7pm, Sun 9am–noon, 4–7pm; bus: Via Nazionale; map p.134 A2
This architectural masterpiece is the work of Bernini, whose genius can be seen throughout. Light from the clerestory windows illuminates the glorious white-and-gold stucco work of the dome and the richly coloured inlaid marble of the walls and floor.

San Carlo alle Quattro Fontane
23 Via del Quirinale; www.san carlino-borromini.it; daily 10am–1pm, 3–6pm, Sun noon–1pm; metro: Barberini, bus: Via Nazionale; map p.134 A2
This tiny church was designed by Bernini's arch-rival, Borromini (1599–1667). Often referred to as San Carlino (little San Carlo), its concave and convex surfaces illustrate Borromini's ingenuity at creating the illusion of space in an awkwardly shaped site. His love for illusion is evident throughout the structure, most notably in the oval dome, designed to give the feel of extra height, and the cloister, which is actually rectangular but appears octagonal.

Piazza di Spagna and Tridente

Santa Maria del Popolo
12 Piazza del Popolo; tel: 06-

Above: funerary monument at Santa Maria del Popolo.

3610 836; Mon–Sat 7am–noon, Sun 8am–7.30pm; metro: Flaminio; map p.133 D3
The 15th-century church of Santa Maria del Popolo is packed with Renaissance masterpieces. The biggest attractions are the two paintings by Caravaggio, *The Conversion of St Paul* and *The Crucifixion of St Peter*, but also worth seeking out are the beautifully detailed frescoes by Pinturicchio, and Guillaume de Marcillat's exquisite stained glass inside the Bramante-designed apse. The small Chigi Chapel was designed by Raphael for influ-

Left: Rome's skyline is scattered with churches.

Dyck crucifix in the sacristy (you need to ask to see it).

The Vatican

Basilica di San Pietro

Piazza San Pietro; www.vatican.va; 06-6988 1662; daily 7am–7pm, until 6pm in winter (no bare legs or shoulders); charge for dome and sacristy; metro: Ottaviano, bus: Piazza Risorgimento; map p.132 A2–B2

Built on the site of St Peter's martyrdom by the Emperor Constantine in around AD 333, the original church was lavishly decorated with mosaics, paintings and statuary, but by the Renaissance it had become dilapidated. In 1506, Pope Julius II commissioned Bramante, the first of a string of architects, to build a new church, but it was almost a century and a half before it was completed. The resulting building is a phenomenal architectural achievement, though it inevitably suffered from the competing visions of all the master architects called in to collaborate.

Michelangelo's 119m high **dome** was inspired by both the Pantheon in Rome and Brunelleschi's dome in Florence. The entrance (daily 8am–6pm, until 5pm in winter, closed during ceremonies; entrance charge) is on the right of the portico. A lift takes you part of the way to the top, the long climb up the remaining 320 steps is rewarded by extensive views across the city.

Inside the basilica, turn right for *La Pietà*, Michelangelo's remarkable statue of the Madonna and dead Christ, which he sculpted in 1499 when only 25. It is an incredibly moving work and the only one Michelangelo ever signed.

In a side street next to the church of Santa Maria in Via Lata (map p.133 E2), which has an impressive façade by da Cortona, is one of Rome's 'talking' fountains, the *facchino* (or water-bearer).

In the days before freedom of speech, the *facchino* and other 'talking statues' were hung with satirical and subversive messages and fulfilled much the same function as a newspaper.

ential banker Agostino Chigi, who commissioned numerous works of art and architecture, including the Villa Farnesina *(see p.98)*. Mosaics in the dome depict God creating the solar system and Chigi's astrological chart. The chapel was completed by Bernini, who added two of his characteristic statues, one of Daniel and one of Habakkuk.

San Lorenzo in Lucina

16a Piazza San Lorenzo in Lucina; tel: 06-6871 494; daily 8am–8pm; bus: Via del Corso or Via del Tritone; map p.133 D2

In a small square about halfway down Via del Corso, this 12th-century church contains some busts by Bernini, and a grille, rumoured to be the very spot where the martyr St Lawrence was burnt to death for his refusal to hand over Church riches to the Roman city government.

San Marcello al Corso

5 Piazza San Marcello; Mon–Fri 7am–noon, 4–7pm, Sat 10am–noon, 4–7pm, Sun 8.30am–noon, 4–7pm; bus: Via del Corso, Piazza Venezia; map p.133 E1

Further along the Corso towards Piazza Venezia, this is another noteworthy church, which has a Van

Below: Michelangelo's glorious dome in St Peter's Basilica.

Above: Santa Maria sopra Minerva's chapel fescoes.

Halfway down the nave, the 13th-century statue of St Peter by Arnolfo di Cambio is so widely venerated that its foot, kissed by devout pilgrims for over seven centuries, is almost worn away.

In the centre of the basilica, directly under the dome is Bernini's *baldacchino* (1633), commissioned by the Barberini Pope Urban VIII. This huge bronze canopy (the largest free-standing bronze structure in the world) rises 26m over the holiest part of the church, the legendary tomb of St Peter.

To the right of the *baldacchino*, stairs lead down to the **grottoes** (daily 7am–7pm, until 6pm in winter) containing the tombs of several popes, including that of the recently deceased Pope John Paul II.

Don't miss the ghoulish **tomb of Alexander VII**, another of Bernini's patrons, to the left of the transept. Just above the door is Bernini's last work, representing a skeletal allegory of death clutching an hourglass.

Piazza Navona and the Pantheon

Santa Maria sopra Minerva

Piazza della Minerva; www. basilicaminerva.it; Mon–Sat 7am–7pm, Sun 8am–7pm; bus:

Largo Argentina; map p.133 D1 Santa Maria sopra Minerva is the only truly Gothic church in Rome. It was built in the 8th century on the site of a Temple of Minerva, but its present form dates from around 1280 when it was rebuilt by Dominicans. The church's most striking feature is the beautiful, Giotto-blue vaulted ceiling.

The tombs of several popes and cardinals are housed here, as are the relics of St Catherine of Siena (the patron saint of Italy who died in the Dominican convent here in 1380). The main treasures date from the Renaissance and include a fresco of *The Assumption* by Filippino Lippi, situated in the last chapel on the right. To the left of the altar stands a Michelangelo sculpture of *Christ the Redeemer*, whose nudity shocked the Church at the time, so much so that a bronze loincloth was ordered to cover his modesty.

San Luigi dei Francesi

Piazza San Luigi dei Francesi; daily 10am–12.30pm and 2.30–7pm, closed Thur pm; bus: Corso Vittorio, Largo Argentina; map p.133 D1

Built in 1589, this is the French national church in Rome. It contains works by

Papal audiences are held in the Vatican on Wednesday at 10.30am, except in the height of summer, when they are at his summer residence at Castelgandolfo outside Rome. Apply for free tickets in writing to the Prefettura della Casa Pontifica, 00120 Città del Vaticano, or go to the office on the preceding Monday or Tuesday (it's through the bronze door watched over by Swiss Guards, to the right of the basilica). For more information, tel: 06-6988 4857.

Giacomo della Porta and Domenico Fontana, but it is the three Caravaggio masterpieces (painted between 1599 and 1602) in the Capella Contarelli that make a visit worthwhile. Showing scenes from the life of St Matthew (*The Calling of St Matthew*, *The Martyrdom of St Matthew* and *St Matthew and the Angel*) these wonderful and moving paintings demonstrate Caravaggio's astounding mastery of light and dramatic realism. Have a euro handy to light the chapel up.

Sant'Agnese in Agone

Piazza Navona; www.santagnese inagone.org; daily 9am–noon, 4–7pm, Sun 10am–1pm, 4–8pm; bus: Corso Vittorio; map p.133 D1

Below: the candle-lit Corpus Domini procession passes through the streets of Rome each year, 60 days after Easter.

Borromini's imposing Baroque church commands attention away from Bernini's sumptuous fountains on Piazza Navona. Here, it is said, the adolescent St Agnes was pilloried and stood naked in the stocks until her hair miraculously grew to protect her from prying eyes. Inside the church there are underground chambers where you can see the ruins of the Stadium of Domitian, a Roman mosaic floor and medieval frescoes.

Above: Bernini's *Ecstasy of St Teresa* depicts the saint just as her heart is pierced by an arrow from heaven.

Campo de' Fiori and the Ghetto

Sant'Andrea della Valle
Corso Vittorio Emanuele II; daily 7.30am–noon, 4.30–7.30pm, Sun 7.30am–12.45pm, 4.30–7.45pm; bus: Largo Argentina; map p.137 D4

This cavernous Baroque church has the second-largest dome in Rome after St Peter's. Designed largely by Maderno, it contains frescoes by Lanfranco and Domenichino, and is the setting for Act I of Puccini's much-loved opera *Tosca*. The church stands over some of the remains of the Teatro di Pompeo, a huge complex built in 55 BC that spread from Campo de' Fiori to the temples at Largo Argentina. You can ask one of the priests to take you downstairs for a look.

Il Gesù
43 Piazza del Gesu, daily 6.45am–12.45pm, 4–7.45pm; bus: Largo Argentina; map p.137 D4

Rome's first Jesuit church, more properly called Santissimo Nome di Gesù, was built between 1568 and 1584 with funds provided by the rich and powerful Cardinal Alessandro Farnese. The flamboyance of its design and decoration look forward to the Baroque churches of the next century. The founder of the Jesuit Order, St Ignatius Loyola, is buried in the opulent Cappella di Sant'Ignazio di Loyola, built by Andrea del Pozzo in 1696. A statue of the saint, framed by gilded lapis lazuli columns, can be seen above the chapel's altar.

Via Veneto and Villa Borghese

Santa Maria della Concezione
27 Via Vittorio Veneto; www.cappucciniviaveneto.it; tel: 06-4871 185; daily, church: 7am–noon, 3–7pm, crypt: 9am–noon, 3–6pm; donation expected; metro: Piazza Barberini, bus: Piazza Barberini, Via del Tritone, Via Veneto; map p.134 A2

At the southern end of the Via Veneto, this Baroque church also goes by the name of *I Cappuccini* (The Capuchins) and has been the home of the Capuchin Order in Rome since 1631.

It has two noteworthy paintings: *The Archangel Michael Slaying the Devil* by Guido Reni and *St Paul's Sight Being Restored* by Pietro da Cortona. But the main draw is in the crypt, which contains the bones and skulls of 4,000 Capuchin friars, ornately displayed *(see box, p.46)*.

Santa Maria della Vittoria
17 Via XX Settembre; Mon–Sat 8.30am–noon, 3.30–6pm, Sun 3.30–6pm; metro: Repubblica, bus: Barberini; map p.134 B2

Begun by Carlo Maderno in 1605, Santa Maria della Vittoria contains Bernini's famous Baroque Cornaro side-chapel, which uses natural lighting effects to highlight the *Ecstasy of St Teresa*, a sculpture of Teresa of Avila, one of the great saints of the Counter-Reformation. Portrayed with open mouth and half-closed eyes at the climax of her vision of Christ, the sculpture has prompted many writers and critics over the centuries to suggest that the love she is experiencing may not be entirely divine.

North of the City

Sant'Agnese fuori le Mura
349 Via Nomentana; www.santagnese.net; tel: 06-861 0840; church: daily 7.30am–noon, 4–7.30pm, catacombs and mausoleum: Mon 9am–noon,

Tue–Sat 9am–noon, 4–6pm; charge for catacombs; bus: 30, 60, 84, 90, 93

This important early Christian church was built over the site of the tomb of St Agnes (martyred in AD 304) in the mid-4th century by Princess Constantina, daughter of the Emperor Constantine. It was rebuilt by Pope Honorius I in the 7th century. The relics of St Agnes are housed in the high altar. Every 21 January, the saint's day, two lambs are blessed and shorn to make woollen robes for the Pope.

The adjoining catacombs are remarkably well preserved. SEE ALSO CATACOMBS, P.39

Trastevere

Santa Maria in Trastevere

Piazza Santa Maria in Trastevere; tel: 06-5814 802; daily 7am–9pm; bus: H, 780, tram: 8; map p.137 C3

The church of Santa Maria in Trastevere is reputedly the oldest in the city. Its foundation can be traced to the 3rd century, but the present structure dates from 1130–43, although the portico was added in 1702. The 12th- and 13th-century mosaics, both inside and outside the church,

are spectacular, and it is worth taking a pair of binoculars to enjoy their details. *The Life of the Virgin* series is by Cavallini (1291). Also worthy of note are the 21 granite columns which divide the nave from the aisles. These were taken from classical buildings including the Baths of Caracalla *(see p.27)*.

San Francesco a Ripa

Piazza di San Francesco d'Assisi; daily 7.30am–1pm, 4–7pm; bus: 780, H, tram: 8; map p.137 C2

Dedicated to St Francis, who stayed in a convent near here, this church is best known for Bernini's quasi-erotic statue of Ludovica Albertoni. Born into a wealthy family, this little-known saint spent her fortune and ruined her health caring for the poor. Her ecstatic expression is reminiscent of his more famous statue of St Teresa in Santa Maria della Vittoria *(see p.45)*.

Santa Cecilia in Trastevere

22 Piazza di Santa Cecilia; tel: 06-5899 289; daily 9.30am–12.30pm, 4–6.30pm, frescoes: Mon–Sat 10.15am–12.15pm; bus: H, 780, tram: 8; map p.137 D3

Nestling in a quiet and secluded part of Trastevere,

Beneath Santa Maria della Concezione *(see p.45)* is an extraordinary crypt which contains the bones of 4,000 monks laid in intricate patterns and tableaux. The origins of this death cult are unclear. The church says that when French Capuchin friars came to Rome they found a shortage of burial space and created this monument. There is also the legend of 'a half-mad monk with time on his hands and a certain passion for tidiness'.

this church is dedicated to the martyr St Cecilia, traditionally regarded as the inventor of the organ and the patron saint of music. Condemned to death for her faith in 230, she was to have been executed by means of suffocation; when this failed, an executioner was despatched to behead her, but she survived the designated three strokes of the axe, living for a further three days. In 1599, her tomb was opened and her body was found in a miraculous state of preservation. The artist Maderno made a beautiful statue of the saint which can be seen

Below: the mosaiced facade of Santa Maria in Trastevere.

beneath the high altar. The adjoining monastery hosts the exquisite frescoes by Cavallini.

Aventino and Testaccio

Santa Maria in Cosmedin
18 Piazza Bocca della Verità; tel: 06-678 1419; daily 9.30am–5.50pm; bus: Circo Massimo; map p.137 D3

First built in the 6th century, with additions made through-out the centuries, the church is a lovely mixture of early Christian, medieval and Romanesque design. The floors were replaced with stunning Cosmati pave-ments, and a belltower was erected in the 12th century. You'll find a Roman bathtub on the altar, used for bap-tisms, and an 8th-century mosaic in the sacristy. Most tourists, however, flock here to stick their hand in the **Boccà della Verità** or Mouth of Truth, which is in the church portico. Legend has it that if you tell a lie while your hand is in the mouth, it will be bitten off.

Santa Sabina and Sant'Alessio
Piazza Pietro d'Illiria; daily 7am–12.30pm, 3.30–7pm; bus: 81, 122, 160, 175, 628, 715; map p.137 D2

This early Christian basilica was built in the 5th century by a priest from Dalmatia, Peter of Illyria, on the site of the house of a martyred Roman matron called Sabina. The broad nave is lined with elegant Corinthian columns, relics of a temple which once stood here. The west door, made of carved cypress wood, depicts biblical scenes, including the earliest known representation of the Crucifixion.

Next door, the church of **Sant'Alessio** has a fine Romanesque *campanile* (bell-

Above: Santa Maria in Trastevere.

tower). A pretty courtyard leads into a Baroque interior with a gilt-covered relic of a staircase, beneath which the poverty-stricken St Alexis is said to have lived and died.

Santa Prisca
11 Via di Santa Prisca; daily 7.30am–noon, 4.30–6.30pm; bus: Santa Prisca; map p.137 E2

This church at the foot of the Aventine Hill is said to occupy the site of a 3rd-century house belonging to Prisca and Aquila, who invited St Peter to dine here. Beneath the church are the remains of a Mithraeum, a grotto to the ancient god Mithras.

San Saba
20 Piazza G. Bernini; tel: 06-5743 352; daily 8.30am–noon, 4.30–7pm; bus: Santa Prisca; map p.138 A1

The pretty 10th-century church of San Saba was

> Rome is an open-air museum, as the government-sponsored 'Tridente' project acknow-ledges. The 'Tridente' refers to the three roads (Corso, Babuino, Ripetta) radiating out from the exquisitely asymmet-rical Piazza del Popolo, taking in the areas' sites, churches and *palazzi*. Maps, leaflets on churches, and suggested itiner-aries can be found at Palazzo Doria Pamphilj.

founded in the 7th century by exiled Palestinian monks. A selection of ancient sculp-tural fragments is displayed in its portico, and the interior has some Cosmatesque work and remains of a 13th-century fresco of St Nicolas.

Celio, Monti and Esquilino

San Giovanni in Laterano
4 Piazza San Giovanni in Later-ano; tel: 06-6988 6433; daily 7am–6.30pm; bus: San Gio-vanni, tram: 3; map p.138 C2

Founded by Constantine the Great, a church has stood on this spot since 313, though it has burnt down twice and been rebuilt several times. The resulting basilica is a mixture of styles from the exquisite 4th-century baptis-tery to the majestic Baroque interior. The east façade, through which you enter, is the work of Alessandro Galilei (1732–5), and Fontana designed the north façade when he was rebuilding the Lateran Palace *(see p.105)*. The central doorway has the original **bronze doors** taken from the Roman Curia of the Forum. The façade is crowned by 15 huge statues of Christ and the Apostles, visible for miles around. Most of the marble-clad interior is the result of remodelling by Borromini (1646), but some of the works of art and church furnishings are far older. They include a fragment of fresco attributed to Giotto (1300) and a 14th-century Gothic *baldacchino* from which only the Pope is allowed to cele-brate Mass. The nave's gilded wooden ceiling was com-pleted in 1567. Also of note are the peaceful 13th-century cloisters *(see box, p.48)*.

The **Battistero Lateran-ense** (Baptistry; daily 8am–12pm, 4–7pm) was part of the original complex, built by Constantine around 320; it was rebuilt in its present octagonal shape in the 5th century. The chapels of San Giovanni Evangelista (St John the Evanglist) and Santi Rufina e Secunda (the original entrance) contain a series of exquisite 5th-century mosaics.

Santi Quattro Coronati
20 Via dei SS Quattro; tel: 06-7047 5427; daily 9am–noon, 4.30–6pm; bus: San Giovanni, tram: 3; map p.138 B3

Originally part of the fortress that protected the Lateran Palace, the 'Four Crowned Saints' belongs to a community of silent Augustine nuns. The present church, built over the remains of a much larger 4th-century edifice, dates from the 11th century.

You will need to ring a bell and ask a kind-hearted nun for the key if you want to see the beautiful 12th-century cloisters, or the Chapel of San Silvestro. This 13th-century chapel contains an endearing fresco illustrating the conversion of Constantine to Christianity by St Sylvester (who was Pope at the time). A mosaic depicts St Helena's discovery of the True Cross, which she found at the same time as the Scala Santa (see p.26).

San Clemente
108 Via S. Giovanni in Laterano; tel: 06-7740 021; www.basilica sanclemente.com; Mon–Sat 9am–12.30pm, 3–6pm, Sun noon–6pm; entrance charge; metro and bus: Colosseo, tram: 3; map p.138 B3

The basilica of San Clemente is one of Rome's most fascinating churches, with some of the finest mosaics and frescoes in the city. Run by an order of Irish Dominicans, it is in fact two churches, one built on top of the other, beneath which are even earlier remains. The present church dates from the 12th century and is built in basilica form, with three naves divided by ancient columns. The apse features a beautifully detailed mosaic depicting the cross as the Tree of Life.

The Chapel of St Catherine has some lovely early Renaissance frescoes depicting the life of St Catherine of Alexandria by Masolino (1383–1447) and Masaccio (1401–28).

To the right nave a staircase leads down to a 4th-century church, with fine 11th-century frescoes of miracles being performed by St Clement, the fourth pope.

An ancient stairway leads deeper underground to a Roman alley and a maze of damp corridors and eerie chambers. Down here is the earliest religious structure on the site, a 2nd-century **Temple of Mithras**, dedicated to the Persian god whose cult spread to Rome.

Santa Maria in Domnica
10 Via della Navicella; tel: 06-7001 519; daily 8.30am–12.30pm, 4.30–7pm; bus: 81, 673; map p.138 B2

The cloisters (daily 9am–6pm) of San Giovanni in Laterano are the star of any tour of the basilica. Completed around 1230, they are the work of Jacopo and Pietro Vassalletto, supreme masters of the Cosmatesque school of mosaic work. The columns are inlaid with chips of coloured glass and marble, which were plundered from ancient remains.

In the apse of this 9th-century church is a magnificent mosaic of the Virgin and Child surrounded by saints and angels in a garden of paradise – the man on his knees at the Virgin's feet is Pope Paschal I, who commissioned the mosaic.

Santi Giovanni e Paolo
13 Piazza Santi Giovanni e Paolo; tel: 06-7005 745; daily 8.30am–noon, 3.30–6.30pm; metro: Circo Massimo, bus: Celio; map p.138 A3

The first church on this site was built in the 4th century, but the present building is mainly 12th-century, with an early 18th-century interior. The 13th-century belltower was built into the remains of a

Below: Roman children take a break after a visit to the church of San Clemente.

Left: 9th-century mosaic in the church of Santa Prassede.

2456; www.santaprassede.org; daily 7.30am–noon, 4–7pm; metro: Termini, bus: Termini, Via Cavour; map p.134 B1

South of Santa Maria Maggiore lies the church of Santa Prassede, built by Pope Paschal I in the 9th century. He commissioned mosaic-workers from Byzantium to decorate the apse, the triumphal arch and the chapel of San Zeno, reintroducing an art that had not been practised in Rome for three centuries – with stunning results.

San Pietro in Vincoli

4 Piazza di San Pietro in Vincoli; tel: 06-488 2865; daily 8am–noon, 3–7pm; metro and bus: Cavour; map p.138 A4

The church of St Peter in Chains was founded in the 5th century as a shrine for the chains said to have bound St Peter during his imprisonment in Jerusalem. They are preserved in a bronze-and-crystal reliquary beneath the high altar. Over the centuries the church was rebuilt and restored many times, but the ancient Doric columns lining the nave remained. The church is also home to Michelangelo's monumental Moses, part of the unfinished tomb that the artist was preparing for Pope Julius II.

Temple of Claudius. The church also gives access to the remains of houses dating back to the 1st century AD (13 Via Chiavio di Scauro; Thur–Mon 10am–1pm and 3–6pm; entrance charge).

San Gregorio Magno

1 Piazza di San Gregorio Magno; tel: 06-7008 227; daily 9am–12.30pm, 3–6.30pm; metro and bus: Circo Massimo, tram: 3; map p.138 A2

Founded by St Gregory in the 6th century, the church is run by Benedictine monks. Inside, the medieval chapels of Santa Barbara and Sant'Andrea are of particular interest, the latter with frescoes by Guido Reni and Domenichino. The chapel of St Sylvia dates from the 17th century.

Santa Maria Maggiore

Piazza Santa Maria Maggiore; www.vatican.va; tel: 06-483 195; daily 7am–7pm; metro: Termini, bus: Cavour; map p.134 B1

According to legend, in August of AD 352, following a vision of the Virgin Mary, Pope Liberius witnessed a snowfall on the summit of the Esquiline Hill. To commemorate the miracle he built the basilica of Santa Maria Maggiore.

The church is the only one of the four patriarchal basilicas in Rome to have retained its paleo-Christian structures. The 18th-century Baroque façade gives no indication of the building's true antiquity, but step inside and its venerable origins become apparent. The striking ceiling and elaborate chapels are 16th- and 17th-century additions, but the mosaics that decorate the triumphal arch and the panels high up on the nave walls date from the 5th century. To the right of the main altar is the burial place of Bernini, Rome's Baroque genius.

Santa Prassede

9 Via Santa Prassede; tel: 06-488

From Santa Maria in Domnica, turn left to reach Via di San Paolo della Croce, which is straddled by the dramatic 1st-century AD **Arco di Dolabella**, part of Nero's great aqueduct *(see p.27)*. Next to the arch, the gateway of **San Tommaso in Formis** is decorated with a 13th-century mosaic showing Christ with two freed slaves, one black and one white.

Essentials

R ome is an Italian city to its core, with a laid-back attitude to just about everything; rather than waste your precious holiday time once you've arrived, it's best to come prepared – book accommodation before you arrive if possible, make copies of important documents in case of emergencies, and find out what's going on during your stay (www.romaturismo.it is an excellent resource) to make the most of your visit. Equip yourself with essential information on money, health and phoning home, and you'll be free to relax and enjoy one of the greatest cities in the world.

Business Hours

In general shops open Mon–Sat 9am–1pm and 3.30–7.30pm. Many shops and restaurants close for two weeks in August. Churches generally open 7am–7pm with a three-hour lunch break. Banks open Mon–Fri 8.30am–1.30pm and 2.45–4pm; a few in the city centre also open Saturday morning. State and city museums are closed on Monday, but there are a few exceptions: the Colosseum, the Roman Forum and the Imperial Fora, and the Vatican Museums.

Crime and Safety

The main problem tourists experience in Rome is petty crime: pickpocketing and bag-snatching, together with theft from parked cars. Leave money and valuables in the hotel safe. If you are carrying a handbag, keep it on the side away from the road; one Roman speciality is the motorbike snatch.

Report a theft *(furto)* to the police as soon as possible: you will need the police report

for any insurance claim and to replace stolen documents. For information on the nearest police station call the central station, the Questura Centrale, 15 Via San Vitale, tel: 06-4686 1.

Disabled Travellers

Rome is a difficult city for people with disabilities. However, things are improving, and the following attractions have installed ramps and lifts: the Vatican Museums, Galleria Doria Pamphilj, Castel Sant' Angelo, Palazzo Venezia, St Peter's and Galleria Borghese. For more information, contact

Below: cards are accepted in the majority of shops in the city.

Roma Per Tutti (tel: 06-5717 7094, www.romapertutti.it), an English-speaking general information line.

Embassies and Consulates

If your passport is lost or stolen you will need to obtain a police report and have proof of your identity to get a new one.
Australia
5 Via Antonio Bosio; tel: 06-8527 21; www.italy.embassy.gov.au; map p.135 D4
Britain
80a Via XX Settembre; tel: 06-4220 0001; www.britain.it; map p.134 B3
Canada
30 Via Zara; tel: 06-8544 41; www.canada.it
Ireland
3 Piazza Campitelli; tel: 06-6979 121; www.ambasciata-irlanda.it; map p.137 D4
New Zealand
28 Via Zara; tel: 06-4417 171; www.nzembassy.com

Emergency Numbers:
Police 113, Carabinieri 112,
Fire 115, Ambulance 118

Left: keep a close eye on your possessions...

You need your passport or identification card when changing money. Travellers' cheques are the safest way to carry money, but banks charge a commission for cashing them, and shops and restaurants give unfavourable exchange rates if they accept them at all.

Major credit cards are accepted most places in Rome but are less easy to use in the countryside. Few petrol stations accept credit cards or travellers' cheques.

Automated cash dispensers (ATMs), called *Bancomat*, can be found throughout central Rome.

Postal Services

Post offices are open Mon–Fri 8.30am–1pm; central post offices are generally open in the afternoon, too.

Stamps *(francobolli)* can be bought at many tobacconists *(tabacchi)*. Italian postboxes are red or yellow, but several blue boxes specifically for foreign letters have been set up in the centre. Postboxes have two slots, *per la città* (for Rome) and *tutte le altre destinazioni* (everywhere else). The main post office is in Piazza San Silvestro, just off Via del Corso (Mon–Sat 8am–7pm).

Visas and Passports

EU passport-holders do not require a visa; a valid passport or ID card is sufficient. Visitors from the US, Canada, Australia and New Zealand do not require visas for stays of up to three months; non-EU citizens need a full passport.

Nationals of most other countries do need a visa. This must be obtained in advance from the Italian Consulate.

Banks and most shops are closed on most holidays, and banks may close early on the preceding day.

South Africa
14 Via Tanaro; tel: 06-8525 41; www.sudafrica.it
United States of America
119A Via Veneto; tel: 06-4674 1; www.usembassy.it; map p.134 A3

Health

EU residents are entitled to the same medical treatment as an Italian citizen. Visitors will need to complete an EHIC form (see www.ehic.org.uk for information) before they go. US citizens are advised to take out private health insurance. Canadian citizens are also covered by a reciprocal arrangement between the Italian and Canadian governments.

Chemists *(farmacie)* can easily be identified by a green cross. Farmacia della Stazione, 51 Piazza dei Cinquecento (corner of Via Cavour), tel: 06-488 0019, and Farmacia Piram Omeopatia, 228 Via Nazionale, tel: 06-488 0754, are both open 24 hours.

If you need emergency treatment, call 118 for an ambulance or to get information on the nearest hospital with an emergency department *(pronto soccorso)*. The most central is Ospedale Fatebenefratelli, Isola Tiberina, tel: 06-6837 1. If your child is sick go to the Ospedale Pediatrico Bambino Gesù, 4 Piazza Sant' Onofrio, tel: 06-6859 1.

Money

The unit of currency in Italy is the euro (€), which is divided into 100 cents.

Below: the Vatican even has its own postal service.

Fashion

Rome is a serious contender for the title of Italian fashion capital. Whereas Milan attracts the label hounds, the capital is the place to seek out young designers, original accessories and gorgeous handcraftsmanship. Despite the cornucopia of one-of-a-kind shops, Roman style tends to conform to the latest trends, and catwalk knock-offs are ubiquitous. Savvier shoppers steer clear of retail chains, save for the staples, and snatch up their extras at the boutiques. The listings below focus on the more original aspects of Italian fashion. For information on department stores and intimate apparel, *see Shopping, p.122–3.*

Hey Big Spender

Label-lovers will get their kicks on and around Via dei Condotti in the Tridente, where Prada, Gucci, Armani and associates cluster. Here's a quick reference of all the big names:

Costume National
106 Via del Babuino; tel: 06-6920 0686; www.costume national.com; Mon–Sat 10am–2pm, 3–7pm; metro: Spagna; map p.133 E3

Dolce e Gabbana
51–52 Via dei Condotti; tel: 06-6992 4999; www.dolceegabbana. com; Mon–Sat 10am–7.30pm, Sun 11am–2pm, 3–7pm; metro: Spagna; map p.133 E2
Also at: 93 Piazza di Spagna, tel: 06-6938 0870; map p.133 E2

Fendi
Men: 36–37A & 39–40 Via Borgognona; tel: 06-696 661; www.fendi.com; Mon–Sat 10am–7.30pm; Sun 11am–2pm, 3–7pm; metro: Spagna; map p.133 E2
Women: 419 Largo Goldoni; tel: 06-696 661; Mon–Sat 10am–7.30pm; Sun 11am–2pm, 3–7pm; metro: Spagna; map p.133 D2

Gianfranco Ferrè
70 Piazza di Spagna; tel: 06-6786 797; www.gianfrancoferre.

com; Mon–Sat 10am–7.30pm, Sun 11am–2pm, 3–7pm; metro: Spagna; map p.133 E2

Gianni Versace
26 Via Bocca di Leone; tel: 06-6780 521; www.versace.com; Mon–Sat 10am–7pm; metro: Spagna; map p.133 E2

Giorgio Armani
77 Via dei Condotti; tel: 06-6991 460; www.giorgioarmani.com; Mon–Sat 10am–7pm; metro: Spagna; map p.133 E2

Gucci
8 Via dei Condotti; tel: 06-6790 405; www.gucci.com; Mon–Sat 10am–7pm, Sun 2–7pm; metro: Spagna; map p.133 E2

Max Mara
17–19A Via dei Condotti; tel: 06-6992 2104; Mon–Sat 10am–7.30pm, Sun 11am–7pm; metro: Spagna; map p.133 E2

Prada
90 Via dei Condotti; tel: 06-6790 897; www.prada.com; daily 10am–7pm; metro: Spagna; map p.133 E2

Roberto Cavalli
7A Via Borgognona; tel: 06-6992 5469; ww.robertocavalli.com; Mon 1–7.30pm, Tue–Sat 10am–7.30pm, Sun 11am–7.30pm; metro: Spagna; map p.133 E2
Also at: Just Cavalli, 82–83

Above: pick up something original at a Rome boutique.

Piazza di Spagna; tel: 06-6792 294; map p.133 E2

Tod's
56A–57 Via Fontanella Borghese; tel: 06-6821 0066; www.tods.com; Mon–Sat 10am–7.30pm; metro: Spagna; map p.133 D2

Even in the glitzy boutiques, try your hand at bargaining. If a button is loose, a seam slightly off, or even if you genuinely aren't quite convinced, play it cool and be discreet, and chances are they'll knock off €10–20.

Left: Dolce & Gabbana for the latest tight and shiny fashions.

A glorious mess of boutique brands, including several independent LA brands in summer, and Rome's funky designer of the moment, Patrizia Pepe. Browse shoes and handbags, dresses, jeans and tops, all tossed together as they might in your own closet (don't you wish). The glam quotient runs high, and customers are a bit prissy, but all bets say you won't leave empty-handed.

Leam
5 Via Bocca di Leone; tel: 06-6787 853; Mon 3.30pm–7.30pm, Tue–Sat 10am–7.30pm; metro: Spagna; map p.133 E2
A veritable men's boutique carrying hot labels like Prada, Gucci, Dior and Ralph Lauren in sporty and elegant versions. Shoes and accessories are also available.

Lei
103 Via dei Giubbonari; tel: 06-6875 432; Mon 3.30–7.30pm, Tue–Sat 10am–2pm, 3.30–7.30pm; bus: 30, 40, H, tram: 8; map p.137 C4
An enviable collection of designer clothing and acces-

Two mega outlet centres are located just outside Rome. Castel Romano (tel: 06-5050 050; www.mcarthurglen.it) and Fashion District (www.fashion district.it) offer nearly 200 stores between them, with discounts reaching 70 percent off. Head to the former for big-name designers and the latter for mid-range labels.

Boutiques
For trends, up-and-coming designers, and unique accessories, peruse the boutique and speciality store circuit.

Arsenale
64 Via del Governo Vecchio; tel: 06-6861 380; Mon 3.30–7.30pm, Tue–Sat 10am–7.30pm; bus: 30, 40, 70, Chiesa Nuova; map p.133 D1
Local stylist Patrizia Pieroni's luscious gowns and funky-shaped shoes and handbags are on display in a museum-esque setting.

Gente
277 Via Cola di Rienzo; tel: 06-3211 516; Mon 3.30pm–8pm, Tue–Sat 9.30am–8pm; bus: 23, 81; map p.133 C3
At Gente they've done all the

work for you, rounding up the best of high- and mid-range designers. Big-name Italian labels share space with brands such as T-Bags Los Angeles, Milly, Seven Jeans and Victoria Beckham. The cut-price outlet is located across the street at No. 246.

Girlish
185 Via Salaria; tel: 06-8535 4422; Mon 4–8pm, Tue–Sat 10am–1pm, 4–8pm; tram: 19, bus: 63; map p.134 B4

Below: take your pick from an amazing array of well-made Italian shoes and accessories.

sories, this is the place to go for striking cocktail dresses in black or red and a great selection of D&G shoes. Delicate dresses by Tara Jarmon come in pretty pastels.

Momento
9 Piazza Cairoli; tel: 06-6880 8157; Mon 4–8pm, 10am–8pm; bus: 30, 40, H, tram: 8; map p.137 C4

This long and narrow boutique houses some of the most original designs in clothing, shoes and accessories in the city. Their signature drop-waisted gowns come in brushed cotton and are dyed in rich pastels, or deep royal reds and purples. Designers from Paris and New York are widely featured, and the shoe and bag selection comprises every colour and texture possible. Momento's scarves, hats, and jewellery will keep a discerning eye occupied for hours.

Nuyorica
36/37 Piazza Pollarola; tel: 06-6889 1243; Mon–Sat 10am–7.30pm; bus: 30, 40, San Andrea della Valle; map p.137 D4

Something of a dream closet, the shop stocks clothing and shoes by Singerson Morrison, Chloe and Pucci to name a few. Pricey and extravagant.

Below: in Rome, do as the Romans do and shop.

Above: these Louis Vuitton bags might look like the real thing, but if the price is too good to be true then the goods are too.

Smalto Shoes and Wine
12 Via Urbana; tel: 06-4882 049; Mon–Sat 10am–8pm; metro: Cavour; map p.138 B4

Find relief for sore feet at this innovative wine bar/shoe boutique in Monti. Sip red or white and slip into sexy heels by Courtney Crawford, Rupert Sanderson, Giorgina Godman and René Gutenberg. A smaller department carries unique clothing pieces for men and women. Complimentary wine from 6–8pm.

Tad
155A Via del Babuino; tel: 06-3269 5122; www.taditaly.com; Sun, Mon noon–7.30pm, Tue–Fri 10.30am–7.30pm, Sat 10.30am–8pm; metro: Spagna; map p.133 E3

A concept store featuring boutique brands of clothing, shoes, and accessories for both men and women, home décor, a fusion restaurant, cosmetics counter and salon.

Tempi Moderni
108 Via del Governo Vecchio; Tel: 06-6877 007; daily 10am–1pm, 4–7.30pm; bus: 30, 40, 70; map p.133 C1

An eclectic, closet-like space filled with retro jewellery, comprising 1950s pieces in Bakelite and an array of Art Deco necklaces and bracelets. Imported silk kimonos and embroidered belts are each one-of-a-kind.

Tipimini
89 Via del Pellegrino; tel: 06-6813 5840; Mon–Sat 10am–1.30pm, 3.30–7.30pm; bus: Chiesa Nuova; map p.133 C1

A baby boutique featuring wool caps and scarves, colourful dresses and trousers in whimsical patterns and whisper-soft fabrics, all as cute as they are luxurious.

One way to get your 'designer' goods cheaply is to buy them from the street vendors who populate the city's most touristy thoroughfares and bridges. Of course, they are selling bags that only look like real Prada, Gucci, Fendi and Louis Vuitton numbers, but at a fraction of the price of the original it can be tempting. Bear in mind that trade in counterfeit goods is actually illegal.

Apparel

Angelo di Nepi
28 Via dei Giubbonari; tel: 06-6893 006; www.angelodinepi.it; Mon 12.30–7.30pm, Tue–Sat 9.30am–7.30pm; bus: 30, 40, H, tram: 8; map p.137 C4

The chilli pepper logo is some indication of the extra punch that designer Angelo Di Nepi packs into his designs. A cross between ethnic and elegant, he utilises smooth satins and embroiders with imported fabrics in eye-popping patterns.

Best Seller
96 Via dei Giubbonari; tel: 06-6813 6040; Mon 3.30–7.30pm, Tue–Sat 10.30am–7.30pm; bus: 30, 40, San Andrea della Valle; map p.137 C4

A great place to pick up pieces by popular designers LiuJo, Miss Sixty, Patrizia Pepe and Fiorucci, all mid-range, though fabulously trendy with the twenty- and thirty-something crowd.

David Mayer
168 Via del Corso; tel: 06-6902 2097; Sun, Mon 11am–8pm, Tue–Sat 10am–8pm; bus: Piazza San Silvestro; map p.133 E2

Club music pours from this trendy men's retail store, with

If you've found the dream bag, and haven't got the cash, or more likely need a second opinion, you can ask sales clerks to leave an *acconto*. This can be as little at €10 – it depends on the store – and they'll set your item aside. The only catch is that you must return to pay the rest, or use your *acconto* towards something else in the store.

chunky, square-toed shoes, trousers and shirts with that urban sheen, and streamlined accessories for the fashion-conscious male.

Miss Sixty
143 Via Cola di Rienzo; tel: 06-3212 0046; Mon–Sat 10am–8pm, Sun 10am–1pm, 4–8pm; metro: Lepanto; map p.132 C3

Urban attire with a feminine twist, Miss Sixty is the home of ultra-skinny jeans and accessories to dress them up.

Patrizia Pepe
1 Via Frattina; tel: 06-6784 698; www.patriziapepe.it; daily 10am–8pm; metro: Spagna; map p.133 E2

Young and punky Florentine designer Patrizia Pepe does jeans and casualwear with a clubbish edge.

Pinko
76/77 Via dei Giubbonari; tel: 06-6830 9446; Mon 3–8pm, Tue–Sun 10am–8pm; bus 30, 40, San Andrea della Valle; map p.137 C4

A playful and subtly glamorous shop for women, where everything is just a bit tighter and a bit shinier. Extremely popular with Roman girls.

Shoes and Accessories

AVC
88 Piazza di Spagna; tel: 06-6992 2355; www.avcbyadriana campanile.com; Mon–Fri 10.30am–2.30pm, 3.30–7.30pm, Sat 11am–2.30pm, 3.30–7.30pm, Sun 3.30–7.30pm; metro: Spagna; map p.133 E3

Roman designer Adriana Campanile has an eye for the trends of the moment, and her inspired imitations come at far less painful prices. (Also at: 141 Via Frattina; tel: 06-6790 891; 1 Largo Pollaro; 06-6821 670.)

Casanita
8 Via del Biscione; tel: 06-6880 4918; www.casanita.it; Mon 3–8pm, Tue–Sat 11am–8pm; bus: 30, 40, San Andrea della Valle; map p.133 D1

Below: the area around the Spanish Steps is prime window shopping territory.

Above: in the more upscale area around Piazza Fiume and the beginning of Via Salaria you'll find some pretty clothes shops.

Above: the big names are never hard to find in Rome.

Specialises in soft-knit tops, mini-dresses and oversized tank tops and sweaters. The shoe department is hidden away on the lower level, a crime considering the selection on offer. Flats, ballets, and low chunky heels come in colours you'll find nowhere else: lime green, aubergine, metallic-tints and patent leather.

Fausto Santini
120 Via Frattina; tel: 06-6784 114; www.faustosantini.it; Mon 11am–7.30pm, Tue–Sat 10am–7.30pm, Sun noon–7.30pm; metro: Spagna; map p.133 E2
Simply elegant and feather-light, Fausto Santini shoes for men and women are hand-made and guaranteed original—they produce two

> There's a well-rounded vintage scene in Rome, with most shops clustered along Via del Governo Vecchio, just off Piazza Navona. For an ultra Roman experience, spend the afternoon trying on 1970s leather jackets and boho dresses, and fuel up at one of the street's copious wine bars.

pairs in each size, per design, per store.

Geox
3A Via Frattina; tel: 06-6994 80; www.geox.it; daily 10am–7.30pm; metro: Spagna; map p.133 E2
The patented breathing system keeps feet fresh and dry, and has helped to bring Geox trainers and sporty everyday shoes to the international scene. The shop also carries more elegant styles for men, women and children, with comfort as the constant selling point.
(Also at: 232A Via Nazionale; tel: 06-4814 518; map p.134 1A–B2)

Joseph Debach
19 Vicolo del Cinque, nr Piazza Trilussa; tel: 06-5562 756; www.josephdebach.com; daily 7.30pm–midnight; bus: 23, 280, H, tram: 8; map p.136 C3
A pair of shoes by Joseph Debauch would look just at home on your mantelpiece as on your feet. Artfully designed and interesting to look at, the men's and women's collection is something worth browsing.

Sermoneta
61 Piazza di Spagna; tel: 06-

6791 960; www.sermoneta gloves.com; daily 9.30am–8pm; metro: Spagna; map p.133 E3
Synonymous with gloves for every occasion, Sermoneta's finely crafted pairs come in every colour under the rainbow, and there are amazing new styles each year.

Talarico
52 Via dei Coronari; tel: 06-6813 1717; daily 10am–1pm, 3–7.30pm; bus: 30, 40, 70; map p.133 D1
A tie by Talarico is something beyond luxury. Each one is handcrafted using the finest Italian, French and English fabrics, to create innumerable designs – there are some 2,500 striped versions alone. Made-to-measure designs start at €80.

Temporary Love
9 Via di San Calisto; tel: 06-5833 4772; www.temporarylove.net; Tue–Thur 11am–1pm, 4–8pm, Fri, Sat 11am–1.30pm, 4–8pm; bus: 780, H, tram: 8; map p.133 D3
This gallery-like shop in the Tridente stocks one-of-a-

kind bags and jewellery by local and international art designers.

Handbags

Artigianato del Cuoio
90 Via Belsiana; tel: 06-6784 435; Mon–Sat 9am–8pm; metro: Spagna; map p.133 E2

Take your dream bag design to these nimble-fingered craftsmen and they'll make it a reality. Choose from hundreds of colours, leathers and synthetics, and garnish with clasps and snaps of your choosing.

Coccinelle
255 Via Cola di Rienzo; tel: 06-3241 749; Mon 4–8pm, Tue–Sat 9.30am–8pm; metro: Lepanto, Ottaviano-San Pietro; map p.132 B3

Above: if the boutiques prove too expensive for your wallet, have a browse of Rome's vintage offerings for something truly unique.

Coccinelle's soft leather bags in neutral colours and unique designs provide a classy alternative to the otherwise ubiquitous trends. A tough competitor to fellow bag maker, Furla.

Furla
22 Piazza di Spagna; tel: 06-6920 0363; www.furla.com; Mon–Sat 10am–8pm, Sun 10.30am–8pm; metro: Spagna; map p.133 E3

Sturdy, solid-coloured bags in basic shapes and smooth, clean leather define Furla worldwide, while yearly trends are reflected in their flashier collections. (Also at: 136 Via Tomacelli; tel: 06-6878 230, map p.133 D2; 54–55 Via Nazionale; tel: 06-4870 127, map p.134 1A; 226 Via Cola di Rienzo; tel 06-6874 505; map p.132 B3)

Mandarina Duck
272 Cola di Rienzo; tel: 06-6896 491; www.mandarinaduck.com; Mon 3.30–7.30pm, Tue–Sat 10am–7.30pm; bus: 23, 81; map p.132 B3

Super-resistant, luxury luggage comes in great colours and synthetic fabrics that will last for life. Day bags come in all sizes, with a pleasantly unisex appeal.

Vintage

Abiti Usati
35 Via del Governo Vecchio; tel: 06-6830 7105; Mon–Sat 10am–8pm, Sun noon–8pm; bus: 30, 40. 70; map p.133 C1

Can't afford a new Gucci purse? Sift through the collection of vintage handbags at this haven for big-name brands with that roughed-up, vintage appeal.

Vestiti Usati Cinzia
45 Via del Governo Vecchio; no phone; Mon 10am–8pm, Sun 2–8pm; bus: 30, 40, 70; map p.133 C1

Glittery catsuits and platform boots aside, the men's and women's clothing and accessories from the 1970s are a wonder to behold. Jackets and halter dresses in prime polyester and fabulously tacky sweaters are in mint condition. The shop is an entertaining browse at the very least.

Below: well-made bags, shoes, belts and other leather goods are worth buying.

Festivals

Rome lays on a generous array of cultural festivals, many of them free, particularly in the summer months, and over the past few years the number of arty events and festivals in the capital has almost tripled. The two most established festivals, which grow in scope every year, are the cultural extravaganzas RomaEuropa and Estate Romana, but a host of smaller, independent events – many music-related – mean that visitors are bound to find something going on in the city at any time of the year. Ask at tourist offices or check www.romaturismo.com for details of current events. *See also Music, Theatre and Dance.*

Public Holidays

New Year's Day *(Capodanno)*: 1 Jan; **Epiphany** *(Befana)*: 6 Jan; **Easter** *(Pasqua)*: variable, Mar–Apr; **Easter Monday** *(Pasquetta)*: variable, Mar–Apr; **Liberation Day** *(Anniversario della Liberazione)*: 25 Apr; **May Day** *(Festa del Lavoro)*: 1 May; **Patron Saints of Rome** *(San Pietro e San Paolo)*: 29 June; **Feast of the Assumption** *(Ferragosto)*: 15 Aug; **All Saints' Day** *(Ognissanti)*: 1 Nov; **Immaculate Conception** *(Immacolata Concezione)*: 8 Dec; **Christmas Day** *(Natale)*: 25 Dec; **Boxing Day** *(Santo Stefano)*: 26 Dec.

February

Carnevale
Late Feb/early Mar
Fancy-dress carnival on the streets of Rome.

March/April

La Festa della Primavera
The arrival of spring is marked with a sea of azaleas at the Spanish Steps.

Giornate Fai
Late Mar/early Apr; www.fondoambiente.it
Private churches, monuments and gardens can be visited for one weekend.

Maratona di Roma
Third or fourth Sun in Mar; www.maratonadiroma.it
Rome's marathon begins and ends in Via dei Fori Imperiali.

Easter
Holy Week *(Settimana Santa)* is huge in the Eternal City. The week culminates on Easter morning with the Pope's *Urbi et Orbi* speech.

Il Natale di Roma
21 Apr
Rome celebrates its legendary founding with fireworks, music and other events.

Settimana della Cultura
Late Apr or May; www.beni

culturali.it

Below: RomeEuropa hosts a wide range of events.

'Week of Culture' all over Italy, when entrance is free to all state-run museums and historical sites.

FotoGrafia
Apr–May; www.fotografia festival.it
Rome's International Photography Festival.

May

May Day
1 May
No buses run today. A huge free concert is held in front of San Giovanni in Laterano.

Italian Open Tennis Championship
2 weeks early May; www.internazionaliBNlditalia.it
Major competition at the Foro Italico.

International Horse Show
End of May; www.piazzadisiena. com
Showjumping event at Piazza Siena.

June

Festival delle Letterature
www.festivaldelleletterature.it
Rome's Literature Festival hosts writers in the Basilica di Massenzio throughout June.

Left: there's always something going on in Rome.

www.altaroma.it
A series of fashion shows against historical backdrops.
Concerti all'Orto Botanico
www.assmusrom.it
Concerts of mainly chamber music take place in Trastevere's Botanic Gardens.

September

La Notte Bianca
Sat night mid-Sept; www.lanotte bianca.it
Many museums, clubs, cinemas and shops stay open all night and offer free entrance.
Enzimi
Usually 2 weeks mid-Sept, sometimes Nov; www.enzimi.com
Music, theatre and arts festival with an emphasis on emerging talent and quirky venues.
RomaEuropa
Mid-Sept to at least mid-Nov; www.romaeuropa.net
A cutting-edge event that covers dance, theatre, readings, cinema and music.

October

RomeFilmFest
www.romacinemafest.org
Rome's international festival of cinema.

November

Giornata dei Defunti
2 Nov
On the 'Day of the Dead', the Pope celebrates Mass at the Verano cemetery.

December

Immacolata Concezione
8 Dec
The Immaculate Conception is celebrated around the statue of the Madonna in Piazza di Spagna.
San Silvestro
31 December
New Year's Eve is celebrated with gusto in Rome, with fireworks and free concerts.

Many festivals are linked to the Catholic Church; religious holidays tend to shut down the entire city and are often an excuse for a slap-up feast.

Regular Summer Events

Cosmophonies
June–mid-Sept;
www.cosmophonies.com
Theatre, dance and music performances in the ancient amphitheatre of Ostia Antica.
Estate Romana
June–Sept; www.estateromana.comune.roma.it
Parks and piazzas host concerts, theatre, outdoor cinema and other events.
Fiesta
June–Aug; www.fiesta.it
Festival of Latin American music, with a sprinkling of international rock and pop.
Jazz and Image Festival
June–Aug; www.villacelimontanajazz.com
Jazz musicians take to the stage in Villa Celimontana.
New Opera Festival
Mid-June–mid-Aug; www.newoperafestivaldiroma.com
Classic Italian operas in the atmospheric setting of the Basilica di San Clemente.
Roma Incontra Il Mondo
Mid-June–early Aug; www.villaada.org
This summer music festival takes place in Villa Ada.
Summer Opera
July–Aug; www.opera.roma.it
The Teatro dell'Opera's summer series is generally held in the Baths of Caracalla.

July

Festa de' Noantri
2 weeks from mid-July
Trastevere's lively two-week street festival.
AltaRomAltaModa
5 days mid-July;

Below: the traditional Good Friday Via Crocis procession.

59

Film

Italian cinema was born in Rome in 1905. The country's first feature, *La Presa di Roma* – a dramatic tale of unification – marked the beginning of the Eternal City's enduring love affair with celluloid. Post-war Rome gave birth to Neo-Realism, an influential movement driven by some of the most acclaimed directors of our time – Rossellini, de Sica and Fellini – bringing a sense of Hollywood glamour to the capital. Today, the once great Cinecittà studios are back in action, and a new star-studded international festival promises to put Rome back on the cinematic map.

Birth of Cinecittà

Mussolini embraced film as the perfect propaganda vehicle for Fascism and, in a characteristic show of bravado, built his own Hollywood-on-the-Tiber at Cinecittà, the largest filmmaking complex in Europe. Directors with the right ideological credentials were bankrolled by the regime, but created little of much merit. Nevertheless, some of Italy's greatest directors learned their trade at the studios, as second-unit directors or writers.

In the 1950s and '60s Cinecittà was synonymous with the epic – titles like *Quo Vadis* (1951) *Ben-Hur* (1959), Taylor and Burton's *Cleopatra* (1963) – but it also made the film that launched a thousand tourist trips, *Roman Holiday* (1953). In its glory years the studios produced over 1,000 films, employing hundreds of actors, extras, technicians and directors.

Cinecittà's Comeback

After years in the wilderness Cinecittà is back. Now that so many film sets are computer-generated, Rome is the place directors go to find the skills and craftsmanship that can create real sets.

In 2002, Martin Scorsese reconstructed entire blocks of 19th-century New York here for *Gangs of New York*. This heralded a slew of international productions, including Mel Gibson's *The Passion of the Christ* (2004), Stephen Soderbergh's *Ocean's Twelve* (2004) and – recalling the scale of the old epics – the lavish HBO/BBC series *Rome* (2005).

Rome's Cinematic Greats

The fall of Fascism marked the emergence of one of the world's great film movements: Neo-Realism. Stimulated by the desperate state of Italy at the end of the war and in response to the fashion for escapist spectacle, the *neorealismo* auteurs set out to record the life of ordinary people.

At their forefront was **Roberto Rossellini**, who began shooting his masterwork, *Rome, Open City* (1945), on Rome's devastated streets even before the

Above: Anita Ekberg exudes glamour in *La Dolce Vita*.

German troops had left. But the signature film of Neo-Realism was **Vittorio de Sica**'s *Bicycle Thieves (*1948); the story of a man and his son in the Rome slums was a huge international success. Other directors influenced by Neo-Realism included **Federico Fellini** and, in the 1960s, **Pier Paolo Pasolini**.

Fellini's devotion to Cinecittà made him the uncrowned king of the studios. He placed his adopted city under a microscope: *Roma* (1972) presented a fantastical vision of Rome, while *La Dolce Vita* (1960)

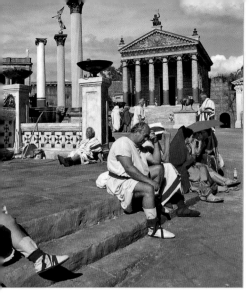

Left: taking a break on the set for the HBO/BBC series, *Rome*.

Cinemas in Rome

Virtually all films on general release are dubbed into Italian. For English-speaking cinema, try the following venues (films are marked VO – *versione originale*):

Alcazar
14 Via Cardinale Merry del Val; tel: 06-5880 099; bus: Trastevere; map p.137 C3
Original versions on Monday.

Casa del Cinema
Villa Borghese, Porta Pinciana; tel: 06-423 601; www.casadelcinema.it; metro: Spagna, bus: Piazzale del Brasile; map p.134 A3
The lovely converted villa just inside the main gates of the Villa Borghese park boasts several screening rooms (showing the occasional film in English), a book and DVD shop, an atmospheric café and a cinema library containing scripts and movie stills.

Metropolitan
7 Via del Corso; tel: 06-3200 933; metro: Flaminio, bus: Via del Corso; map p.133 D3
Multi-screen cinema with one screen devoted to original-version movies.

Nuovo Olimpia
16G Via in Lucina; tel: 06-6861 068; bus: Piazza Venezia, Via del Corso; map p.133 D2
Arthouse movies, as well as original-language films.

Warner Village Moderno
44 Piazza della Repubblica; tel: 06-4777 911; metro: Repubblica, bus: Via Nazionale; map p.134 B2
Frequent original-version films.

Nuovo Sacher
1 Largo Ascianghi; tel: 06-5818 116; bus: Trastevere; map p.137 C2
Nanni Moretti's own cinema club in Trastevere occasionally screens original-language films.

The Venice Film Festival has a new rival. In October 2006, Rome had its first film festival, held right after the Lido festival in September. The 2007 edition was a star-studded event, opened by Oscar-winning actor, Cate Blanchett, thus confirming its intention to join the ranks of Cannes, Sundance and Venice as a big-budget, high-profile cinematic event (www.romacinemafest.com).

---

satirised the idle rich who hung around the then glamorous Via Veneto, and left us the enduring image of Anita Ekberg cooling off in the Trevi Fountain.

Today, Rome's most acclaimed film-maker is **Nanni Moretti**, Italy's Woody Allen. The city is often centre stage in his films, notably *Caro Diario* (1994), where he scooters around the concrete suburbs in search of the essence of Rome. In 2001, his film *The Son's Room* was awarded the coveted Palme d'Or at Cannes. With a distinctively languid, ironic style, Moretti returned to film-making in 2006 after a long gap with *Il Caimano* (The Caiman), an acid satire on the Italy of Silvio Berlusconi.

The Next Generation

A new generation of actors and directors are working hard at putting Italian cinema back on the world map. Many regions now have active film commissions generating new movie-making in Campania, Ischia, Capri and Catania, while Rome's new film festival hopes to become a serious contender to the Venice Film Festival *(see left)*.

Below: the Rome Film Festival pulls in big Hollywood names.

Food and Drink

'*A Rome Se Magna*'. As the local dialect proudly dictates. 'In Rome, you eat.' When not eating, Romans are generally talking about eating, cooking, or planning the next meal. Culinary traditions run deep in Rome, from the exotic fancies of the emperors and popes to the earthy and genuine dishes of the *cucina povera*, 'cuisine of the poor'. Roman cooking traditionally follows seasonal produce. While supermarkets are slowly invading the city shoppingscape, most Romans, when possible, enjoy shopping around for ingredients from speciality stores and their favourite stands at the market.

La Cucina Romana

Much local cuisine involves offal, the so-called *quinto-quarto* (fifth quarter) of the animal. Long-time favourites include *rigatoni con pajata* (pasta with veal intestines) and *trippa alla romana* (tripe with tomato sauce, mint and pecorino), both of which are savoury and delicious, if the thought doesn't get in the way. Most restaurants in the centre of town offer a varied menu of pan-Italian cuisine, featuring dishes visitors are more familiar with, like lasagne, pesto sauce and risotto.

Pasta

High cuisine serves up all manner of tempting combinations, but typical Roman establishments tell a less complicated story. Try spaghetti *alla carbonara* (with bacon, egg and pecorino cheese), *cacio e pepe* (with pecorino and black pepper) or *all'amatriciana* (with bacon or *guanciale*, cured pork jowl, and tomato), and *bucatini alla gricia* – tubular spaghetti in *amatriciana* sauce minus the tomato. Pasta shows up in

Above: typical starters utilise fresh local ingredients, such as this rocket salad with roasted fig and pecorino cheese.

Roman soups: *pasta e ceci* (chickpea soup flavoured with rosemary) and *broccoli e arzilla* (clear soup of broccoli and skate). *Gnocchi alla romana* (larger, softer potato dumplings in a meat sauce) are traditionally prepared on Thursday.

Fish and Meat

Simplicity sums up fish dishes as well: clams tossed with spaghetti and olive oil become spaghetti *alle vongole*, calamari and shrimp are often fried or grilled (ask for a *fritto misto* or *grigliata mista*).

Popular meat dishes are *saltimbocca alla romana* (veal escalope, pan-fried with prosciutto and sage) and the arch-Roman *coda alla vaccinara* ('oxtail butcher's style', slow-braised in a garlic, pepper, tomato and celery sauce). Try *abbacchio* (milk-fed lamb), which is usually roasted with herbs and garlic or served *alla scottadito* (as grilled chops).

Vegetable Dishes

Vegetarians revel in Rome, as most restaurants stock up on seasonal produce from the

Left: spaghetti *alla carbonara*.

wines from all regions of Italy. For the connoisseurs, choose a wine bar or *enoteca*, where an expert staff pairs food and wine accordingly.

Pizza

The Neapolitans are credited with inventing pizza, but Romans eat their fair share. In an answer to their southern pizza brothers, Rome's pizza is characterised by a paper-thin, crispy crust, and heaped with toppings. Look for a wood-burning stove *(forno a legna)*, and be sure to order a *fritto misto* appetizer. The pizzeria version comes with *supplí* (fried rice balls), fried zucchini blossoms, fried mozzarella balls, olive *ascolane* (stuffed and fried green olives), and potato croquettes.

On the Go

Ice cream is an all-day, all-ages treat, and accordingly, *gelaterie* are easy to find and stay open late. Other treats that can be picked up from street vendors all over town

local markets. Most come simply steamed, grilled, fried or sautéed. November to April is the season for another Roman speciality, artichokes. Try them pressed open and fried *carciofi alla giudea* ('Jewish-style' and typical of the Ghetto), or *alla romana* (stuffed with garlic and mint, and stewed).

A typical winter salad is *puntarelle*, made by shredding the stalks of locally grown chicory and serving them with a vinegar-anchovy dressing. Summer brings roasted peppers, aubergines

Below: a patriotic *gelato*.

and courgettes *(zucchini)*, and tomatoes stuffed with herbs and rice, while in spring you'll see asparagus and *fave con pecorino* (raw broad beans with pecorino cheese).

Starters and Desserts

If you can manage an appetizer and dessert, a few common starters are melon or figs with prosciutto and *fiori di zucca* (deep-fried zucchini flowers filled with mozzarella and anchovies). Popular desserts are *torta della nonna ricotta* (ricotta tart topped with pine nuts), *panna cotta* (eggless, firm creamy custard with a fruit sauce) and tiramisu.

Wine

Local wines still dominate the wine selections of most Roman restaurants, especially those from Frascati, which are constantly improving. Vinophiles predict a DOCG *(Di Origine Controllato e Garantita)*, or highest-quality, Frascati wine in the near future. The sweeping wine trend has restaurants scrambling to provide a comprehensive wine list, including

The gastronomically curious may like to visit the **Museo Nazionale delle Paste Alimentari** (Trevi Fountain; Piazza Scanderberg; tel: 06-6991 120; daily 9.30am–5.30pm), for fascinating displays of all kinds of pasta. Better yet, visit an *alimentari*, the small grocery shops that sell a bit of everything and often prepare sandwiches. Ask for a slice of local cheese, *pecorino romano*, a hard, *grana* variety, similar to Parmesan, or *ricotta di pecora*, brought in fresh from the farms. You'll also find *porchetta* (whole roasted pig, sliced to order), a speciality of the hill towns around Rome.

are roasted chestnuts in the autumn and winter, and refreshing *grattachecca* (shaved ice with syrup) and watermelon wedges in summer.

Romans often stop at the local bar a couple of times a day, first for a breakfast of espresso or cappuccino and a *cornetto* (the Italian version of the croissant), then another espresso or perhaps a snack, such as a *panino* or *tramezzino* (small sandwiches) later in the day.

Pizza a taglio (by the slice) is also easy to find. Thicker than pizzeria pizza and topped with dozens of imaginative combinations, *pizza a taglio* is always sold by weight; an *etto* (100 grams) is a small portion. Many of the same shops also sell *supplì* and olive *ascolane*.

Open-Air Markets

Shop as the Romans do, and peruse the stands at a *mercato rionale* near you. Markets typically open by 6.30am, and close up just

---

That most popular of Italian drinks, cappuccino, is named after the garb worn by Capuchin monks. The colour of the milky coffee is reminiscent of their brown robes and their pointed hoods of the peaks of the milky foam. The word cappuccino literally means 'little hood' or 'monk's cowl'.

---

after lunch. These are the biggest and the best.

Mercato Campo de' Fiori
Campo de' Fiori; no phone; bus: Largo Argentina; map p.137 C4
Devastatingly charming fruit and vegetable market, despite the tourist-targeted prices, and the swarms of tourists themselves.

Ex-Piazza Vittorio
Via Lamarmora; no phone; metro: Vittorio; map p.138 C4
This market once filled Piazza Vittorio Emanuele, but following complaints of disorder and dirt, it took up residence in a former barracks nearby. This is the place for exotic spices and rices, Halal meat and imported crafts.

Mercato Trionfale
Via Andrea Doria; no phone; metro: Cipro-Musei Vaticani, bus: 490, 492; map p.132 A3
Five minutes' walk north of the Vatican Museums, the market takes up both sides of an entire city block.

Mercato San Cosimato
Piazza San Cosimato; no phone; bus: 780, H, tram: 8; map p.137 C3
Get there early to beat the tourist rush and join the local restaurant owners as they choose the day's produce.

Delicatessens, Speciality Food and Wine Shops

Rome abounds with tempting bakeries, food shops and treats of all dimensions. Here's a sampling. Wine-lovers should look for an *enoteca*: they're everywhere. *See also Bars and Cafés, p.33 (Buccone) and p.34 (Centro Vini Arcioni).*

Ai Monasteri
72 Corso Rinascimento; tel: 06-6880 2783; www.monasteri.it; Mon–Wed, Fri, Sat 9am–1pm, 2.30–7.30pm, Thur 9am–1pm;

Below: Roman nuns peruse the fresh produce on offer at the city's bustling Campo de' Fiori market.

Above: patisserie is an art form.

Above: fruity red wine.

bus: Corso Rinascimento; map p.133 D1

Browse the retro-packaged honey, preserves, liqueurs, tinctures, and curious cures (elixir of good humour, or long life, for example), all made by monks throughout Italy.

Castroni
196 Via Cola di Rienzo; tel: 06-6874 383; www.castroni.com; Mon–Sat 8am–8pm; metro: Ottaviano; bus: Piazza Risorgimento, tram: 19; map p.132 C3

Foodies tend to get lost inside this shop, which roasts its own espresso beans and sells Italian regional specialities in cute gift sizes, as well as imported foodstuffs.

Costantini
16 Piazza Cavour; tel: 06-3213 210; www.pierocostantini.it; Mon 4.30–8pm, Tue–Sat 9am–1pm, 4.30–8pm; bus: Cavour; map p.138 A4

Wine collectors will spend hours in the downstairs cellar, while foodies and aspiring chefs won't leave without a package of pasta or gourmet sauces.

Forno del Ghetto
1 Via Portico d'Ottavia; tel: 06-6878 637; Mon–Thur 8am–7.30pm, Fri 8am–sunset; bus: Largo Argentina; map p.137 D4

Three ladies run this tiny shop, which often runs out of their sumptuous cakes and pies by noon. Black cherry ricotta and chocolate ricotta pies are the best-sellers. Purchase whole or by the slice.

Innocenzi
31 Via Natale del Grande; tel: 06-5812 725; Mon–Wed, Fri, Sat 7am–2pm, 4.30–8pm; bus: 780, H, tram: 8; map p.137 C3

A great selection of grains, beans, dried fruit, and spices, as well as imported food items.

Josephine's Bakery
56–57 Piazza del Paradiso; tel: 06-6871 065; Mon, Tue 2–8pm, Wed–Sun 9am–8pm; bus: Sant' Andrea della Valle; map p.137 C4

An ex-London model, Josephine opened this pastry shop to soothe her cravings for cheesecake, chocolate fudge cake, carrot cake, cupcakes and sugar cookies.

Panella
54 Via Merulana; tel: 06-4872 344; Mon–Fri 8am–2pm, 5.20–8pm; metro: Vittorio Emanuele; map p.138 B4

A bread and pastry wonderland, serving something for both sweet and savoury tastes. Make a sandwich on crispy *pizza bianca* (focaccia), or sample a few biscotti with their famous coffee.

Trimani
20 Via Goito; tel: 06-4469 661; Mon–Sat 9am–1.30pm, 3.30–8.30pm; metro: Termini; bus: 75, 86, 92; map p.134 B3

The oldest wine shop in Rome, stocking thousands of bottles. Try some wine paired with fancy cooking in the adjoining bar.

Volpetti
47 Via Marmorata; tel: 06-5742 352; www.volpetti.com; Mon–Sat 8am–2pm, 5–8.15pm; metro: Piramide, bus: 23, 30; map p.137 D1

You can smell the cheese through the display windows at this amazing deli and food shop. Sample products and choose from Italy-wide regional cheese and cured meats.

Although supermarkets are competing hard, there are a number of reasons why the tradition of buying fresh produce from markets will be hard to extinguish. Not least of these is the importance human contact and personalised service plays in the life of many, especially older, Roman shoppers.

65

Gay and Lesbian

When the centre-left government headed up by Romano Prodi took control of the Parliament, the civil union question made it back to the table, and gay and lesbian couples are hoping to make strides in civil rights in the coming years. Slowly but surely, the capital is inching its way toward becoming a more tolerant and gay-friendly city. A number of bars, restaurants and clubs have opened up within the city centre, and welcome a mixed crowd, no longer banishing homosexuality to the far edges and dark corners of the city. The listings below provide information on some of the best services and the varied nightlife scene.

Associations

Arcigay Roma
35B Via Goito; tel: 06-6450 1102; www.arcigayroma.it; Thur (Welcome Night) 7–9pm, Fri (Living Room) 6–9pm; metro and bus: Termini; map p.134 B3
The Rome branch of the Italian Arcigay association serves as a meeting and information point, as well as a centre for social activism. Many clubs and social centres require an Arcigay membership card, which can be purchased on site (€15 annual, €8 for visitors).

Casa Internazionale delle Donne
19 Via della Lungara; tel: 06-6840 1720; www.casainternazionale delledonne.org; bus: 23, 280; map p.132 C1
An ex-convent, the structure is now a swank, modern facility hosting several women's organisations, as well as a pristine, women-only hostel (see Accommodation below).

Circolo Mario Mieli di Cultura Omosessuale
2A Via Efeso; tel: 06-5413 985; www.mariomieli.org; Mon–Fri 10am–6pm; metro: San Paolo,

Above: Rome's colourful Gay Pride parade.

bus: 23
Rome's most respected gay, lesbian and transgender organisation, its website is a viable resource for all things gay in the city. The structure itself serves as a cultural and counselling centre.

Accommodation

B&B In and Out
97 Via Arco del Monte; tel: 06-9799 8676; www.inandout-rome.com; bus: 30, 40, 64;
A gay and lesbian-owned hotel with a sleek, modern interior, styled with Japanese-inspired accents.

La Forestera Orsa Maggiore
1A Via San Francesco di Sales; tel: 06-6840 1724; www.casa internazionaledelledonne.org; bus: 23, 280; map p.136 B4
Located inside an ex-convent, the hostel still sticks to a women- (and children) only policy. A communal kitchen is available for guests' use.

Gay Open
44 Via Statuto; tel: 06-4820 013; metro and bus: Piazza Vittorio; map p.138 B4
Primarily aimed at gay visitors, lesbians are also welcome. Located near the Termini station, in the heart of Rome's most ethnic neighbourhood.

Health Clubs and Saunas

Europa Multiclub
40 Via Aureliana; tel: 06-4823 650; daily 1pm–midnight; metro and bus: Piazza Repubblica; map p.134 B4

The ubiquitous rainbow flags do not always necessarily signify gay-friendly. The rainbow flag is also the Italian symbol for peace and anti-war movements.

Left: two women enjoy a drink in one of Rome's bars.

Gay Village
Location changes yearly; www.gayvillage.it; June–Sept
A cool, outdoor setting in the summer for a mixed, gay and lesbian crowd. Dancing, film, live music and shows.

Hangar
69 Via in Selci; tel: 06-4881 3971; www.hangaronline.it; Mon, Wed–Sun 10.30pm–2.30am; metro: Cavour, bus: 75, 84; map p.138 B4
A friendly bar; weekly events include porno-video and strip-tease. With an ingenious tunnel between two bars.

Locanda Atlantide
22B Via dei Lucani; tel: 06-4470 4540; www.locandatlantide.it; events vary by month; tram: 19; map p.139 D4
One of the city's most vibrant venues for local live music, dance and art shows.

Muccassassina
212 Via di Portonaccio; tel: 06-5413 985; www.muccassassina. com; Fri 11pm–4am; metro: Tiburtina, bus: 409
Fridays are the Muccassassina gay night at popular disco Qube. This will always be the first mention on Rome's mixed gay nightlife list.

Sky Line
26 Via degli Aurunci; tel: 06-4441 417; www.skylineclub.it; Mon–Sat 10.30pm–4am, Sun 5pm–4am; metro: San Giovanni, bus: 360; map p.139 D4
Two floors of fun at this popular gay club. The atmosphere is easy-going and energised, with plenty to do. Naked party every Monday.

Venus Rising – Goa
13 Via Libetta; tel: 06-5748 277; Last Sun of month midnight–4am; metro: Garbatella, bus: 769
This ladies-only event attracts thousands of girls. One of lesbian Rome's coolest venues.

Arcigay covers everyone, but a sub-branch of Arcigay is yet another resource for lesbians. Arci-Lesbica Roma; 15 Viale G. Stefanini; tel: 06-4180 211; www.arcilesbica.it; metro: Santa Maria del Soccorso.

A men's gym and sauna, complete with whirlpool, bar and private rooms.

Mediterraneo
3 Via Villari; tel: 06-7720 5934; www.saunamediterraneo.it; daily 1pm–midnight; metro: Manzoni, bus: 85, 87; map p.138 C3
For visitors of all nationalities and ages, this clean and welcoming sauna features a Turkish bath and jacuzzi, as well as a bar, video room and a series of relax rooms.

Bars and Clubs

L'Alibi
40–44 Via di Monte Testaccio; tel: 06-5743 448; Thur–Sun 11.30pm–5am; metro: Piramide, bus: 23, 30, 95; map p.137 D1
Two floors, plus a summertime rooftop terrace, provide space aplenty for dancing, cruising, drinking and shows.

Coming Out
8 Via San Giovanni in Laterano; tel: 06-7009 871; www.coming out.it; daily 7pm–3am; metro and bus: Colosseum; map p.138 B3
Karaoke and a lively scene ensure a faithful following, not just from the gay community.

Garbo
1A Vicolo S. Margherita, off Via della Lungaretta; tel: 06-5832 0782; Tue–Sun 10pm–2am; bus: 23, 280, tram: 8; map p.136 C3
A tiny, kitschy place with chandeliers and velvet couches. A mixed, friendly crowd; attracts all ages.

Below: Rome's gay population is coming out of the shadows.

History

753 BC
Roman historian Livy records 21 April 753 BC as the date on which Romulus founded Rome.

509 BC
Rome's last Etruscan king is driven into exile, and Rome becomes a Republic ruled by a Senate.

264–146 BC
The Punic Wars fought against Carthage. By 146 BC Rome dominates the entire Mediterranean.

58–44 BC
Julius Caesar conquers Gaul, invades Britain, then leads his army back into Italy, challenging the Senate. He defeats Pompey and is made dictator of Rome, only to be assassinated in 44 BC.

44–AD 96
Octavian defeats Caesar's assassins and then Mark Antony to become Augustus, the first Roman Emperor. Rome's cultural apex, producing Virgil, Ovid and Livy. Augustus' dynasty ends with the extravagant Nero, who builds the Golden House in AD 64, but commits suicide four years later. Followed by the effective Flavian Dynasty. Titus completes the Colosseum.

98–117
The Roman Empire achieves its greatest extent under Emperor Trajan, extending from northern England to the Persian Gulf.

161–80
Reign of philosopher-emperor Marcus Aurelius. With his predecessors, Trajan and Hadrian, he led Rome to the height of its power in the 2nd century.

284–305
Emperor Diocletian divides Empire into two halves, East and West. Intense persecution of Christians.

324
Christianity is officially recognised.

395
The Roman Empire is divided into East and West.

476
Following the sack of Rome by Visigoths, then Vandals, the Western Roman Empire falls and Byzantium becomes the seat of the Empire.

536–68
Rome and most of Italy recaptured by the Eastern Empire, but the Byzantine armies are overwhelmed by another invasion, by the Lombards.

590–604
Pope Gregory the Great strengthens the papacy and makes peace with the Lombards.

750
Pepin, king of the Franks, lays the foundations of temporal sovereignty of the papacy.

1309
Clement V removes the seat of the papacy to Avignon in the south of France.

1377
The papacy returns to Rome under Gregory XI, but rival popes still contest claims of his successors.

15TH CENTURY
With the election of Pope Martin V in 1417, Rome enters a new phase of prosperity during the Renaissance. The popes commission great works from the likes of Bellini, Botticelli, Bramante, Donatello, Michelangelo and Raphael.

1527
Emperor Charles V – ruler of Spain and Austria – sacks Rome.

1585–90
Pope Sixtus V orders major public works, including the restoration of aqueducts and fountains.

1626
Consecration of St Peter's.

1796–1814
The French Revolutionary armies under Napoleon take Rome and make it a Republic. Rome becomes part of the French Empire, but the Papal States are restored to Pope Pius VII at the Congress of Vienna.

1848–50
Pope Pius IX gives the Papal States a constitution but refuses to support Italian unification. Radicals declare a Roman Republic, but Rome is besieged by the French, who restore papal rule.

1870
Italian troops take over Rome, which is declared capital of the Kingdom of Italy.

1871–1910
New Italian government undertakes massive building works, including the Tiber embankments.

1922
Mussolini marches on Rome and seizes power. More new building, with broad avenues and monuments, and suburbs around the city.

1940–45
Italy enters World War II in 1940. On 4 June 1944, the Allies liberate Rome. Mussolini hanged in 1945. After the war Italy becomes a Republic.

1957
The European Economic Community is established by the Treaty of Rome; Italy is one of its six founder members.

1960
La Dolce Vita is released; Rome holds the Olympics.

1978
Cardinal Karol Wojtyla becomes the first Polish pope as John Paul II.

1993
Corruption scandals rock Italy; national unity government formed.

2000
Millions flock to Rome for Holy Year celebrations after a frenzy of restoration work.

2001
Silvio Berlusconi becomes prime minister for the second time. Walter Veltroni of the centre-left wins Rome's mayoral elections.

2005
Pope John Paul II dies: Cardinal Joseph Ratzinger is elected Pope Benedict XVI.

2006
Berlusconi loses power by the narrowest of margins to a centre-left coalition led by Romano Prodi.

69

Hotels

Traditionally Rome has always been an expensive city to stay in, with price often a poor reflection of quality. In recent years the accommodation options have begun to broaden so that, while still expensive, you can now choose to avoid the peeling *pensione* of old. Conventional façades now hide avant-garde interiors, while at the grander end of the scale, gracious, timeless hotels like Hotel de Russie retain their cachet. But for those not on an imperial budget there are plenty of welcoming guesthouses and family-run hotels, while self-catering apartments and bed and breakfasts are increasingly popular options.

Forum and Colosseum

Capo d'Africa
54 Via Capo d'Africa; tel: 06-772 801; www.hotelcapodafrica.com; €€€; metro: Colosseo; map p.138 B3

This hotel's dramatic, palm-tree-lined entrance bodes well, and its 65 rooms are comfortable and contemporary. Views are delightful, especially from the stunning glass-walled rooftop breakfast room.

Celio
35C Via dei Santissimi Quattro; tel: 06-7049 5333; www.hotel celio.com; €€–€€€; metro: Colosseo; map p.138 B3

This delightful hotel a few streets from the Colosseum has 20 rooms, named after great Italian artists of the Renaissance and lavishly decorated to match, and a lovely rooftop terrace.

Domus Sessoriana
10 Piazza Santa Croce in Gerusalemme; tel: 06-706 151; www.domussessoriana.it; €€; metro: San Giovanni; map p.139 D3

Attached to the monastery of the church of Santa Croce in Gerusalemme, this hotel offers elegant, simple accommodation to a largely business clientele. Request a room overlooking the monastery's garden. The roof terrace has great views of San Giovanni in Laterano and beyond.

Hotel 47
47 Via Petroselli; tel: 06-6787 816; www.47hotel.com; €€€–€€€€; bus: 170; map p.137 D3

This plush modern hotel is set in an austere 1930s building which has been tastefully converted and filled with repro furniture and contemporary artworks. The views are wonderful, especially from the rooftop bar-restaurant.

Inn at the Roman Forum
30 Via degli Ibernesi; tel: 06-6919 0970; www.theinnatthe romanforum.com; €€€–€€€€; bus: 75; map p.138 A4

This new boutique hotel offers spacious, luxurious rooms with canopied beds, antique furnishings, a prime

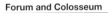

Above: breakfast on the terrace at the Inn at the Roman Forum.

location and even its own ancient Roman crypt, currently being excavated on the ground floor.

Lancelot
47 Via Capo d'Africa; tel: 06-7045 0615; www.lancelothotel.com; €€; metro: Colosseo; map p.138 B3

This ultra-friendly, family-run hotel has light, airy rooms and enjoys an enviable position, a few minutes' walk from the Colosseum. Ask for one of the rooms with terraces looking towards the Palatine. Half-board is also available.

Prices for an average double room in high season:
€ under €100
€€ €100–€180
€€€ €180–€350
€€€€ €350 and up

Left: the science-fictionesque reception area at Hotel Art.

area is contained within two futuristic pods, while the sleek lounge area is laid out in the former chapel beneath frescoed vaulted ceilings.

Casa Howard
18 Via Capo le Case and 149 Via Sistina; tel: 06-6992 4555; www.casahoward.com; €€–€€€; metro: Spagna; map p.133 E2

Each of the 10 rooms in this stylish hotel in two locations has a different theme; those in the newer Via Sistina location all have bathrooms en suite and are slightly more luxurious. Turkish bath available at both sites. This is *residenza* accommodation: there is no reception – guests are given a set of keys.

Fontanella Borghese
84 Largo Fontanella Borghese; tel: 06-6880 9504; www.fontanellaborghese.com; €€–€€€; metro: Spagna; map p.133 D2

This elegant hotel, once the residence of the noble Borghese family, is well located for shopping in the Piazza di Spagna and Via Condotti area. Rooms overlooking the internal courtyard are quieter.

Gregoriana
18 Via Gregoriana; tel: 06-6794 269; www.hotelgregoriana.it; €€; metro: Spagna; map p.133 E2

Fans of Art Deco will adore the striking retro interior of this ex-convent, with its wonderful gold-and-black lift and original 1930s room numbers by the Russian fashion designer Erté.

Hassler
6 Piazza Trinità dei Monti; tel: 06-699 340; www.hotelhassler roma.com; €€€€; metro: Spagna; map p.133 E2

This historic establishment is still one of Rome's most alluring luxury hotels, its old-

The Trevi Fountain and Quirinale

Daphne Trevi
20 Via degli Avignonesi Trevi, off Via delle Quattro Fontane; tel: 06-8745 0087; www.daphne-rome.com; €€; metro: Barberini; map p.134 A2

This hotel in two central locations excels in its level of service – friendly, knowledgeable staff, and laptops (one per floor) and mobile phones (one per room) are provided – an unexpected bonus in this price bracket.

Residenza Cellini
5 Via Modena; tel: 06-4782 5204; www.residenzacellini.it; €€–€€€; metro: Repubblica; map p.134 B2

With rooms that are unusually large for the price, this hotel

is deservedly popular. The décor is classic, with parquet floors, wood furnishings and fabrics in flouncy florals. All bathrooms have jacuzzis or hydro-massage showers. On a new floor three of the rooms have balconies.

Piazza di Spagna and Tridente

Hotel Art
56 Via Margutta; tel: 06-328 711; www.hotelart.it; €€€€; metro: Spagna; map p.133 E3

Set in a converted seminary, this upmarket hotel is a blend of old and new. The reception

Below: one of Celio's Renaissance-inspired rooms.

Left: designer Salvatore Ferragamo's Portrait Suites.

€€€–€€€€; metro: Spagna; map p.133 E2

Opened in 2006, this boutique hotel has become a favourite with the fashion set – it's owned by the Italian couturier Ferragamo. Rooms are as stylish as you'd expect, and there's plenty of fashion memorabilia from the designer's archives. The decked terrace is great for an *aperitivo*.

Hotel de Russie

9 Via del Babuino; tel: 06-328 881; www.hotelderussie.it; €€€€; metro: Flaminio; map p.133 D3

This is Rome's original designer hotel, housed in a *palazzo* by Valadier. It is chic, modern and understated. The internal courtyard is magical, and the luxurious spa is one of the best in town. Ask for a room with a view of Piazza del Popolo.
SEE ALSO PAMPERING, P.107

Suisse

54 Via Gregoriana; tel: 06-6783 649; www.hotelsuisserome. com; €€; metro: Spagna; map p.133 E2

This charming hotel has been in the same family since 1921. Rooms are large, with sturdy wooden furnishings, parquet floors and classic décor. Breakfast is served in the rooms. Great value for money.

Valadier

15 Via della Fontanella, off Via del Babuino; tel: 06-3611 998; www.hotelvaladier.com; €€€–€€€€; metro: Spagna; map p.133 D3

This attractive hotel has

world glamour a real contrast with the sleek minimalism of some of the city's new 5-stars. Imàgo, the newly renovated restaurant, offers breathtaking views over the city.

Inn at the Spanish Steps

85 Via dei Condotti; tel: 06-6992 5657; www.atspanishsteps. com; €€–€€€€; metro: Spagna; map p.133 E2

The stunning rooms at this luxury boutique hotel are a mix of carefully selected antiques and bold fabrics; some boast 17th-century frescoes. A sister hotel, the View at the Spanish Steps, along the same road at No.

95, is similarly luxurious, though slightly more pared-down in style.

Modigliani

42 Via della Purificazione; tel: 06-4281 5226; www.hotel modigliani.com; €€; metro: Spagna; map p.134 A2

A lovely hotel with great views from top-floor rooms and a garden in an inner courtyard. Two apartments with independent entrances are also available.

Pensione Panda

35 Via della Croce; tel: 06-6780 179; www.hotelpanda.it; €; metro: Spagna; map p.133 E2

A rare budget option a stone's throw from the Spanish Steps, its rooms, though small and pretty basic, have been attractively decorated, and some have wood-beamed ceilings. There's no breakfast, but you'll find plenty of places nearby. Book early.

Portrait Suites

23 Bocca di Leone; tel: 06-6938 0742; www.lungarnohotels.com;

Hotels in Rome are rated by stars, but these ratings correspond to quantity of facilities and services and not to quality, which is often disappointing compared with what you would expect from similarly rated hotels in other major European cities.

Prices for an average double room in high season:
€ under €100
€€ €100–€180
€€€ €180–€350
€€€€ €350 and up

recently been revamped. The rooms are grandly styled, with luxurious furnishings and marble bathrooms. The new 'Bamboo' rooms have a sleek, designer feel, while the suites are more traditional.

The Vatican and Prati

Bramante

24 Vicolo delle Palline; tel: 06-6880 6426; www.hotelbramante.com; €€; metro: Ottaviano; map p.132 B2

This 15th-century former inn on a tranquil side street near St Peter's is now a charming hotel. All the wood-beamed rooms are quiet and elegantly furnished. The small terrace makes a pleasant place to unwind after a busy day.

Cavalieri Hilton

101 Via Cadlolo; tel: 06-350 91; www.cavalieri-hilton.it; €€€€; bus: 991

Luxury hotel situated on top of Monte Mario, just north of the Vatican. Quiet and spacious, it offers amenities that more central hotels lack – tennis courts and indoor and outdoor swimming pools among them – as well as one of Rome's best restaurants, La Pergola. SEE ALSO RESTAURANTS, P.114

Colors

31 Via Boezio; tel: 06-6874 030; www.colorshotel.com; €–€€; metro: Ottaviano; map p.132 C3

Above: the restaurant at the elegant Hotel Hassler has great views over the city.

Bright, clean hotel, with rooms with or without en suite bathroom, and dormitory accommodation. The third-floor rooms are slightly pricier but offer extras such as breakfast, satellite TV and air-con. Fully equipped kitchen, laundry facilities and a roof terrace. Helpful staff.

Farnese

30 Via Alessandro Farnese; tel: 06-3212 553; www.hotelfarnese.com; €€–€€€; bus: 70; map p.133 C3

This upmarket 4-star occupies a grand old aristocratic residence. Attention to detail makes it special: the reception desk is a 17th-century altar from a deconsecrated church.

Rooms are elegant with antiques, marble bathrooms and Murano lamps. The breakfast is excellent, and there is a pretty roof terrace.

Franklin

29 Via Rodi; tel: 06-3903 0165; www.franklinhotelrome.it; €€–€€€; metro: Ottaviano; map p.132 A4

This modern hotel has airy, pleasant rooms, all with a musical theme. There are CD players in all rooms, with an extensive collection of music for guests to borrow in the reception area, plus bicycles for guests' use.

Sant'Anna

133 Borgo Pio; tel: 06-6880 1602; www.hotelsantanna.com; €€;

Below: the grand reception area at the Cavalieri Hilton.

Rome offers countless places to stay, but the area around Piazza Navona, the Pantheon and Campo de' Fiori offers perhaps the best introduction to the city, since you are right in its medieval heart and within easy reach of most main sights. However, there are relatively few hotels in the area, and these tend to be booked up early, so try to plan ahead if possible.

metro: Ottaviano; map p.132 B2
Housed in a 16th-century building, this hotel has comfortable rooms with a slightly old-fashioned feel. Breakfast is taken in the small courtyard at the back or the mural-decorated breakfast room. Service is friendly.

Piazza Navona and the Pantheon
Due Torri
23 Vicolo del Leonetto, off Via dell'Orso; tel: 06-6880 6956; www.hotelduetorriroma.com; €€; bus: 70; map p.133 D2
A delightful hotel – in a former cardinal's palace tucked away down a narrow cobbled street – and quiet by Roman standards. Rooms are small and cosy with dark wood furniture and traditional décor; those on the top floor have terraces.

Below: the view from the Campo de' Fiori roof terrace.

Grand Hotel de la Minerve
69 Piazza della Minerva; tel: 06-695 201; www.grandhoteldela minerve.com; €€€€; bus: 40; map p.133 D1
Hotel in a 17th-century *palazzo* on the *piazza*. Vast expanses of Venetian glass create spectacular public spaces, and there are splendid views from the roof terrace. All rooms are airy and elegant, but if you're looking to blow the budget, book the gloriously frescoed Stendhal Suite.
Navona
8 Via dei Sediari; tel: 06-6864 203; www.hotelnavona.com; €€; bus: 64; map p.133 D1
This family-run hotel on the second floor of an attractive *palazzo* was built on the site of the ancient baths of Agrippa – the ground floor dates back to AD 1. Good value for the location.
Raphael
2 Largo Febo, off Piazza Navona; tel: 06-682 831; www.raphael hotel.com; €€€€; bus: 116; map p.133 D1
A distinctive ivy-covered exterior, antique furnishings, artworks and stunning views. The Richard Meier-designed 'Executive' rooms on the third floor are sleek and modern, while the rest of the hotel has a classic feel. Some rooms don't quite live up to expectations, but facilities, rooftop restaurant, bar and views do.
Relais Palazzo Taverna
92 Via dei Gabrielli; tel: 06-2039 8064; www.relaispalazzotaverna.com; €€; bus: 70; map p.133 C1
Rooms at this smart new guesthouse near the antiques shops of Via dei Coronari have stylish, modern décor. Excellent value for this part of town. With tiled floors and frescoes.
Teatro Pace 33
33 Via del Teatro Pace; tel: 06-6879 075; www.hotelteatro pace.com; €€; bus: 40; map

p.133 D1
This 17th-century building on a quiet, cobbled alley near Piazza Navona boasts a magnificent Baroque spiral staircase (there's no lift) and wood-beamed rooms decorated in classic style, with marble bathrooms. Breakfast is served in the rooms.

Campo de' Fiori and the Ghetto
Barrett
47 Largo Torre Argentina, off Corso Vittorio Emmanuele II; tel: 06-6868 481; www.pensione barrett.com; €€; bus: 40 map p.137 D4
Located between Campo de' Fiori and the Pantheon, this great-value hotel has been run by the same family for over 40 years. The knick-knacks and quirky antiques which cram every room provide character. Breakfast can be arranged for an extra fee. No credit cards.
Campo de' Fiori
6 Piazza del Biscione; tel: 06-6880 6865; www.hotelcampo defiori.com; €€; bus: 64; map p.137 C4
This hotel has a beautiful roof terrace and intimate, individually decorated rooms with bijou en suite bathrooms. The hotel management also rents several upmarket apartments in the area.

Below: the doormen can assist with your many purchases.

entranceway and bedrooms to its soothing 'Paradise Spa' in the basement. Unusual features such as an outsize backgammon set in the inner courtyard give the hotel a quirky appeal.

Bernini Bristol
23 Piazza Barberini; tel: 06-488 931; www.berninibristol.com; €€€–€€€€; metro: Barberini; map p.134 A2
From the imposing entrance hall, with its chandeliers and acres of marble flooring, to the elegant rooms, this is a classy hotel, but more afford-able than the megahotels that line Via Veneto. It also houses a spa and a prestigious restaurant, L'Olimpo.

Daphne Veneto
55 Via di San Basilio; map p.134 A2; *see Daphne Trevi, p.71.*

Eden
49 Via Ludovisi; tel: 06-478 121; www.starwoodhotels.com; €€€€; bus: 116; map p.134 A3
This discreet, ultra-refined hotel rejects ostentatious opulence in favour of classic, pared-down elegance. Excellent, un-snooty service, and a gourmet roof garden restaurant, La Terrazza dell' Eden, with views that are among the best in the city.
SEE ALSO RESTAURANTS, P.117

Lord Byron
5 Via Giuseppe De Notaris; tel: 06-3220 404; www.lordbyron hotel.com; €€€–€€€€; bus: 52
Built into a former monastery, this small hotel has the atmosphere of a private club, and enjoys a serene location

Ponte Sisto
64 Via dei Pettinari; tel: 06-686 310; www.hotelpontesisto.it; €€–€€€; bus: 23; map p.137 C4
Once the residence of a noble Venetian family, this hotel enjoys an excellent, central location. The rooms are elegant and simple, with luxurious marble bathrooms. The peaceful, palm-tree-lined courtyard is a pleasant spot for an early evening *aperitivo*.

Residenza in Farnese
59 Via del Mascherone, off Via Giulia; tel: 06-6889 1388; www.residenzafarneseroma.it; €€€; bus: 23; map p.137 C4
Rooms in this converted convent vary from simple and basic to spacious and luxurious. Ask for a room overlooking the gardens of Palazzo Spada or, on the other side, the magnificent French Embassy. Breakfast is a feast of home-made goodies.

Teatro di Pompeo
8 Largo del Pallaro; tel: 06-6830 0170; www.hotelteatrodipompeo. it; €€; bus: 116; map p.137 D4
This charming, friendly hotel was built on the site of the ancient Theatre of Pompey (the remains of which can still be seen in the vaulted breakfast room). The comfortable rooms have wood beams and terracotta floors.

Via Veneto and Villa Borghese

Aldrovandi Palace
15 Via Ulisse Aldrovandi; tel: 06-3223 993; www.aldrovandi.com; €€€€; bus: M
Sumptuous rooms and suites at this beautiful hotel. The lovely gardens, spectacular outdoor pool and restaurant (Baby), run by a Michelin-starred chef, are further draws.

Aleph
15 Via di San Basilio; tel: 06-422 901; www.boscolohotels.com; €€€€; metro: Barberini; map p.134 A2
This stylish hotel has an intriguing 'heaven and hell' theme, from its flame-red

Prices for an average double room in high season:
€ under €100
€€ €100–€180
€€€ €180–€350
€€€€ €350 and up

In its *dolce vita* heyday, the Westin Excelsior *(see below)* on Via Veneto played host to some of the most glamorous stars of the day. Many a tempestuous scene between hot-headed lovers Frank Sinatra and Ava Gardner was played out within its walls.

away from the city centre. Sumptuous décor, with supremely tasteful rooms and a fabulous restaurant.

Parco dei Principi

5 Via G. Frescobaldi; tel: 06-854 421; www.parcodeiprincipi.com; €€€€; bus: 910

This hotel is a great choice if you want tranquillity and luxury. Rooms are opulent, and there's a large outdoor swimming pool – a rarity in Rome. The excellent restaurant, Pauline Borghese, overlooks the park and the city.

Westin Excelsior

125 Via Vittorio Veneto; tel: 06-4708 1; www.starwood.com; €€€€; metro: Barberini; map p.134 A3

Part of the 1950s *dolce vita* scene and always the grandest of Via Veneto's 5-stars, the Excelsior offers the ultimate in opulence and glamour, with staggeringly luxurious, antiques-laden rooms and Europe's largest suite (1,100sq m, it boasts its own cinema, pool and gym).

Trastevere and the Gianicolo

Antico Borgo Trastevere

7 Vicolo del Buco; tel: 06-5883 774; www.hotelanticoborgo.it; €–€€; bus: H; map p.137 D3

In a good location on the quieter, eastern side of Trastevere, this hotel's rooms are for the most part tiny, but tastefully decorated. Breakfast is served at nearby sister hotel the Domus Tiberina, on a *piazza* overlooking the river.

Arco del Lauro

27 Via dell'Arco de' Tolomei, off Via del Salumi; tel: 06-9784 0350; www.arcodellauro.it; €€; bus: 125; map p.137 D3

Mini-hotel, with just four rooms, in a tranquil residential part of Trastevere. The fresh, simple and excellent-value rooms here are a welcome addition to the area. Breakfast is served in a nearby bar.

Residenza Arco de' Tolomei

26C Via dell'Arco de' Tolomei; tel: 06-5832 0819; www.inrome.info; €€; bus: 125; map p.137 D3

This beautifully decorated guesthouse on a quiet alley has just five rooms, three with terraces. Decorated in country-house style, rooms have a homely feel. Breakfast is a real event here, with homemade baked goods and jams served in a light-filled breakfast room.

San Francesco

7 Via Jacopa de' Settesoli; tel: 06-5830 0051; www.hotelsan francesco.net; €€; bus: 44; map p.137 C2

Set back a little from the bustle of central Trastevere, rooms are good-sized and comfortable; ask for one of the rooms overlooking the internal courtyard of the adjacent convent. Breakfast is served on the roof terrace in warm weather.

Santa Maria

2 Vicolo del Piede; tel: 06-5894 626; www.htlsantamaria.com; €€; bus: H; map p.136 C3

Gated, refurbished 16th-century cloister. Rooms are large and comfortable, with a view out onto a large, sunny central courtyard planted with orange trees. Bikes are available for guests' use. One room has been adapted for those with disabilities.

Trastevere

24A–25 Via L. Manara; tel: 06-5814 713; www.hoteltrastevere. net; €–€€; bus: H; map p.136 C3

With clean, simple rooms overlooking Piazza San Cosimato market square, this

Below: the Radisson SAS Hotel.

Left: the lounge at the elegant Hotel Eden.

sunny patio. Breakfast can be provided on request.

Exedra
47 Piazza della Repubblica; tel: 06-489 381; www.boscolo hotels.com; €€€€; metro: Repubblica; map p.134 B2

Among the most opulent of the city's 5-star hotels, the Exedra is chic and glamorous, with luxurious, no-expense-spared rooms and stunning suites that are a favourite with visiting film stars. There's also a rooftop bar, restaurant, pool and a swanky spa.

Montreal
4 Via Carlo Alberto; tel: 06-4457 797; www.hotelmontrealrome. com; €€; metro: Termini; map p.134 B1

The Montreal's 27 rooms are bright, cheery and spacious, and its small, flower-filled patio makes a lovely spot for breakfast in the summer months. This is an ever-popular mid-range option, so book ahead.

Radisson SAS Hotel
171 Via Filippo Turati; tel: 06-444 841; www.radissonsas. com; €€€; metro: Termini; map p.134 C1

This cutting-edge-design hotel has a spectacular decked rooftop terrace with a restaurant and a pool (in summer). Its location – right opposite the station – is convenient but far from picturesque.

St Regis Grand
3 Via V.E. Orlando; tel: 06-47091; www.starwood.com/stregis; €€€€; metro: Repubblica; map p.134 B2

The St Regis Grand provides a taste of 19th-century *belle époque* grandeur, with individually designed rooms of undreamt-of luxury and a butler service. If you can't afford to stay here, try to drop in for high tea or cocktails.

charming, down-to-earth little hotel is a great deal for the area, with several good-value apartments for rent nearby.

Aventino, Testaccio and EUR

Sant'Anselmo
2 Piazza Sant'Anselmo; tel: 06-570 057; www.aventinohotels. com; €€–€€€; metro: Circo Massimo; map p.137 D2

Nestling in a peaceful garden on the leafy and exclusive Aventine Hill, each room in this hotel has been given its own imaginative theme. Details such as four-poster beds, free-standing baths and frescoes make it a very special place to stay.

Villa San Pio
19 Via di Santa Melania; tel: 06-570 057; www.aventinohotels. com; €€; metro: Circo Massimo; map p.137 D2

This hotel consists of three separate buildings which share the same attractive gardens. It has elegant, spacious rooms with antique furnishings and generous bathrooms with jacuzzis.

Celio, Monti and Esquilino

Des Artistes
20 Via Villafranca, off Via Vicenza; tel: 06-4454 365; www.hoteldesartistes.com; €; metro: Termini; map p.134 C2

Quality of accommodation tends to dip around the station, but Des Artistes is an exception: though the rooms are simple, they're comfortable and clean, and staff are friendly and helpful. The hotel also has spotless dorms.

The Beehive
8 Via Marghera; tel: 06-4470 4553; www.the-beehive.com; €; metro: Termini; map p.134 C2

Rooms at this appealing budget option all have shared bathroom, but are clean and stylishly decorated. There's also a small organic restaurant, a yoga space and a

Prices for an average double room in high season:
€ under €100
€€ €100–€180
€€€ €180–€350
€€€€ €350 and up

Language

Italian is a beautiful language, and one that is relatively easy to pick up if you have any knowledge of French (or a grounding in Latin). Most hotels have staff who speak some English, and unless you go well off the beaten track, you should have little problem communicating in shops or restaurants. However, there are places not on the tourist circuit where you will have the chance to practise your Italian, and local people will think more of you for making an effort. It is well worth buying a good phrase book or dictionary, but here are a few basics to help you get started.

Pronunciation

Italian pronunciation is fairly straightforward: you pronounce it as it is written. There are a couple of important rules to bear in mind: **c** before **e** or **i** is pronounced **ch**, e.g. *ciao, mi dispiace, la coincidenza*. **Ch** before **i** or **e** is pronounced as **k**, e.g. *la chiesa*. **Sci** or **sce** are pronounced as in sheep or shed respectively. **Gn** is rather like the *ni* sound in onion, while **gl** is softened to resemble the *li* sound in bullion.

Nouns are either masculine (*il*, plural *i*) or feminine (*la*, plural *le*). Plurals of nouns are most often formed by changing an **o** to an **i** and an **a** to an **e**, e.g. *il panino: i panini; la chiesa: le chiese*. As a rule, words are stressed on the penultimate syllable unless an accent indicates that you should do otherwise.

Useful Phrases

Yes *Sì*
No *No*
Thank you *Grazie*
Many thanks *Mille grazie/ Tante grazie*
You're welcome *Prego*

Above: it helps to learn some menu basics.

All right/That's fine *Va bene*
Please *Per favore/Per cortesia*
Excuse me (to get attention) *Scusi*
Excuse me (in a crowd) *Permesso*
Could you help me? (formal) *Potrebbe aiutarmi?*
Certainly *Ma, certo/ Certamente*
Can you show me…? *Può indicarmi…?*
Can you help me, please? *Può aiutarmi, per cortesia?*
I need… *Ho bisogno di…*
I'm lost *Mi sono perso*
I'm sorry *Mi dispiace*
I don't know *Non lo so*
I don't understand *Non capisco*

Do you speak English/French? *Parla inglese/francese?*
Could you speak more slowly? *Può parlare più lentamente, per favore?*
Could you repeat that please? *Può ripetere, per piacere?*
How much does it cost? *Quant'è, per favore?*
this one/that one *questo/quello*
Have you got…? *Avete…?*

At a Bar/Restaurant

I'd like to book a table *Vorrei prenotare un tavolo*
Have you got a table for… *Avete un tavolo per…*
I have a reservation *Ho fatto una prenotazione*
lunch/supper *il pranzo/ la cena*
I'm a vegetarian *Sono vegetariano/a*
May we have the menu? *Ci dia la carta?*
What would you like? *Che cosa prende?*
I'd like… *Vorrei…*
a bottle of fizzy/still mineral water *una bottiglia di acqua minerale gasata/ naturale*

Left: no fly-posting allowed.

il pesce spada swordfish
il risotto di mare seafood risotto
le vongole clams
i crostacei shellfish
le cozze mussels
il fritto misto mixed fried fish
i gamberi prawns
il granchio crab
il merluzzo cod
i contorni side dishes
insalata caprese fresh tomato, basil and mozzarella salad

Getting Around
What time do you open/close? *A che ora apre/chiude?*
Closed for the holidays (typical sign) *Chiuso per ferie*
ferry terminal *la stazione marittima*
Where can I buy tickets? *Dove posso fare i biglietti?*
What time does the train/ferry leave? *A che ora parte il treno/vaporetto?*
Can you tell me where to get off? *Mi può dire dove devo scendere?*
Where is the nearest bank/hotel? *Dov'è la banca/l'albergo più vicino?*
right/left *a destra/a sinistra*
Go straight on *Va sempre diritto*

Italian has formal and informal words for 'you'. In the singular, *tu* is informal while *lei* is more polite. For visitors, it is simplest – and safest, to avoid giving offence – to use the formal form.

On the Menu
antipasto misto mixed hors d'oeuvres: cold cuts, cheeses, roast vegetables (ask for details)
arrosto roast
al forno baked
alla griglia grilled
involtini stuffed meat rolls
il maiale pork
il fegato liver
il manzo beef
il pollo chicken
affumicato smoked
alle brace charcoal-grilled
alla griglia grilled
fritto fried
ripieno stuffed
il pesce fish

red/white wine *vino rosso/bianco*
beer *una birra*
milk *latte*
pastry/brioche *una pasta*
sandwich/roll *un tramezzino/un panino*
the dish of the day *il piatto del giorno*

Below: you will find plenty of opportunities to try out your Italian, from seeing a film (the majority are dubbed into Italian), ordering your pastry, to attempting to decipher the local grafitti.

79

Literature

Rome's literary pedigree stretches right back to the days of the Republic, when Cicero penned his hugely influential philosophical works and speeches, and the city has been inspiring dazzled writers ever since. Though traditionally the Romans have always been more interested in the visual arts than the printed page, the new trend for book bars and some thriving local bookshops are signs of a renewed interest, and the city's Literature Festival *(see p.58)* draws world-renowned authors and hordes of literature-hungry Romans alike. This section provides an overview of the literary scene in Rome, past and present.

History

Literature flourished under the Emperor Augustus, a patron of the arts, bringing Ovid, Horace and Virgil to prominence; the latter's epic *Aeneid*, a mix of legend and history, traces the story of the Trojan ancestors of Rome.

The 18th century was also a period of much literary activity, when a fashion for all things classical brought Europe's Grand Tourists to Rome in their droves, among them Goethe and the English Romantic poets Keats, Byron and Shelley. In the 19th century, home-grown poets Trilussa and Gioacchino Belli wrote bitingly satirical verse in Roman dialect, and in the 20th century, a burst of postwar literary activity included works by Alberto Moravia and his wife Elsa Morante. In recent years, ancient Rome has become a popular backdrop for contemporary novelists such as Lindsey Davis, Michael Dibdin and Iain Pears.

Recommended Reading

Augustus, by Allan Massie (Sceptre). This exploration of

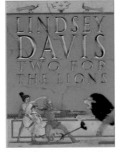

Above: Davis writes comedic thrillers set in Ancient Rome.

the life of the first emperor is fresh and readable thanks to its unexpectedly modern voice.

History: A Novel, by Elsa Morante (Penguin). Morante spent a year hiding from the Germans in mountain villages outside Rome, and chronicled the impact the war had on the ordinary people she met.

Open City: Seven Writers in Postwar Rome, by William Weaver (ed.; Steerforth Press). A rewarding introduction to the writing of Italy's foremost contemporary Italian novelists, including Moravia, Bassani and Ginzburg.

The Raphael Affair, by Iain Pears (HarperCollins). First in a series of art history-themed crime novels, this is a holiday page-turner with plenty of local colour.

That Awful Mess on Via Merulana, by Carlo Emilio Gadda (New York Review of Books). Often described as an Italian *Ulysses*, Gadda combines intrigue and black humour in this exceptional philosophical crime novel, set in Mussolini's Rome.

A Traveller in Rome, by H.V. Morton (Methuen). This evocative and often funny book, written by seasoned traveller Morton in the 1930s, is full of wry observations on the city and its occupants.

Two for the Lions, by Lindsey Davis (Arrow Books). Davis's entertaining thrillers, set in ancient Rome, provide useful background history; here, detective Falco delves into the world of gladiators.

A Violent Life, by Pier Paolo Pasolini (Carcanet Press). Renowned film-maker and poet Pasolini's novel about the inhabitants of Rome's post-

Left: a 1st-century fresco of a scene from Virgil's *Aenid*.

Sun 10am–7.30pm; metro: Spagna; map p.133 D3
Particularly strong on fiction and with a well-stocked children's section and a café, plus knowledgeable staff, this bookshop is deservedly popular.

Book Bars
Bar à Book
23 Via dei Piceni; tel: 06-4544 5438; www.barabook.it; Tue–Thur 4pm–midnight, Fri–Sat 4pm–2am, Sun 11am–8pm; bus: 492; map p.135 D1
In the studenty San Lorenzo district, this bar has towering shelves crammed with books, a good selection of wines, readings, and occasional DJs.
Caffè Letterario
83 Via Ostiense; tel: 06-9346 0; www.caffeletterarioroma.it; Mon–Fri 10am–2am, Sat–Sun 3pm–2am; bus: 23
In an area near trendy Testaccio that's being transformed into a 'City of the Arts', this cutting-edge bar and bookshop is a stylish place to browse as you sip.
Lettere Caffè
100 Via San Francesco a Ripa; tel: 06-6456 1916; www.lettere caffe.org; daily 5pm–2am; bus: H; map p.137 C3
With delicious homemade cakes supplementing the drinks menu, and a lively programme of literary, arty and musical events, this Trastevere bar is always buzzing.
Salotto 42
42 Piazza di Pietra; tel: 06-6785 804; www.salotto42.it; Tue–Sat 10am–2am, Sun 10am–midnight; bus: 62; map p.133 1E
A slick, stylish bar in the heart of the historic centre, where you can lounge on impeccably trendy designer sofas and leaf through glossy design, art and photography tomes.

Book bars are a relaxing alternative to the city's slew of noisy cocktail bars: great places to while away an evening, flick through a book or take in a literary event *(see right)*.

war slum suburbs is a bleak but compelling read.

The Woman of Rome, by Alberto Moravia (Steerforth Press). Fascist Rome is the backdrop to Moravia's delicately woven tale of the trials of a Roman prostitute.

Bookshops
The Almost Corner Bookshop
45 Via del Moro; tel: 06-5836 942; Mon–Sat 10am–1.30pm, 3.30–8pm, Sun 11am–1.30pm, 3.30–8pm; bus: H; map p.137 3C
This tiny bookshop, a Trastevere institution, stocks plenty of fiction, as well as books on Roman history and art.
Feltrinelli International
84 Via V.E. Orlando; tel: 06-4827 878; Mon–Sat 10am–8pm, Sun 10.30am–1.30pm, 4–8pm; metro: Repubblica; map p.134 B2
An extensive range of litera-

ture, magazines and guidebooks in English and other languages.
Libreria del Viaggiatore
78 Via del Pellegrino; tel: 06-6880 1048; Mon 4–8pm, Tue–Sat 10am–2pm, 4–8pm; bus: 40; map p.133 C1
This cosy space is dedicated to travellers, with travel literature, guidebooks and maps, appealingly presented in vintage suitcases.
The Lion Bookshop
33 Via dei Greci; tel: 06-3265 4007; www.thelionbookshop. com; Mon 3.30–7.30pm, Tue–

Below: Gadda's novel is a scathing attack on fascist Italy.

THAT AWFUL MESS ON VIA MERULANA

With a new Introduction by Italo Calvino

Monuments

R ome's monuments have awed and inspired visitors for centuries. Today, only a tiny fraction of ancient Rome is visible, let alone visitable. The main cluster – reminders of Roman power and politicking (the Forum) or sites of amusement (the Colosseum) – are in the historical centre. More recently, domestic sites such as markets and dwellings have been restored and opened up. The Roman Empire gave way to Christendom, and its former glories were reinvented, temples as churches, mausoleums as prisons and palaces, stadiums as *piazze*, and aqueducts feeding elaborate fountains.

The Capitoline Hill

Il Vittoriano
Piazza Venezia; daily summer 9am–5.30pm, winter 9.30am–4.30pm; free; bus: Piazza Venezia; map p.133 E1

In the 19th century, a whole swathe of medieval streets was razed to make way for this hulking white monument erected in honour of Victor Emmanuel II of Savoy, the first king of the newly unified Italy. Romans refer to it irreverently as the typewriter, the wedding cake or even Rome's false teeth. However, entrance is free, and visitors can climb the steps for wonderful views of the city.

Below the equestrian statue of Victor Emmanuel is the Tomb of the Unknown Soldier, flanked by perpetually burning flames and two armed guards. The monument also has a permanent museum complex. The **Museo del Risorgimento** recounts the history of the *Risorgimento* (literally 'Resurrection'), a turbulent period of war and political wrangling that led to the reunification of Italy. However, few of the exhibits are labelled in English, and it's of limited appeal to those with only a passing interest in military history.

Around the back of the building, facing the Forum, is a space used for high-profile international exhibitions.

The Forum

The Imperial Fora
6 Largo Salara Vecchia; tel: 06-3996 7700; daily 9.30am–7.30pm; free; metro: Colosseo, bus: Piazza Venezia, Colosseo; map p.84–5, p.137 E4

On the south side of the Via di Fori Imperiali are the remnants of **Caesar's Forum** (Foro di Cesare), the first of the Fora, built in 51 BC by Julius Caesar when the original became too small for Rome's increasing population. The **Forum of Augustus** (Foro di Augusto) across the street was built to celebrate his victory and revenge over the army of Cassius and Brutus, who had led the conspiracy to assassinate Julius Caesar, his adoptive father.

Trajan's Forum (Piazza della Madonna de Loreto)

Above: the Temple of Antoninus and Faustina at the Forum.

was a massive complex of temples, libraries and markets, surrounded by colonnades, that outdid the other Fora in size and splendour. It was designed in AD 106 by Apollodorus of Damascus, the best architect of his time.

Trajan also commissioned his architect to build the **Mercati di Traiano** (Trajan's Markets; entrance 94 Via IV Novembre; Tue–Sun 9am–sunset; entrance charge), the ancient equivalent of a multi-storey shopping mall. Its remains reveal a complex system of streets on various levels, with shops, administrative offices

Left: the imposing Vittoriano monument.

ing from the 2nd century BC. On the steps, you can see the remains of a temple to Venus, nicknamed Cloacina because the small circular building marks the spot where the Cloaca Maxima (the city's main sewer, built in the 1st century BC) empties into the valley of the Forum.

Beyond the Basilica Aemilia is the **Curia**, the ancient Senate House that was the centre of political life in Republican Rome.

Behind looms the imposing **Arco di Settimio Severo** (Arch of Septimius Severus). The triple arch was built in AD 203 to celebrate the 10th anniversary of the emperor's ascent to the throne. The reliefs on the arch depict the victorious campaigns Septimius Severus and his two sons, Geta and Caracalla, fought in the east.

Beside the arch is the **Umbilicus Urbis**, a navel-shaped piece of stone that marked the centre of the city. Beside it stood the **Rostra**, the orators' platform where speeches were made and public ceremonies took place.

After their deaths, many emperors were automatically deified and had temples consecrated to them. All that remains of the **Temple of Vespasian** (AD 69–79) are three Corinthian columns.

In the north-western corner of the Forum stands the **Tempio di Saturno** (Temple of Saturn), which housed the Roman state treasury. All that remains of this, the most venerated temple of Republican Rome, consecrated in 498 BC, are eight Ionic columns on a podium.

Heading eastwards along the Via Sacra (with your

Avoid the refreshment stands dotted around the major tourist sites unless you're absolutely desperate for a drink. They're overpriced and prey on thirsty tourists. If you don't want to be ripped off, it's worth stocking up on a supply of bottled mineral water or filling up from one of the *fontanelle* (drinking fountains) on Rome's streets.

and spaces reserved for the distribution of grain.

The magnificent **Colonna Traiana** (Trajan's Column) nearby was erected in AD 113 to celebrate Trajan's victory over the Dacians (inhabitants of today's Romania). The minutely detailed friezes spiralling around the column are a veritable textbook on Roman warfare.

The Foro Romano
6 Largo Salara Vecchia; tel: 06-3996 7700; daily summer 8.30am–7.15pm, winter 8.30am–4.30pm; free; metro: Colosseo, bus: Piazza Venezia, Colosseo; map p.137 E3

From the main entrance on Via dei Fori Imperiali a path leads down to the **Via Sacra**

(Sacred Way), the oldest street in Rome, which once ran through the Forum from the Arch of Titus up to the Capitol. Triumphal processions of victorious generals in horse-drawn chariots parading their prisoners and spoils of war, and followed by their soldiers, would pass along the street to the Temple of Jupiter on the Capitol.

Walking westwards in the direction of the Capitoline, to the right lie the remains of the **Basilica Aemilia**, a massive assembly hall for politicians, businessmen and traders dat-

Below: a corner of the Mercati di Traiano (Trajan's Markets).

Above: the eight floodlit columns of the Temple of Saturn.

back to the Capitol), to your left stands the Corinthian **Colonna di Foca** (the Column of Phocas), erected in 608 by a Byzantine governor, in honour of the Eastern Emperor Phocas who donated the Pantheon to the Church.

On the other side of the Via Sacra stood the **Basilica Giulia**, originally the largest building in the Forum (101m long and 49m wide). All that remains of this two-storeyed, marble-faced structure are its pillared foundations. The basilica housed four courts of law, was the seat of the

Roman office of weights and measures, and was a meeting place for bankers.

Heading in the direction of the Colosseum, you'll come to the three surviving columns of the **Tempio di Castore e Polluce** (Temple of Castor and Pollux), built in 448 BC to commemorate the decisive battle of Lake Regillus fought between Latins and Romans in 499 BC. A block of marble from this temple was used by Michelangelo as the base for the equestrian statue of Marcus Aurelius he made for the Piazza del Campidoglio.

Beyond this temple, the **Tempio di Cesare** (Temple of Caesar) occupies the site where Caesar's corpse was cremated after his assassination on the Ides of March in 44 BC.

Directly opposite, 20 Corinthian columns surround the remains of the circular **Tempio di Vesta**, goddess of the hearth and patron of the state. Here the Vestal Virgins kept the eternal flame of Rome burning and watched over the sacred image of Minerva (daughter of Jupiter and Juno). The Vestals entered divine service as young girls and lived a chaste life for at least 30 years in the **House of the Vestal Virgins**, the rectangular structure next to the temple, a once luxurious building.

Back near the main entrance of the Forum, a broad flight of steps leads up to the **Tempio di Antonino e Faustina** (Temple of Antoninus and Faustina), built in AD 141 by the emperor in memory of his wife and converted to a church in the 12th century.

The eastern half of the Forum is dominated by the **Basilica di Massenzio e Constantino**, a three-aisled

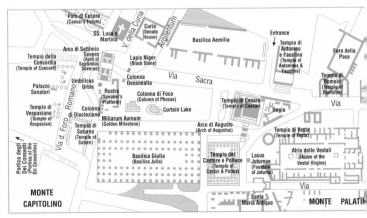

One of the most venerated of Roman deities was Saturn, god of agriculture. Each year in December the festival of Saturnalia was celebrated. Masters and their slaves briefly traded places; generous banquets were held and gifts exchanged. Scholars widely agree that Christmas was established around this time of year to coincide with the widespread pagan holiday.

Above: A Banquet in Nero's Palace, by Henryk Sienkiewicz (1846–1916), *see p.86.*

basilica that was begun by Emperor Maxentius (303–12) and completed by his successor, Constantine (306–30). Only the northern nave remains.

With its colourful brickwork, the Romanesque belltower of the church of **Santa Francesca Romana** will catch your eye. The present building is 13th-century, though the façade was added in 1615.

Beyond the church, marking the end of the Via Sacra, stands the majestic **Arco di Tito** (Arch of Titus), the oldest triumphal arch in Rome, built by Domitian to celebrate the capture of Jerusalem in AD 70 by his brother Titus and father Vespasian.

The Palatine Hill
30 Via di S. Gregorio; tel: 06-3996 7700; daily summer 8.30am–7.15pm, winter 8.30am–5.30pm; entrance charge; metro: Colosseo, bus: Piazza Venezia, Colosseo; map p.86 and p.137 E3

From the Arch of Titus, the road goes up to the Palatino, where Rome's Imperial rulers lived in luxury. Paths and steps lead up to the **Orte Farnesiani** (Farnese Gardens). These pleasure gardens were laid out in the 16th century for Cardinal Farnese, over the ruins of the Palace of Tiberius. They end at a viewing terrace with a fine panorama over the Forum.

A subterranean vaulted passageway leads to the **Casa di Livia** (House of Livia; closed for restoration), famous for its frescoed walls.

In the south-west corner of the hill, excavations have revealed the oldest traces of a settlement in the city (8th century BC). The Iron Age hut known as the **Capanna di Romolo** (Hut of Romulus) was supposedly the dwelling of a shepherd who raised Romulus and Remus, after they were suckled by the wolf in a nearby cave.

South of the gardens lay the **Domus Flavia**, built by Emperor Domitian. The room with a pattern traced on its floor was the courtyard; behind that was the dining room, and the room to the right was the nymphaeum, where diners retired for breaks during banquets.

Next to this palace was the **Domus Augustana** (House of Augustus), private residence of the emperor. To the south are the impressive ruins of the **Terme Severiane** (Baths of Septimius Severus). The tall grey building sandwiched between the Domus Flavia and the Domus Augustana is the **Museo Palatino.**
SEE ALSO MUSEUMS AND GALLERIES, P.91

Forum (Foro Romano)

ilica di Massenzio e Constantino
silica of Maxentius
& Constantine)

Santa Francesca Romana

Templo di Venere e Roma
(Temple of Venus & Rome)

Antiquarium Forense

Sacra

Arco di Tito
(Arch of Titus)

Via Sacra

Colosseo

Nova

Palatino

0   50m

N

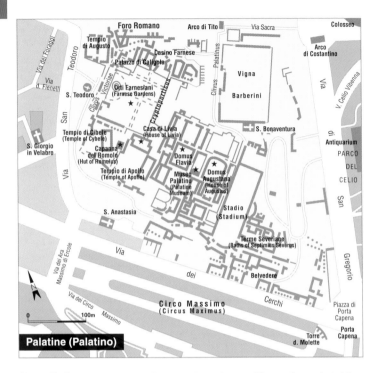

Palatine (Palatino)

Circus Maximus

The remains of the Palatine palaces overlook the Circo Massimo, one of the oldest Roman arenas. Not much of this 6th-century BC stadium remains, but you can make out the track, which was used mainly for chariot races. There are traces of seating to the south (the tower is a medieval addition). In its heyday the arena held around 300,000 spectators, and not only hosted chariot races, but also staged sea battles, which required the pumping of gallons of water into the stadium.

The Colosseum

Piazza del Colosseo; tel: 06-3996 7700; daily: 8.30am–one hour before sunset; entrance charge; metro/bus: Colosseo; map p.138 A3

Work on the construction of the Colosseum began in AD 72 under Vespasian and was completed by his son Titus. The vast amphitheatre measured 190m long and 150m wide, had 80 entrances and could seat between 55,000 and 73,000 spectators. It opened in AD 80 with a three-month programme of games to satisfy a bloodthirsty audience. Christians fought lions, gladiators fought each other and wounded contestants lived or died according to the emperor's whim, expressed by the Imperial thumb, which pointed either up or down. Today, the walls of the various dungeons, cages and passageways, gruesome reminders of the centuries-long slaughter that took place here, can be seen through the caved-in floor of the arena. The **Ludus**

Magnus, the nearby training ground of the gladiators, was connected to the arena by a tunnel.

Gladiatorial combat was banned in AD 438, and over time the amphitheatre became a quarry supplying material for many of Rome's buildings, including Palazzo Venezia and St Peter's.

Between the Colosseum and the Palatine Hill is the **Arco di Constantino** (Arch of Constantine), built to commemorate Constantine I's victory over Maxentius at the Ponte Milvio in AD 312.

Nero's Golden House

Viale della Domus Aurea; www.pierreci.it; tel: 06-3996 7700; Tue–Fri 10am–4pm; entrance charge, advance booking required; metro/bus Colosseo; map p.138 B4

A short walk uphill from the

Colosseum is Nero's Golden House (Domus Aurea). Work began here in AD 64 immediately after a fire had devastated a large chunk of Rome.

Made up of a series of pavilions surrounded by a small artificial lake (on which the Colosseum now stands), pastures, woods and vineyards, it originally extended from the Palatine to the Caelian and Oppian Hills. The enormous complex was filled with Greek statues and monumental fountains. But Nero did not have long to enjoy it. He committed suicide in AD 68 after he was condemned to death by the Senate. Almost immediately the house began to be stripped, demolished or built on by his successors.

Some 30 rooms are open to the public; many more are either off-limits or awaiting excavation. It is hard to get an idea of the opulence and size of the extraordinary 250-room mansion, built on an estate that covered a third of ancient Rome; only the skylit Octagonal Hall gives any real idea of its former architectural grandeur.

Fontana di Trevi and Quirinale

The Trevi Fountain
Piazza Fontana de Trevi; bus: Via

> According to the Latin biographer Suetonius, Nero's palace was the height of ancient Roman opulence. Covered in gold and decorated with precious gems and mother-of-pearl, it had dining rooms from which rotating panels showered guests with flowers, while fitted pipes sprinkled them with perfume.

del Tritone; map p.133 E2
The flamboyant rococo-style fountain was designed in 1762 by Nicola Salvi. Its central figure is the sea god Neptune standing astride a giant shell drawn by winged horses led by Tritons. One horse is placid, the other agitated, symbolising calm and stormy seas. In the niches on either side are statues of Health (right) and Abundance (left). Above the latter, a marble relief shows Agrippa commissioning the aqueduct in 19 BC which still supplies the fountain to this day.

Piazza di Spagna and Tridente

Column of Marcus Aurelius
Piazza Colonna, Via del Corso; bus: Via del Corso, Via del Tritone; map p.133 E2
The 30m Colonna di Marco Aurelio dominates the Piazza Colonna. It dates from AD 180,

and the bas-relief around the shaft depicts the campaigns of Marcus Aurelius against the Germanic tribes and the Sarmatians. Stairs lead to the top, where the original statue of the emperor was replaced with one of the Apostle Paul in 1589.

Ara Pacis
Lungotevere in Augusta; www. arapacis.it; tel: 06-0606 08; Tue–Sun 9am–7pm; entrance charge; metro: Flaminio, bus: Piazza Venezia, Flaminio; map p.133 D2
The Ara Pacis, a finely carved sacrificial altar built in 13 BC to commemorate the era of peace *(pax romana)* that followed Augustus' victories in Gaul and Spain, was painstakingly pieced together by archaeologists from original and reconstructed fragments, and erected in its current location by Mussolini in 1938. The altar is enclosed by a white marble screen decorated with reliefs illustrating mythological and allegorical scenes. After years of neglect and botched restorations, the altar is now the principal exhibit in a new complex, designed amid great controversy by US architect Richard Meier. His striking glass-and-travertine design is the only work of modern architecture in the *centro historico*.

Below: the Trevi Fountain.

Below: the Colosseum.

Above: the Portico d'Ottavia – above the arch, there is a Latin inscription demanding that all fish exceeding the length marked have to be decapitated and their heads given to Conservatori.

Mausoleum of Augustus

Behind the altar is the Mausoleo di Augusto, built between 28 and 23 BC, long before it was intended for use. The first person buried here was Augustus' nephew Marcellus, then Augustus himself in AD 14. It's hard to believe now that this overgrown ruin was one of the most magnificent sights in Rome, covered as it was with marble pillars and statues.

The Vatican and Prati

Castel Sant'Angelo

50 Lungotevere Castello; www.castelsantangelo.com; tel: 06-3996 7600; Tue–Sun 9am–8pm; entrance charge; metro: Lepanto, bus: Piazza Cavour; map p.132 C2

Construction of the castle began in AD 123, and 16 years later it became Hadrian's mausoleum. It has since been a fortress, a prison and the popes' hiding place in times of trouble, thanks to the *passetto*, the corridor that connects the Vatican Palace with the castle. The castle houses artefacts from all periods of Roman history, and many of the rooms, such as the Sala Paolina painted by del Vaga in 1544, are beauti-

fully frescoed. The papal chambers and other rooms are accessible via the spiral ramp inside, which is still in an excellent state of preservation. The gigantic bronze statue of the Archangel Michael that crowns the citadel was placed here in 1753.

Piazza Navona and the Pantheon

The Pantheon

Piazza della Rotonda; tel: 06-6830 0230; Mon–Sat 8.30am–7.30pm, Sun 9am–6pm; free; bus: Largo Argentina; map p.133 D1

The magnificent Pantheon (also known as the Basilica di Santa Maria ad Martyres) is

Below: the intricately carved Ara Pacis, *see p.87.*

ancient Rome's best-preserved monument. Originally built as a temple to the gods, its subsequent conversion into a church in 609 saved it from being torn down. As the inscription over the portico informs us, the statesman Marcus Agrippa, son-in-law of Augustus, built the original Pantheon in 27 BC in honour of the victory over Antony and Cleopatra at Actium. Agrippa's building, however, was severely damaged by fire in AD 80 and was completely rebuilt by Hadrian (AD 117–38), who has been credited as the building's architect, not just its patron.

The portico is stately and imposing: 16 massive Corinthian columns support a roof with a triangular pediment (the notches cut into the portico columns are said to have supported stalls for a fish and poultry market in the Middle Ages). The walls are 6m thick and the huge bronze doors 8m high. But the most striking aspect of the building is the magnificent coffered dome. Over 43m in diameter (exactly equal to its height), it is even wider than the mighty cupola of St Peter's. Held up without

At the top of the ramp in the Castel Sant' Angelo are the terraces and café, both with superb views of the Dome of St Peter's and the rest of Rome. It was from this parapet that Puccini's heroine, Tosca, plunged to her death.

any sustaining columns or flying buttresses, its is a great feat of engineering. On fine days, a shaft of light illuminates the windowless vault through a circular hole (the oculus) in the dome.

The Pantheon contains the tombs of painters and kings; Raphael (1483–1520) is buried here.

Campo de' Fiori and the Ghetto

Portico d'Ottavia

Bus: Corso Vittorio; map p.137 D4

Erected in 27 BC by Augustus, this portico was dedicated to his sister, Octavia, the abandoned wife of Mark Antony. In the Middle Ages, the ruin was used as a covered fish market.

Theatre of Marcellus

29 Via di Portico Ottavia; tel: 06-6710 3819; 9am–7pm; bus: Marcello; map p.137 D4

What looks like a smaller version of the Colosseum attached to a Renaissance *palazzo* is in fact the remains of the Teatro di Marcello. The once-glorious performance space was completed under the reign of Emperor Augustus, who named if after his nephew Marcellus. In its heyday, the 20,000-seat theatre flaunted three tiers, each supported with a different style of column, from the basic Doric to the extravagant Corinthian, and the top level, which has collapsed, was adorned with decorative theatre masks.

Statue of Giordano Bruno

Campo dei Fiori; bus: Corso Vittorio or Largo Argentina; map p.137 C4

With its reputation for being a carnal, pagan place, the Campo de' Fiori was a natural spot to hold executions. Of all the unfortunate victims, Giordano Bruno was the most important figure to be burnt at the stake here, in 1600. A priest and philosopher, he was found guilty of freethinking, claiming that the earth was not the centre of the universe but revolved round the sun, a belief which cost him his life. He is commemorated with a statue on the Campo de' Fiori.

Trastevere and the Gianicolo

Bramante's Tempietto

Tue–Sun 9.30am–12.30pm, 2–4pm; bus: Gianicolo; map p.136 C3

Donato Bramante's Tempietto di San Pietro in Montorio (1502) is the first monument of the High Renaissance style. It possesses a gravity all of its own – not surprising, considering its location: it marks the spot that was believed to be the site of St Peter's crucifixion. Too small to fit a congregation (5m in diameter), the circular temple supports a classical entablature, which lends further weight and severity. These features, combined with the perfect classical proportions, make the Tempietto a brilliant homage to antiquity.

Aventino and Testaccio

Temples of Hercules and Portunus

Piazza della Bocca della Verità; bus: Circo Massimo; map p.137 D3

In the Piazza della Bocca della Verità are two well-preserved Republican-era temples. The

round one was recently restored and determined by archaeologists to be the oldest marble structure in the city, built in the 1st century BC and dedicated to Hercules. The nearby square temple is dedicated to Portunus, the god of harbours.

Celio, Monti and Esquilino

Terme di Caracalla

52 Viale delle Terme di Caracalla; www.pierreci.it; tel: 06-3996 7700; Tue–Sun 9am until one hour before dusk, Mon 9am–2pm; entrance charge; metro: Circo Massimo, bus: 160, 628; map p.138 A1

In AD 212 these were the most luxurious baths of Rome and the city's largest until the completion of the Baths of Diocletian *(see p.99)* a century later. Built to accommodate 1,600 people, visitors could enjoy the use of libraries and lecture rooms, a gymnasium and a stadium, quite apart from the complex of saunas and pools.

The interior was sumptuously decorated with marble, gilding and mosaics. The unearthed statues are now scattered among various collections, but the buildings are still impressive, their vaults rising 30m.

Below: fragments from the Baths of Caracalla.

89

Museums and Galleries

The last 10 years have seen a quiet revolution in Rome's museums and galleries, both state-run and private, with extended opening hours, improved facilities and impressive refurbishments. Unlike galleries in other countries, many of the masterpieces are *in situ*, on the walls of the villa for which they were commissioned or purchased. While the main attractions remain ancient Roman, Renaissance and Baroque, the general overhaul includes new exhibition spaces and the creation of centres focusing on contemporary art.

The Roma Pass

The Roma Pass costs €20 (three days) and gives free entrance to the first two museums or archaeological sites you visit (most major sites are included in the scheme; call 06-8205 9127 or see www.romapass.it for details); the card entitles you to reduced admission on any further sites you visit. Full access to the public transport system is also included in the price. An extra €5 gives you the **Roma & Più Pass**, including transport and entrance to selected sites in the province.

A €22 **Roma Archeologia Card**, valid for seven days, covers the sites of the Museo Nazionale Romano, the Colosseum, the Palatine, the Baths of Caracalla, the Tomb of Cecilia Metella, the Balbi Crypt and the Villa of the Quintili. They can be bought from any participating site.

The Capitoline Hill

The Musei Capitolini
Piazza del Campidoglio; tel: 06-0608; www.museicapitolini.org; Tue–Sun 9am–8pm; entrance charge; bus: Piazza Venezia; map p.137 D4

Above: the tunnel linking the two Capitoline *palazzi*.

The Capitoline Museums' collection is the oldest public collection of classical sculpture in the world – the first exhibits were bequeathed to the people of Rome by Pope Sixtus IV in 1471. It is divided between two palaces on either side of the Campidoglio, the **Palazzo dei Conservatori** and the **Palazzo Nuovo**. They are connected via a passage lined with artefacts that runs underneath the square.

PALAZZO DEI CONSERVATORI

A visit to the museums begins in the Palazzo dei Conservatori (to the right of the Michelangelo staircase as you face the statue of Marcus Aurelius), where the ticket office and cloakrooms are. Here you can see one of the museum's most iconic exhibits, the much-copied she-wolf wet-nursing **Romulus and Remus**, symbol of Rome (it's even the emblem of the Roma football team). The wolf is Etruscan, dating from the 5th century BC, but the twins were added in the 15th century by Florentine artist Pollaiuolo. You can also get a close-up view of the original equestrian statue of Marcus Aurelius (the one on the square is a copy). Other

Left: Constantine's giant toes, in the Palazzo dei Conservatori.

This palace now holds the Museo di Palazzo Venezia, with displays of medieval paintings, sculptures and artefacts, terracotta models (some by Bernini), ceramics, bronze sculptures, and glass, silver and ivory objects. The museum has a permanent collection of Renaissance arts and crafts, and also hosts regular exhibitions.

The Forum and the Colosseum

Museo Palatino
Palatine Hill; tel: 06-3996 7700; www.pierreci.it; Mon–Sat 9am–1.30pm, 2.30–5pm; entrance charge; metro: Colosseo, bus: Circo Massimo; map p.137 E3
This museum on the Palatine Hill houses a fine collection of artefacts found during the course of excavations.
SEE ALSO MONUMENTS, P.85

The Trevi Fountain and Quirinale

Accademia di San Luca
77 Piazza dell'Accademia; tel: 06-679 8850; www.accademia sanluca.it; Mon–Sat 10am–12.30pm; free; bus: Via del Tritone; map p.133 E2
Housed in the Palazzo Carpegno, the Accademia di San Luca (Academy of St Luke), was founded in 1577

> Most museums are closed on Monday, although there are some exceptions. Important art exhibitions are usually open daily.

highlights include a graceful 1st-century BC figure of a boy removing a thorn from his foot, an earlier Venus, a fine collection of Renaissance and Baroque art, and fragments of a huge statue of Constantine.

PALAZZO NUOVO

This second museum in the Capitoline duo is filled with row upon row of portrait busts of Roman emperors, but the first floor contains some exquisite examples of Roman statuary. The most fabulous piece here is the *Dying Gaul*, a beautifully evocative statue of a fatally wounded warrior. Other artworks worth singling out include the voluptuous *Capitoline Venus* and the red marble *Satyr Resting*. More earthly subjects on display include a drunken woman and children with various animals. Look out also for the *Mosaic*

of the Doves from Hadrian's villa and the 2nd-century mosaic of theatre masks.

Museo di Palazzo Venezia
118 Via del Plebiscito; tel: 06-6999 4319; Tue–Sun 8.30am–7.30pm; entrance charge; guided tours to apartments Sat, Sun 11.30pm; bus: Piazza Venezia; map p.133 E1
Built by Cardinal Barbo in 1455 and enlarged when he became Pope Paul II, the Palazzo Venezia was later handed over to the Venetian ambassadors and then to the Austrians, until Mussolini decided it would make a perfect office and addressed the crowds from its balcony.

Below: the poignant statue of the *Dying Gaul* in the Palazzo Nuovo.

to train artists in the Renaissance style. Bernini and Domenichino were both former directors of this august institution.

The academy's gallery, which has recently been extensively renovated, has a collection of portraits, drawings and landscapes of Rome spanning the centuries, including works by Titian, Guido Reni and Van Dyck. There's also an impressive ramp, designed by Borromini, which spirals up to the top floors of the *palazzo*.

Free exhibits are held by art students, and the academy organises a prestigious architecture prize.

Museo Nazionale delle Paste Alimentari
117 Piazza Scanderbeg; tel: 06-6991 120; www.pastain museum.com; daily 9.30am–5.30pm; entrance charge; bus: Via del Tritone; map p.133 E1
Here at the Pasta Museum you will find a whole wealth of information about this Italian staple. The gift shop sells all kinds of pasta-related paraphernalia.

Scuderie del Quirinale
Piazza del Quirinale; tel: 06-3996 7500; www.scuderie

Titian's *Salomé* has been dazzling audiences since the 16th century. One theory behind the power of Titian's depiction suggests that John the Baptist's head is a self-portrait of the artist and Salomé that of a lover who rejected him.

quirinale.it; daily 10am–8pm, Fri–Sat until 10.30pm; entrance charge; metro: Barberini, bus: Via Nazionale; map p.134 A1
Part of the complex on the opposite side of the Quirinal Palace, the former palace stables, or *scuderie*, have recently been converted into a bright and spacious two-level museum space, which hosts important exhibitions all year round. The stairs leading from the top floor back to the lobby offer fine views of the city.

Palazzo Barberini
18 Via Barberini, entrance on Via Quattro Fontane; tel: 06-481 4591; Tue–Sun 9am–7pm; entrance charge; metro: Barberini, bus: Via del Tritone; map p.134 A2
The Barberini Palace displays works from the early Renaissance to the late Baroque, including *The Annunciation*

by Lippi, canvases by Caravaggio, Raphael's celebrated *La Fornarina*, a Tintoretto, Pietro di Cosimo's *Maddalena*, a portrait of Henry VIII by Holbein and a fine ceiling fresco by da Cortona. Parts of the palace are closed for restoration which is not due for completion until 2009, but the masterpieces are usually kept visible.

Palazzo delle Esposizioni
194 Via Nazionale; tel: 06-3996 7500; www.palazzoesposizioni.it; Tue–Fri 10am–8pm, Sat–Sun 10am–10pm; entrance charge; bus: Via Nazionale; map p.134 A1
Reopened in 2007 following a five-year restoration after a ceiling caved in, this imposing 19th-century building, designed by Pio Piacentini, is the city's answer to New York's MoMA. Run by the same team who manage the *scuderie (see left)*, it houses a dynamic cultural centre with an imaginative programme of art exhibitions and events, including film and children's events, and the bookshop is one of the largest and best-stocked in the city.

Galleria Colonna
66 Piazza SS Apostoli, entrance on Via Pilotta; tel: 06-6784 350; www.galleriacolonna.it; Sept–July Sat 9am–1pm; entrance charge; bus: Via Nazionale; map p.133 E1
This charming art gallery within the part-residential Palazzo Colonna is only open on Saturday mornings, but worth a visit if you happen to be in the area. It features richly vaulted, frescoed ceilings, one of which portrays Marcantonio Colonna's victory at the battle of Lepanto (1571). Artists represented here include Lorenzo Monaco, Veronese, Jacopo and Domenico Tintoretto, Pietro da Cortona and Guer-

Below: Caravaggio's *Judith and Holofernes*, housed in the Palazzo Barberini.

Above: the Keats-Shelley House, by the Spanish Steps.

Above: the interior of the Galleria Colonna, housed in a part residential *palazzo*.

cino. Be sure to look out for Bronzino's sensuous *Venus and Cupid*, and Annibale Caracci's *Bean-Eater*, the gallery's most prized work.

Piazza di Spagna and Tridente

Casa di Goethe
18 Via del Corso; tel: 06-3265 0412; www.casadigoethe.it; Tue–Sun 10am–6pm; entrance charge; metro: Flaminio; bus: Via del Corso or Flaminio; map p.133 D3

Not far from the Piazza del Popolo is the apartment where German poet Goethe lived for two years in the late 18th century. He shared the house with painter Hans Tischbein, whose depictions of the poet are on display.

You can peruse the writer's journals and a room dedicated to all his works either written in, or inspired by, the Eternal City. Among them are *Iphigenia*, *The Roman Elegies*, *Faust*, *The Roman Carnival* and *Italian Journey*.

SEE ALSO LITERATURE, P.80

Galleria Doria Pamphilj
2 Piazza del Collegio Romano; tel: 06-6797 323; www.doria pamphilj.it; Fri–Wed 10am–5pm; entrance charge (free audioguide); bus: Piazza Venezia; map p.133 E1

The Galleria Doria Pamphilj contains one of the best art collections in Rome, with over 400 paintings from the 15th to 18th centuries. The 17th-century palace was the residence of the once-powerful Doria Pamphilj dynasty (it is still the property of the Pamphilj family, who live in the opposite wing). Every inch of wall space in the ornate **State Apartments** is taken up with paintings, in keeping with the interior fashions of the time. The finest room here is the 18th-century **Gallery of Mirrors** – a Versailles in miniature. The light pouring in from the windows on both sides is reflected in the mirrors and gold frames to dazzling effect. One of the museum's prize possessions is the portrait of Innocent X by Velázquez (painted in 1649), depicted with a penetrating gaze and a certain ruthlessness in his expression. Nearby is a bust of the Pope by Bernini. Other important works include Titian's *Salomé*, a double portrait by Raphael, and two masterpieces by a young Caravaggio – *Rest on the Flight to Egypt*, much lighter than the rest of his oeuvre, and the *Magdalene*.

Keats-Shelley House
26 Piazza di Spagna; tel: 06-6784 235; www.keats-shelley-house.org; Mon–Fri 9am–1pm, Sat 11am–2pm; entrance charge; metro: Spagna, bus: Via del Corso; map p.133 E2

Keats spent the last few months of his life in a small room overlooking the Spanish Steps; he died of consumption there in 1821, aged just 25. In 1906, the house was bought by an Anglo-American association and turned into a museum and library dedicated to Keats and his fellow Romantics who had made Rome their home. The Keats-Shelley House has an intriguing collection of personal objects and documents relating to the lives of Shelley and Byron, but the main focus is on Keats – his prints, paintings, books and even his death mask are on display.

The Vatican and Prati

The Vatican Museums
100 Viale Vaticano; tel: 06-6988 4947/4676; www.vatican.va; summer Mon–Fri 8.45am–4.45pm, Sat and last Sun of month 8.45am–1.45pm, winter Mon–Sat and last Sun 8.45am–1.45pm, last admission 90 minutes before closing, closed Catholic holidays; no bare legs

93

Above: the ornate ceiling of the Gallery of Maps, situated in the Vatican Museums.

or shoulders; entrance charge, last Sun in month free; metro: Ottaviano-San Pietro, bus: Piazza Risorgimento, tram: 19; map p.132 A3–B2

The Vatican Museums house one of the biggest and most important art collections in the world. They merit a lifetime's study, but for those who have only a few hours, there are some sights that simply should not be missed.

No visit to the Vatican is complete without a look inside the **Sistine Chapel**. The walls, depicting scenes from the lives of Christ and Moses, were painted by some of the greatest masters of the Renaissance: Botticelli, Perugino, Ghirlandaio and Signorelli. It is Michelangelo's sublime frescoes, however, which have made the chapel universally famous.

The four **Raphael Rooms** are the second star attraction. They were decorated by Raphael in the 16th century at the request of Pope Nicholas V. In the central and most visited **Stanza della Segnatura** are two masterly frescoes, the *Dispute over the Holy Sacrament* and the famous *School of Athens (see box, right).*

The **Museo Pio-Clementino** contains some of the greatest sculptures of antiquity. The **Pinacoteca** picture gallery houses an extensive collection of paintings from Byzantine times to the present, with works by Giotto, Bellini, Titian, da Vinci, Raphael, Caravaggio and many others. The **Vatican Library** contains a priceless collection of illuminated manuscripts and early printed books. The **Chapel of St Nicholas** has some exquisite frescoes by Fra Angelico; and frescoes by Pinturicchio can be seen in the **Borgia Apartment**.

More recent artwork is not neglected, either, and the **Modern Religious Art Collection**, adjoining the apartment, displays works by Paul Klee, Francis Bacon, Max Ernst and Henri Matisse, among others.

The **Etruscan Museum**, meanwhile, contains many artefacts found in tombs of the mysterious pre-Roman civilisation. The **Gregoriano Profano Museum** houses finds from the Baths of Caracalla, on the old Via Appia.

Museo Storico Nazionale dell'Arte Sanitaria
3 Lungotevere in Sassia; tel: 06-6787 864; Mon, Wed, Fri 10am–noon; bus: Piazza Risorgimento or Corso Vittorio; map p.132 B2
Within the Ospedale Santo Spirito, near the Vatican, is a small but fascinating museum of medical artefacts displaying an array of medical paraphernalia, and two beautifully frescoed wards.

Piazza Navona and the Pantheon

Museo di Roma
10 Piazza San Pantaleo; tel: 06-8205 9127; www.museodiroma. comune.roma.it; Tue–Sun 9am–

Below: a detail of Aristotle and Plato from the *School of Athens*.

7pm; entrance charge; bus:
Corso Vittorio; map p.133 D1

The Palazzo Braschi was built
by Cosimo Morelli in the closing years of the 18th century
as a papal residence for Pius
VI; the chapel and staircase
are by Valadier. It houses a
sizeable collection of art and
artefacts which document the
daily life of Roman nobility
from medieval times to the
beginning of the 20th century.

Part of the collection is
housed in the Museo di
Roma in Trastevere *(see
p.98)*, and the rest is shown
in rotation.

Museo Napoleonico
1 Piazza di Ponte Umberto; tel:
06-6880 6286; www.museo
napoleonico.it; Tue–Sun 9am–
7pm; entrance charge; bus:
Corso Vittorio; map p.133 D2

In the 1820s Rome was
home to members of the
Bonaparte family, and this
museum contains an array of
family memorabilia. Among
the eclectic collection of personal effects is a cast of the
right breast of Napoleon's
sister, Pauline, made by
Canova in 1805, when he
started work on the reclining
nude in the Galleria Borghese
(see p.96). For Napoleon
enthusiasts only.

**Museo Nazionale
Romano: Palazzo Altemps**
48 Piazza di Sant'Apollinare; tel:
06-3996 7700; www.archeo
roma.beniculturali.it; Tue–Sun
9am–6pm; entrance charge
(combination ticket valid for

Raphael's *School of Athens*
fresco in the Vatican portrays
ancient characters as contemporary heroes. The bearded
figure of Plato in the centre is
da Vinci; Bramante appears as
Euclid in the foreground, and
the thoughtful figure of
Heraclites on the steps is
Michelangelo.

three days includes Palazzo
Massimo alle Terme, the Baths
of Diocletian and Crypta Balbi);
bus: Corso Vittorio; map p.133
D2

Comprised of tranquil rooms
set around a central courtyard, this airy museum contains many treasures of
classical statuary and art,
most of which come from the
priceless collection amassed
by Cardinal Ludovisi. The
prize exhibit is the **Ludovisi
Throne**, a decorative Greek
sculpture, thought to date
from the 5th century BC,
which Mussolini sold to Hitler
in 1938, and which is now
believed to be one of a pair.
Upstairs, the vaulting of the
loggia is intricately painted
with a vine-covered pergola
full of winged *putti*, flowers,
fruits and exotic birds,
inspired by the flora and fauna
imported by the explorers of
the New World. It is lined with
busts of the 12 Caesars.

Other masterpieces here
include an incredibly well-preserved carved sarcophagus
from the 3rd century and the
moving *Galata Suicide*, said
to have been commissioned
by Julius Caesar.

The *palazzo* also contains
many frescoes and bas-
reliefs, a private chapel, and
parts of the ancient Roman
houses on which its foundations can be seen.

Campo de' Fiori and the
Ghetto

Museo Barracco
166 Corso Vittorio Emanuele; tel:
06-6880 6848; www.museo
barracco.it; Tue–Sun 9am–7pm;
entrance charge; bus: Corso
Vittorio; map p.137 C4

Built for a French prelate,
Thomas Leroy, in 1523 and
decorated with fleurs-de-lis,
this elegant Renaissance
palace houses the newly
restored Museo Barracco,

Above: the courtyard of the
Palazzo Altemps.

which holds a fine collection
of ancient sculpture. Artworks
on display include Assyrian
bas-reliefs, Attic vases, rare
examples of Cypriot art and
exceptional Phoenician,
Etruscan and Roman pieces.

Crypta Balbi
31 Via delle Botteghe Oscure;
tel: 06-6780 167; Tue–Sun 9am–
7pm; entrance charge; bus:
Corso Vittorio; map p.137 D4

This huge courtyard, originally annexed to a theatre built
for Augustus at the end of
the 1st century AD, was
excavated in 1981 and forms
the basis for the fascinating
Crypta Balbi Museum.

The museum combines
state-of-the-art technology
with the preservation and
interpretation of archaeological finds on the site itself,
tracing the development of
Roman society from antiquity
to modern times. The ruins
beneath the structure can be
visited once an hour (on the
hour) for short periods, and
reveal the expansive lobby of
the theatre, built by Cornelius
Balbus, a friend of Augustus.

Museo Ebraico
Tempio Maggiore, Lungotevere
Cenci; tel: 06-6840 0661;
www.museoebraico.roma.it;
Sun–Thur 10am–5pm, June–
Sept until 7pm; entrance
charge; bus: Corso Vittorio; map
p.137 D4

Above: Carlo Bilotti, art collector and museum founder.

The Synagogue, consecrated in 1904, was built to a great height to send a message to the Vatican across the Tiber. Attached to the Synagogue (make sure you carry some form of ID, as security is strict) is the Museum of Jewish Culture. Reopened in 2006 after careful renovations, the museum recounts the story of Rome's Jewish population through art, relics and a documentary film. Six new exhibition spaces contain treasures from the community, including Renaissance-era embroidery, stunning ritual items and original marble blocks from some of the Cinque Scole, Rome's five ancient synagogues.

Galleria Spada

13 Via Capo di Ferro; tel: 06-6874 896; www.galleriaborghese.it; Tue–Sun 8.30am–7.30pm; entrance charge; bus: Corso Vittorio; map p.137 C4

The Spada family bought the palace in 1632 and Borromini restored it, adding the ingenious corridor to the courtyard.

On 13 April 1986, Pope John Paul II and Rabbi Elio Toaff held a historic meeting at the Synagogue, marking the first time that a Bishop of Rome had prayed in a Jewish house of worship.

Borromini raised the floor and shortened the columns to create a false sense of perspective, making the corridor appear much longer than it actually is. At the end, a statue was placed against a painted garden backdrop. The statue is less than 1m tall, but from afar it seems to be life-size.

The *palazzo* is home to the Galleria Spada, which has a fine collection of paintings, including work by masters including Rubens, Domenichino, Guercino, Tintoretto, Reni and Artemisia.

Villa Borghese

Galleria Borghese

5 Piazzale Scipione Borghese; tel: 06-328 101; www.galleria borghese.it; Tue–Sun 9am–7pm, controlled entry every two hours on the hour until 5pm; reservations advisable in high season; entrance charge; bus: Via Veneto; map p.134 A4

The Galleria Borghese is housed in an early 17th-century *palazzina* built for Cardinal Scipione Borghese. The cardinal was a great patron of the arts, and laid the basis for the remarkable collection of paintings and sculptures on view today.

Some of Bernini's best work is on display here, including his dramatic statue of *David*, caught just as he is about to release his slingshot, *Apollo and Daphne* and *Pluto and Persephone*.

Scipione was one of the few cardinals to appreciate Caravaggio, and the collection includes several of his paintings, alongside works by other great Italian masters including Raphael, Correggio, Titian, Perugino, Lotto, Domenichino, Giorgione, Dossi and Bassano, as well as by Rubens and Cranach, among others.

Between 1801 and 1809 the Galleria Borghese's sculpture collection was severely depleted, when more than 500 pieces were sold to Napoleon; these now make up the Borghese Collection of the Louvre in Paris. But there are still some marvellous pieces on show.

Museo Carlo Bilotti

Viale Fiorello La Guardia, Villa Borghese; tel: 06-8205 9127; www.museocarlobilotti.it; Tue–Sun 9am–7pm; entrance charge; metro: Flaminio, bus: Via Veneto; map p.133 E4

The old orangery *(aranceria)* in the Villa Borghese gardens has been restored and transformed into a museum containing a collection of works from Carlo Bilotti, an Italo-American collector who favoured modern art. The core of the collection is made up of 22 paintings and sculptures by Giorgio de Chirico. There is also a portrait of the larger-than-life arts patron Larry Rivers and one of his wife and daughter, the *Portrait of Tina and Lisa Bilotti* (1981) by Andy Warhol. Other key works include *Summer* by Gino Severini and the large bronze *Cardinal* by Giacomo Manzù. The complex regularly houses important modern and contemporary art exhibitions.

Museo Etrusco di Villa Giulia

9 Piazzale di Villa Giulia; tel: 06-3200 562; Tue–Sun 8.15am–7.15pm; charge; tram: 3, 19

Rome's Museum of Etruscan Art gives a unique insight into the life and art of the enigmatic pre-Roman civilisation of the Etruscans. Among the many outstanding exhibits are the sweet 6th-century BC sarcophagus of a married couple – *degli Sposi* – from the excavations in Cerveteri, and a 6th-century bronze statue of Apollo of Veio. These and other pieces form one of the finest collections of Etruscan art in the world, rivalled only by that of the Vatican.

Some of the collection is on show in the restored, 16th-century Villa Ponia-towski nearby. Once part of the Villa Giulia complex, it was renovated in the early 19th century by the Polish Prince Stanislao Poniatowski.

Galleria Nazionale d'Arte Moderna
131 Viale delle Belle Arti; tel: 06-3229 8221; www.gnam.arti.beniculturali.it; Tue–Sun 8.30am–7.30pm; entrance charge; tram: 3, 19; map p.133 E4

A permanent collection of 19th- and 20th-century pieces (dating until the 1960s) by Italian and foreign artists including de Chirico, Van Gogh, Modigliani, Degas, Cézanne, Courbet, Kandin-sky, Mondrian, Klimt, Henry Moore and others. The gallery frequently hosts trav-elling exhibitions of inter-national importance.

SEE ALSO BARS AND CAFÉS, P.36

Above: a carving from the 1st–3rd century, Galleria Spada.

North of the City

MACRO
54 Via Reggio Emilia; tel: 06-6710 70400; www.macro.roma.museum; Tue–Sun 9am–7pm; entrance charge; bus: Nomen-tana; map p.134 B4

At the beginning of Via Nomentana, set in a former Peroni brewery, is the **Museo di Arte Contemporanea di Roma** (MACRO). One of two sites (the other is in Testaccio), it houses artworks by the key figures in Italian contemporary art. The site is currently being expanded (hence the reduced entrance fee) and connected

with glass walkways to other buildings behind it. The expanded venue should be ready in 2009.

Villa Torlonia
70 Via Nomentana; tel: 06-0608; www.museivillatorlonia.it; 1 Apr–30 Sept Tue–Sun 9am–7pm, Mar and Oct 9am–5.30pm, 1 Nov–28 Feb 9am–4.30pm; entrance charge; bus: 36, 60, 84, 90; map p.135 D4

Further east, on Via Nomen-tana, the Villa Torlonia was the last great villa built in Rome. In the early 19th cen-tury, the aristocratic Torlonia family contracted French architect Valadier to design the villa, which had a small lake, guesthouse, sports field and Temple of Saturn. The splendid three-storey resi-dence, the Casino Nobile, was Mussolini's home from 1924 until 1943. It was then occupied by Allied forces, who used it as a military command base, but after the war it was left to disintegrate. Following 50 years of neglect the palace has been restored to something of its former glory. The rooms are lavishly decorated – the chandeliered ballroom is the grandest –

Below: the former home of the powerful Borghese family is now a world-class museum.

While you're in the Villa Torlonia grounds, the *Casina delle Civette* (Owl House) is also worth a visit. The Swiss chalet-style residence was built in 1840 and restored in the 1920s in Art Nouveau style, with stained-glass windows featuring idyllic scenes of flora and fauna.

though furnishings are sparse, as so much was looted or destroyed. You can also visit the network of bunkers Mussolini had built in case of attack.

MAXXI

2 Via G. Reni; tel: 06-3210 181; www.maxximuseo.org; Tue–Sun 11am–7pm (for exhibitions); free; metro: Flaminio, bus: Flaminia

Just across Via Flaminia, west of the auditorium, the **Museo Nazionale delle Arti del XXI Secolo** (MAXXI) is taking shape. The impressive new centre for contemporary arts and architecture, designed by Zaha Hadid, is not due for completion until the end of 2008, but if you want to visit, small temporary exhibitions are held in a dedicated space

throughout the year.
SEE ALSO ARCHITECTURE, P.31

Trastevere
Museo di Roma in Trastevere

1B Piazza Sant'Egidio; tel: 06-5897 123; Tue–Sun 10am–4pm; free; bus: Trastevere; map p.136 C3

This museum is dedicated to the life and customs of Romans under the papacy. The exhibition on the upper floor begins with a collection of watercolours by Ettore Roesler Franz (1845–1907), known as 'Lost Rome'. They present a rose-tinted Rome as it was before the urban restructuring of the 1870s.

At the far end of the floor is a series of life-size reconstructions of Roman life in the 18th century, and a room of objects from the studio of popular Trastevere poet Carlo Alberto Salustri (1871–1950), known as Trilussa.

The staircase features casts of the so-called 'Talking Statues' *(see box p.43).* The ground floor of the museum is used for temporary exhibitions, often focusing on photography and new media.

Villa Farnesina

230 Via della Lungara; tel: 06-6802 7268; Mon–Sat 9am–1pm and first Sun of month, Apr–Oct 9am–4pm; entrance charge; bus: 125; map p.136 C4

This sumptuous villa was built between 1508 and 1511 for the fabulously wealthy papal banker, Agostino Chigi. Renowned for his lavish banquets, Chigi was also a noted patron of the arts, and had his villa decorated with a series of beautiful frescoes by some of the best artists of the time. The highlights of the downstairs rooms are Raphael's sensual *Triumph of Galatea* and *Three Graces*. Upstairs is a fine *trompe l'œil* depicting contemporary views of Rome by Peruzzi, and Sodoma's magnificent *Wedding of Roxanne and Alexander*.

Palazzo Corsini

10 Via della Lungara; tel: 06-6880 2323; www.galleria borghese.it/corsini; Tue–Sun 8.30am–1.30pm, entrance at allotted times of 9.30, 11.30 and 12.30; entrance charge; bus: Trastevere; map p.136 C4

Built in the 15th century for a wealthy cardinal, this *palazzo* opposite the Villa Farnesina

Below: a painting in the Terme di Diocleziano.

Above: Pope Innocent III (1160–1216), Museo di Roma.

now houses part of the **Galleria Nazionale d'Arte Antica** collection, which includes works by Fra Angelico, Rubens, Van Dyck, Caravaggio and Luca Giordano, whose *Christ among the Doctors* is one of the collection's key works. *(The rest of the collection is in the Palazzo Barberini, see p.92).*

Aventino and Testaccio

MACRO al Mattatoio
4 Piazza Orazio Giustiniani; tel: 06-6710 70400; www.macro. roma.museum; Tue–Sun 4pm–midnight; free; metro: Piramide; map p.137 C1
This is one of two sites occupied by the Museo d'Arte Contemporanea di Roma (The other main site is in the process of expansion, *see p.97*). The Mattatoio gallery hosts impressive art shows and installations, often in collaboration with the big guns on the contemporary art scene, including New York's MoMa and PS1.

Centrale Montemartini
106 Via Ostiense; tel: 06-5748 042; www.centralemontemartini.org; Tue–Sun 9am–7pm; entrance charge; metro: Piramide
Just a 10-minute walk from the Piramide di Caio Cestio in the old industrial district of Ostiense, the Centrale Monte-

martini is worth a detour. What began as a temporary solution to the overcrowding of the Capitoline Museums has become a delightful landmark museum. Four hundred pieces of Roman sculpture are on permanent display in a converted electricity power plant. The juxtaposition of statues with machinery, tubes and furnaces make this a highly unusual venue.

Celio, Monti and Esquilino

Museo Nazionale d'Arte Orientale
249 Via Merulana; tel: 06-4874 413; Mon, Wed, Fri and Sat 8.30am–2pm except 1st and 3rd Mon of month, Tue, Thur and Sun 8.30am–7.30pm; entrance charge; metro: Vittorio E, bus: C3, 16, 714; map p.138 B4
The 19th-century Palazzo Brancaccio houses the Museum of Oriental Art, a small but impressive collection ranging from 6,000-year-old Middle Eastern pottery to 18th-century Tibetan fans and ancient artefacts from the Swat culture in Pakistan. In the gardens are remains of Nero's water cistern, the Sette Sale, built for his private house and used to feed Trajan's Baths.

Museu Nazionale Romano: Terme di Diocleziano
79 Via Enrico de Nicola; tel: 06-3996 7700; www.archeorm.arti. beniculturali.it; daily 9am–1.30pm, 2.30–5pm; entrance charge; metro: Termini, bus: 36, 40, 64, 170; map p.134 B2
Early in the 4th century, these baths – then the largest and most beautiful of the city's 900 bath-houses – were a buzzing centre of social activity. They fell into ruin after the aqueduct that fed them was destroyed by invading Goths.

Above: a Raphael fresco in the Villa Farnesina.

In the 16th century, the church of Santa Maria degli Angeli (www.santamariadegliangeliroma.it; tel: 06-4880 812) was built inside the *tepidarium* (warm bath) to a design by Michelangelo. The interior exploits the massive vaulting of the ancient building to dramatic effect. Highlights include a painting by Domenichino of the *Martyrdom of St Sebastian* and an elaborate timepiece on the nave floor.

The splendid **Aula Ottagona** (Octagonal Hall; Tue–Sat 9am–2pm, Sun 9am–1pm; free) round the corner displays sculptures from the museum collection.

Museo Nazionale Romano: Palazzo Massimo alle Terme
1 Largo di Villa Peretti; tel: 06-3396 7000; Tue–Sun 9am–7.45pm; entrance charge; metro, bus: Termini; map p.134 B2
There's a stunning array of statuary on the ground floor from the Republican age (2nd–1st century BC) to the late Imperial age (4th century AD), but best of all are the splendid floor mosaics and wall paintings from the houses of wealthy Romans, seen at their best in the delicate frescoes from the Villa di Livia, the house of Augustus' wife that once stood on the Via Flaminia.

Music, Theatre and Dance

Rome is constantly developing its cultural programme. The Auditorium Parco della Musica hosts much of the city's high-quality performing arts. Most theatre is performed in Italian, with the exception of the English Theatre of Rome. World-famous performers regularly frequent the city's venues as part of the concert series; the music and theatre season runs from June to October. For contemporary dance, check out the calendar of festivals. Alternative music venues are listed in Nightlife, see p.102.

Classical Music

There is a wide range of venues for classical music. With special summer concerts and year-round music festivals, there's usually something on.

Auditorium Parco della Musica

30 Pietro de Coubertin; tel: 06-8024 1281; www.auditorium.com; metro: Flaminio, bus: M from Termini, tram: 2

A music and arts complex designed by Renzo Piano, it features three concert halls with excellent acoustics, along with exhibition spaces and a café and restaurant-bar. While classical music packs the calendar, dance festivals, jazz, and visiting pop stars all feature on the programme.

The **Festival Equilibrio** runs throughout the year as part of the Auditorium's *(see above)* regular series and focuses on developments in contemporary dance. The Auditorium opens its season in September with **Metamorfosi**, a series of performances which blur the lines between dance and circus.

During July, the Auditorium hosts the **Luglio Suona Bene** (July Sounds Good) festival in an outdoor arena.

The high-profile **Accademia di Santa Cecilia** (www.santacecilia.it) also holds concerts of its symphonic and chamber orchestras inside the Auditorium.

Il Tempietto Cultural Association

June–Sept at Teatro di Marcello; bus: Marcello; map p.137 D4; Dec–Mar at Sala Baldini; 9 Piazza Campitelli; bus: 64; map p.137 D4; tel: 06-8713 1590; www.tempietto.it

This vibrant cultural association organises world-class performances of classical music. The ticket for the summer programme at the **Teatro di Marcello**, referred to as *Notte Romane*, includes a trip to the archaeological area of the ancient theatre. SEE ALSO MONUMENTS, P.89

Dance

Rome has yet to blossom as a hub for dance in all its forms. The most stimulating performances happen in smaller venues, attached to *associazioni culturali* (cultural associations) and dance schools. Festivals throughout the year bring big names in dance and choreographers to major Roman venues, and the **Auditorium** arts complex hosts the annual **Equilibrio** festival of contemporary dance *(see box)*.

Teatro Olimpico

17 Piazza Gentile da Fabriano; tel: 06-3265 991; www.teatroolimpico.it; ticket office: daily 11am–7pm; bus: 280, 310, tram: 2, 19

The main venue for international and contemporary

Below: a dance performance at the RomaEuropa festival.

Left: the Montalvo-Hervieu dance company at RomaEuropa.

val, with contemporary interpretations of everything from dance to literature; and **Roma Incontra Il Mondo**, Rome's premier world music festival.
SEE ALSO FESTIVALS, P.59

Opera and Ballet

While local opera troupes perform in churches and the occasional piazza, Teatro dell' Opera dominates the scene.

Teatro dell'Opera

1 Piazza Beniamino Gigli; tel: 06-4816 0255; www.opera roma.it; ticket office Tue–Sat 9am–5pm, Sun 9am–1.30pm; metro: Repubblica, bus: 40, 60, 70; map p.134 B2

The city's hub for opera and ballet puts shows on virtually every night of the season. The outdoor summer opera series has been held in various venues in past years, including the Baths of Caracalla *(see p.89)*. Rome's **New Opera Festival** (tel: 06-5611 519; www.newoperafestival diroma.com) puts on classic Italian operas in the atmospheric setting of the **Basilica di San Clemente**, near the Colosseum, most nights mid-June to mid-Aug.
SEE ALSO CHURCHES, P.48; FESTIVALS, P.59

For the most comprehensive listings of what's on in Rome, pick up *Roma C'e*, a weekly booklet with an abbreviated section in English. The fortnightly English magazine *Wanted in Rome* also has listings.

---

dance is the Teatro Olimpico, which welcomes companies from around the world for a series of festivals. The theatre also hosts most of the concerts and performances associated with the **Rome Philharmonic** (www.filarmonica romana.org).

Teatro Palladium

8 Piazza Bartolomeo Romano; tel: 06-5706 7761; www.teatro-palladium.it; metro: Garbatella

Teatro Palladium is an architectural landmark, legacy of a Mussolini-led project to revive the working-class neighbourhood of Garbatella. The theatre puts on a varied series of dance, music and film, all with the goal of promoting cultural awareness. The Palladium is a key venue during the **RomaEuropa** festival.
SEE ALSO FESTIVALS, P.59

Festivals

Every year brings a new festival of music and dance to the city. Many festivals take place outside of city limits. Check out the festival of Latin music and culture, **Fiesta** (www.fiesta.it) and **Rock and Pop** festival (www.romarock.it), both of which take place south of town. Festivals within the city limits include **Equilibrio** and **Metamorfosi** *(see box)*; **La Notte Bianca** – a great chance to see local and emerging dancers, musicians and performance artists; **RomaEuropa Festi-**

Below: pop star Pink performs at the Auditorium.

Theatre

The English Theatre of Rome

Teatro Larciliuto: 5 Piazza Montevecchio, off Via dei Coronari; tel: 06-6879 419 (after 4pm); www.rometheatre.com; bus: Corso Rinascimento; map p.133 D1

This young and vibrant company of locals perform their favourite plays, along with production and world premières by new playwrights. Visiting writers, actors, and comedians enrich the programme.

101

Nightlife

Roman nightlife takes place most frequently around the dinner table: languishing multi-course meals are a typical night out. However, bar-hoppers will find a plethora of drinking holes, from riotous, student-packed pubs and music bars, to tranquil wine bars *(see Bars and Cafés)*. A lounge atmosphere can be found in the early part the of the evening before the discos get pumping. Once midnight strikes, the hordes pour in, and the night gives over to the beats of house, hip hop and electronic – Rome's favourite dance club soundtracks. For a more relaxed scene, check out a live music venue. For a list of cinemas, *see Film, p.61.*

Music Venues

For a night of animated conversation and good music, try one of the city's little jazz clubs, or one of the budding alternative and internationally themed music establishments.

Alexanderplatz
9 Via Ostia, off Via Leone IV; tel: 06-3974 2171; www.alexander platz.it; 8.30pm–1.30am; metro: Ottaviano San Pietro; bus: 23, 70; map p.132 B3

When the big names come to town, they often play at this tiny, yet established jazz club and restaurant which runs the summer jazz series at the **Villa Celimontana** (www.villa celimontanajazz.com).

Below: barman at the trendy SupperClub.

Beba do Samba

8 Via dei Messapi; tel: 339-878 5214; www.bebadosamba.it; daily 10pm–2am; tram: 19

A lively jazz and occasional world music venue in the heart of the bohemian university area, San Lorenzo.

Big Mama
18 Via San Francesco a Ripa; tel: 06-5812 551; www.bigmama.it; Thur–Sat 10pm–4.30am; bus: 23, 280, tram: 8; map p.137 C3

A great blues club, regularly featuring American and other visiting musicians, and some rock and jazz.

Brancaleone
11 Via Levanna, off Via Nomentana; tel: 06-8200 4382; www. brancaleone.it; Thur–Sat 10pm–4.30am; bus: 60 or 90 express

One of the liveliest of Rome's *centri sociali*, attracting high-quality DJs and live acts of all genres of music.

Gregory's
54 Via Gregoriana; tel: 06-6796 386; Tue–Sun 6pm–3.30am; metro: Spagna, Barberini; map p.133 E2

Dine or drink at this tiny, two-level jazz club with a dark, old-school feel – complete with black-and-white photos

and low, clustered couches.

Micca Club
7A Via Pietro Micca, off Via di Porta Maggiore; tel: 06-8744 0079; www.miccaclub.it; Wed–Sun 10pm–2am, later on weekends; bus: Porta Maggiore, tram: 19; map p.139 D3

A multi-function music venue, magazine, website and radio station, Micca is Rome's most varied music venue. Funk, blues, jazz, indie and even burlesque performances grace the stage, which is surrounded by a spacious seating area.

The Club Scene

For those in the mood to dance, Rome is hardly lacking on the disco front. Do be prepared for battle, however. Most nightclubs don't get going until at least midnight and may not even open their doors until then. At swankier establishments doormen are paid to select a well-dressed and female-majority crowd. You'll often be asked if you're 'on the PR list' in which case, unless you're dressed like a millionaire, or manage to seduce the bouncers, you'll be asked to wait, or turned away.

Left: a typically-packed Roman dance floor.

6880 2029; Mon, Tue, Thur–Sat 7pm–3am; bus: Chiesa Nuova or Corso Rinascimento; map p.133 D1

A chic sushi bar and cocktail lounge, this is a gathering place for the visiting and local style set. The best bet is to book a table for dinner, and keep it through the night.

Caruso
36 Via di Monte Testaccio; tel: 06-5745 019; www.carusocafe doriente.com; Tue–Thur, Sun 10.30pm–3.30am, Fri, Sat 11pm–4.30am; metro and bus: Piramide; map p.137 D1

One of the city's premier salsa clubs. Come for live Latin American music, a great dance floor, and the pleasant roof terrace in the summer.

La Maison
4 Vicolo dei Granari; tel: 06-6833 312; Wed–Sat 11pm–4am; bus: Chiesa Nuova or Corso Rinascimento; map p.133 D1

Quite hip, with a 1970s-retro feel to the décor and ambience, and a good mix of commercial, hip hop and house.

RialtoSantAmbrogio
4 Via Sant'Ambrogio; tel: 06-6813 3640; www.rialtosantambrogio. org; opening times vary; bus: Largo Argentina; map p.137 D3

An extremely popular *centro sociale* offering everything from art exhibitions and DJs to live music and theatre. Be prepared to queue.

Supperclub
14 Via de' Nari, off Via Monterone; tel: 06-6830 1011; www.supperclub.com; Mon, Tue, Thur–Sun 8.30pm–3.30pm; bus: Largo Argentina; map p.133 D1

This futuristic restaurant with a clubby feel serves creative cuisine is devoured on sleek white couches. The after-dinner club scene is hopping, and cocktails are great.

You may encounter what is referred to as a *centro sociale*. These themed club-venues often require a simple membership subscription, the cost of which covers entry to the show.

Trastevere is still a reliable destination for Romans in search of a good time. **Testaccio** and **Ostiense** are home to most of the city's favourites, as well as a decent gay scene, and a sprinkling of salsa clubs.

Piazza Navona clubs are frequented by a thirsty American student crowd, whereas **Via Veneto** caters to a moneyed, would-be jet set.

SEE ALSO GAY AND LESBIAN, P.66–7

AKAB
69 Via di Monte Testaccio; www.akabcave.com; tel: 06-5725 0585; Tue–Sat midnight–5am; metro and bus: Piramide; map p.137 D1

Popular club with two floors and a terrace garden. Mainly commercial dance music.

Alpheus
36 Via del Commercio; tel: 06-5747 826; www.alpheus.it; Fri–Sun 10.30pm–4am; metro

and bus: Piramide

Everything from R&B and hip hop to house, with live music and performances that vary from rock and blues, to Middle Eastern. Tango is the latest craze to hit this eclectic club.

Anima
57 Via di Santa Maria dell'Anima; tel: 347-850 9256; daily 6pm–4am; bus: Chiesa Nuova or Corso Rinascimento; map p.133 D1

This trendy, narrow bar and disco with mezzanine sofas and a crowded dance floor, serves cocktails to an R&B, dance and soul soundtrack.

Bloom
30 Via del Teatro Pace; tel: 06-

Below: Rome's bar staff are as glamourous as the clientele.

Palazzi

The palaces *(palazzi)* flanking modern Rome's traffic-laden streets tell the stories of the great families and heads of the Church that helped carve out the magnificence of today's city. Their wealth and fame allowed them to patronise the finest artists and architects around, and today a great many of their lavish palaces are open to the public as museums and galleries. What follows is a selection of those *palazzi* not covered in *Museums and Galleries*, but worth visiting none the less. Many are now government offices, private dwellings and businesses, so they have erratic hours or may only be viewed from the outside.

The Quirinale

Palazzo del Quirinale
Piazza del Quirinale; www.quirinale.it; tel: 06-4699 1; Sept–June Sun 8.30am–noon (depending on state visits – check website); charge; metro: Barberini, bus: Quirinale; map p.134 A1

Between Piazza Barberini and the Imperial Fora, and dominating the summit of the highest of the seven hills of ancient Rome, is the Baroque Palazzo del Quirinale. Since 1947, it has been the official residence of the President of the Republic.

Piazza di Spagna and Tridente

Palazzo di Montecitorio
24 Piazza del Parlamento; www.senato.it; first Sun every month 10am–7.30pm (check website); free; bus: Piazza Venezia; map p.133 D2

Behind Piazza Colonna, Palazzo di Montecitorio is where the Chamber of Deputies has met since 1871. Before that, it was the Papal Tribunal of Justice. Virtually all that remains of Bernini's 17th-century design is the convex curve of the façade – designed to make the building look even bigger than it is – and the rusticated columns.

The Egyptian obelisk in front of the *palazzo* dates from the 6th century BC. It was used by Emperor Augustus as an enormous sundial.

Piazza Navona and the Pantheon

Palazzo Madama
11 Piazza Madama; www.senato.it; first Sat every month 10am–6pm (check website); free; bus: 71, 81, 87, 492; map p.133 D1

The Senate has occupied the Palazzo Madama since 1870. The palace was built for the Medici family in the early 16th century, and several of its members lived here before becoming Pope, including Leo X (1513–21) and Clement

> Those *palazzi* that are visitable frequently offer free tours, all-night openings (the September Notte Bianca), special open days (FAI 'Spring Day' in March) or banks opening (October). Check at the Tourist Information for further details.

Above: Palazzo Madama, seat of the Senate.

VII (1523–34). Catherine de' Medici lived here until she married Francis I of France in 1533. The palace gets its name from the Habsburg Madama Margherita (1522–86), the illegitimate daughter of Emperor Charles V and the wife of Alessandro de' Medici.

Palazzo Massimo alle Colonne
141 Corso Vittorio Emmanuele; tel: 06-6880 1545; 16 Mar only, call for times; bus: Corso Vittorio or Largo Argentina; map p.133 D1

Next door to the Palazzo

Left: the Baroque interior of the Palazzo Lateranense.

now the American Embassy; metro: Barberini, bus: Via Veneto; map p.134 A3
One of the Ludovisi princes had this gigantic building constructed as a substitute for his lost garden, but his money ran out and he had to sell it to the Savoy royal family, who moved the queen mother in. It bears her name to this day.

Celio, Monti and Esquilino

Palazzo Lateranense
Piazza di San Giovanni in Laterano; no phone; metro and bus: San Giovanni; map p.138 C3
The original papal residence, the Lateran Palace was founded in the 4th century, but damaged by fire and fell into ruin. In 1586, Pope Sixtus V commissioned Domenico Fontana to build a new palace as a papal summer residence, though it was never used as such. Fontana's Baroque palace now houses the offices of the diocese of Rome (of which the Pope is bishop). It was the site of the historic meeting that led to the 1929 Lateran Treaty, which established the Vatican's relationship with the Italian state.

Below: the Palazzo Lateranense.

Braschi, home of the Museo di Roma *(see p.95)*, this palace was designed in 1536 by Baldassare Peruzzi for the Massimo family, who occupy it to this day. The building is screened by a fine curved portico of Doric columns visible from the Via del Paradiso.

Campo de' Fiori and the Ghetto

Palazzo della Cancelleria
Piazza della Cancelleria; not open to public; bus: Largo Argentina; map p.133 D1
This splendid Renaissance palace, not far from the Campo de' Fiori, was built between 1485 and 1527. The architect is unknown, but the beautiful courtyard is attributed to Bramante, who also modified the adjoining 4th-century basilica of San Lorenzo in Damaso.

The palace was built for Cardinal Raffaele Riario, who is said to have financed it from the proceeds of one night's gambling, before being confiscated by the Pope and used as the Apostolic Chancery. It is not usually open to the public (it is

still Vatican property), but is occasionally used as a venue for classical concerts.

Palazzo Farnese
Piazza Farnese; tel: 06-6889 2818; www.france-italia.it; Mon and Thur 3pm, 4pm and 5pm; free; bus: Corso Vittorio; map p.133 D1
A masterpiece of High Renaissance architecture, the Palazzo Farnese was commissioned by Cardinal Alessandro Farnese in 1517 but only completed in 1589. The palace cost so much that for a while even the Farnese finances were strained. The original designs were by da Sangallo, but Michelangelo took over the work. When he died, Vignola and della Porta finished it off. Annibale Caracci frescoed the main salon over the central doorway. In 1874 Palazzo Farnese became the French Embassy. Visits in Italian and French must be booked well in advance (email: visitefarnese@france-italia.it).

Via Veneto and Villa Borghese

Palazzo Margherita
119A Via Veneto; tel: 06-4741;

Pampering

Romans have been tending to their bodies and minds for millennia, from poolside gossip sessions and steam-room lawmaking to the use of oils and essences designed to create glistening, perfumed skin. Big fans of make-up, fashion and elaborate wigs, Romans gave great attention to physical appearance. These days, a drop-in visit to the make-up counter or beauty parlour is far more common than a day at the healing spa. Luckily, for those in search of a body-beautifying experience, Rome offers plenty of options. For *profumerie* stocking cosmetics and beauty products *see Shopping, p.124–5*.

Roman Baths

The original Roman bath experience consisted of three rooms. In the *tepidarium*, a warm and slightly steamy area which inspired the Turkish bath, clients lounge about, rub themselves with oils and creams, and then enjoy a thorough scrub down. The *caldarium* is the antecedent to the steam room, where essential oils are poured on hot stones to clear the sinuses and induce relaxation. The *frigidarium* is the refreshing pool to rejuvenate the senses and stimulate circulation. You'll likely encounter a steam room, massage and a variety of masks, treatments and miracle cures at the city day spas, which are generally located within the city's grandest hotels. Several spas include a Hammam, the original, Roman three-part spa route, as part of their list of services.

Spas

Acqua Madre Hammam
17 Via di S.Ambrogio, off Piazza Mattei; tel: 06-6864 272; www.acquamadre.it; Mon, Wed, Fri 11am–9pm (women only), Tue 2–9pm, Thur, Sat 11am–9pm (mixed); bus: Largo Argentina; map p.137 D4

It's hard to believe that this underground, arched setting was not originally a Roman bath. Recently opened and incredibly received, the Hammam offers the traditional three-part spa route and scrub, along with a relaxation and tearoom and a full list of massage and spa treatments.

El Spa
15C/D Via Plinio; tel: 06-6819 2869; www.elspa.it; Mon–Thur, Sun 10am–9pm, Fri and Sat 10am–10pm; metro: Lepanto, bus: Via Cola di Rienzo or Via Cicerone; map p.132 C3

The spa offers a Hammam, ritual baths, Ayurvedic treatments, and their speciality: the Mandi Lulur, an ancient Indonesian beauty scrub, followed by a yogurt body mask and a flower-scented bath.

Hammam
87 Via della Maratona; tel: 06-3629 8573; www.hammam roma.it; Tue–Sun noon–7.30pm; bus: 301, 411, 446

A bit far afield, but worth the trek, this Hammam is styled

Above: a hot stone treatment at Spa Saint Peters.

in purely Moroccan fashion, with mosaic massage tables, low lights and exotic-coloured curtains. In addition to the traditional Hammam and a range of specialty oriental massages, the 'bridal' treatment involves a bath in water scented with flower petals and aromatic massage.

Saint Peter's Spa
415 Via Aurelia Antica; tel: 06-6642 740; www.saturniaspa. com; daily 9am–9pm; bus: 870

A brand new spa and fitness centre complete with Turkish bath, poolside relaxation area with fireplace and tea infu-

Left: the luxurious spa at Hotel di Russie.

tial oils, and full salon and spa service. Try a massage with relaxing or stimulating oils, catering to your skin's needs.

Centro Estetico Malò
120 Piazza Tavani Arquati, off Via Renella; tel: 06-5898 950; Mon 3–8pm, Tue–Sat 10am–8pm; bus: 23, 271; map p.137 C3
This is the Trastevere neighbourhood hotspot for waxing, facials, manicures and pedicures, and relaxing, full-body skin treatments.

Femme Sistina
75A Via Sistina; tel: 06-67 80 260; www.femmesistina-roma.com; Mon–Sat 10am–7pm, Sun 11am–7pm; metro: Spagna; map p.133 E2
This full-service salon has a legacy of luxury. It opened in 1959, catering to the *dolce vita* beauties on the prowl on Via Veneto. Stars still find their way here for everything from cut and style to waxing, facials and manicures.

Sheherazade
6 Via Bu Meliana; tel: 06-3903 1105; Mon–Fri 9.30am–6.30pm; Sat 9.30am–1pm; bus: 23, 70
This tiny, Moroccan-run place does an amazing bikini wax and eyebrow shaping, relaxing facials, and a long-lasting, curative pedicure.

Satisfaction is only guaranteed if you and your beautician know what you're talking about. An essential lexicon: **bikini** – *inguine*; **haircut** – *taglio di capelli*; **facial** – *pulizia del viso*; **highlights** – *colpi di sole*; **legs** – *gambe*; **manicure** and **pedicure** are used in Italian; **shave** – *fare la barba*; **spa** – *centro benessere*; **trim** – *spuntare*; **wax** – *ceretta*

sion tastings and a mile-long list of face and body treatments for men and women.

Hotel de Russie Spa
9 Via del Babuino; tel: 06-3600 6028; www.hotelderussii.it; daily 9am–9pm for guests, visiting clients are advised to book in advance; metro: Spagna; map p.133 E3
Located within the luxurious Hotel de Russie, this sleek, contemporary spa offers a Finnish sauna, steam baths and a saltwater whirlpool. Hair and skin treatments utilise exclusive products by Carita and Décleor. Specialities of the house: coffee-based products and hot stone massage.
SEE ALSO HOTELS, P.71

Wonderfool
39 Via Banchi Nuovi; tel: 06-6889 2315; www.wonderfool.it; Sun noon–8pm, Tue–Sat 10am–8pm; bus: 30, 40, 70; map p.133 C1
A new concept in pampering for men, Wonderfool blends the retro charm of a barbershop shave with the sleek, day-spa experience. Book a shave with warm towels and soothing aftershave products, or indulge in a massage, skin and body treatments, or a consultation with a personal trainer.

Beauty Parlours and Hairdressing
Rome abounds with miniature beauty parlours, *centri estetici*, which take care of nails and waxing. Haircare comes under the name *parrucchiere* (unisex) or *barbiere* (barber).

Aveda
9 Rampa Mignanelli; tel: 06-6992 4257; www.avedaroma.com; Mon 3.30–7.30pm, Tue–Sat 10am–8pm; metro: Spagna; map p.133 E2
The standby in all-natural products, expert use of essen-

Below: Rome's spas offer a wide range of treatments.

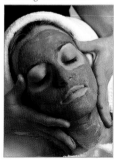

Parks, Gardens and Beaches

It may be hard to believe when you're lost in the twisting alleys of the *centro storico*, but Rome harbours a wealth of green spaces. Once the gardens of *palazzi* belonging to the city's princes, popes and kings, today these parks provide welcome respite from the hectic pace of Roman life. Vast public parks – like Villa Borghese and Villa Pamphili – offer a wealth of activities, from on-site museums to bike rides along the leafy thoroughfares. Others are simply a pleasant spot to have a wander and soak up the sun.

Villa Veneto and Villa Borghese

Villa Ada
Main entrance Via di Ponte Salario; daily dawn–dusk; bus 86, 92, 63

To the north-west, vast Villa Ada is the former hunting grounds of the Savoy royal family. It's a lovely, peaceful park, shaded by centuries-old holm oaks, and has a wilder feel than most Roman parks, with few attractions, but plenty of scope for walks. A set of 2nd-century AD catacombs, the **Catacombe di Priscilla**, extend under the park.
SEE ALSO CATACOMBS, P.39

Villa Borghese
Main entrance Via Pinciana; www.villaborghese.it; daily dawn–dusk; metro: Spagna, bus: Piazzale del Brasile; map p.134 A3

The most popular of Rome's central parks, leafy Villa Borghese offers so many enticing attractions that you could easily spend a day here. Its status as Rome's 'park of the arts' was secured long ago, thanks largely to its founder, Cardinal Scipione Borghese Caffarelli, a nephew

of Pope Paul V, a fanatic of the arts who turned the family estate into a spectacular pleasure garden, amassing a vast collection of art in the 17th century. In 1901, the state bought the villa and, two years later, gave it to the people. The park comes to life on Sundays, when most of Rome seems to head to its grassy hills to picnic and play.

Villa Borghese is home to a handful of important museums. Unmissable is the **Galleria Borghese**; others include **Villa Giulia**, the **Galleria Nazionale d'Arte Moderna** and the **Museo Carlo Bilotti**.

There's also a cinematic cultural centre (**Casa del Cinema**), a zoo (**Bioparco**) and an exact replica of Shakespeare's **Globe Theatre** (Largo Acqua Felix; tel: 06-8205 9127; www.globetheatreroma.com; June–Sept), a touch incongruous in this very Italian setting. Bicycles and go-karts are available for hire at stands around the park, there's a mini-boating lake, the dreamy **Giardino del Lago**, complete with reproduction Greek tem-

Above: an inquisitive statue in Villa Sciarra park.

ples and a colony of terrapins, as well as some lovely cafés in which to relax and watch the world go by.
SEE ALSO FILM, P.61; MUSEUMS AND GALLERIES, P.96–7

Pincio Gardens
Villa Borghese; map p.133 E3

A number of green spaces, including Villa Borghese, Villa Ada, Villa Pamphili and Villa Torlonia, are wireless hotspots, meaning that even those with work to do can enjoy the city's parklife.

Left: an elegant water feature in the Pincio Gardens.

late 18th century, transforming its orchards, vineyards and open fields into a verdant oasis dotted with sumptuous *palazzi*. An array of architects and landscape gardeners have left their mark over the years. Torlonia commissioned Valadier to work on the north section of the park in the late 18th and early 19th centuries; his classical layout was dominated by symmetrical avenues of oaks, some of which still remain. The southern section was the work of landscape gardener Giuseppe Jappelli, whose romantic style extended to the whimsical buildings in this part of the park. During the war, the gardens were used both for Mussolini's social functions and as a vegetable garden.

After decades of neglect, the park has only recently been restored to its former glory, its lawns newly tended and its various buildings open to the public.

SEE ALSO MUSEUMS AND GALLERIES, P.97–8

Trastevere and Gianicolo
Villa Sciarra
Main entrance Via Calandrelli;

A number of parks extend their opening hours on warm summer evenings for open-air concerts. For details of events in Villa Ada, Villa Celimontana and the Orto Botanico, *see Festivals, p.59.*

Technically part of Villa Borghese, these formal gardens occupying a corner of the park were designed by Valadier in the 19th century. Look out for the fanciful water clock and the **Casina Valadier**, once an elegant café visited by the intellectuals of the Roman *belle époque*. Nowadays, it is an expensive restaurant with a fabulous view from its terrace (tel: 06-6992 2090; www.casinavaladier.it; Tue–Sat 12.30am–3pm, 8pm–11pm, Sun lunch only). Outside, the romantic terrace of the Pincio overlooks Piazza del Popolo and offers a splendid vantage point to view the city. Further down the Pincio hillside is the majestic **Villa Medici**. Rebuilt in the 16th century for the Crescenzi family, it was then passed to the Medicis, before being confiscated by

Napoleon in 1803 and made the home of the French Academy, open for occasional exhibitions and concerts. There are guided tours of the gardens (in Italian and French only) on Saturday and Sunday morning (advance booking, tel: 06-67611; www.villamedici.it).

Villa Torlonia
70 Via Nomentana; tel: 06-8205 9127; www.museivillatorlonia.it; park: daily dawn–dusk; bus: 60; map p.135 D4
Towards the east, Villa Torlonia was the last great villa built in Rome. Giovanni Torlonia bought the land in the

---

Below: an agave plant in the desert garden of the Orto Botanico.

Left: the fountain in the Villa Medici gardens.

century by Prince Camillo Pamphili, Villa Pamphilj is now the city's biggest park, a sprawling expanse of wooded green crisscrossed by picturesque walkways. Beloved of dog-walkers and strollers, it's also a favourite with children, thanks to the turtles in its mini-lake and its pony rides.

Aventino, Testaccio, EUR

Roseto Comunale

Via di Valle Murcia; tel: 06-574 6810; May–June daily 8am–6.30pm; metro: Circo Massimo; map p.137 E2

On the Aventine Hill, the Roseto was Rome's Jewish cemetery for centuries, before being given to the city in the 20th century. The garden layout pays tribute to the site's history, with paths forming a candelabra shape. The rose garden opens to the public during the flowering season, displaying an extensive and wonderfully fragrant collection of roses, rambling over pergolas on the upper slopes.

Celio, Monti and Esquilino

Villa Celimontana

Main entrance Via della Navicella; daily dawn–dusk; bus: 60; map p.138 B2

This charming walled garden near the Colosseum is too small for serious walkers, but there are plenty of benches for weary sightseers, and it's a pleasant spot for a picnic. Seek out its Egyptian obelisk, tucked away and somewhat forgotten at the park's southern end.

Parco degli Acquedotti

Main entrance Viale Appio Claudio; always open; metro: Giulio Agricola

Rome's 'aqueduct park' near

---

daily 7am–sunset; bus 75; map p.136 B2

A walled green space nestling above the hill of the Gianicolo, this tiny gem of a park has lovely landscaped gardens, 18th-century fountains and children's rides. A walk up a steep flight of steps from Trastevere, it's a haven of peace that feels a long way from central Rome.

Orto Botanico

24 Largo Cristina di Svezia; tel: 06-4991 7135; Apr–Oct Mon–Sat 9.30am–6pm, Nov–Mar Mon–Sat 9.30am–5.30pm; entrance fee; bus: H; map p.136 C4

In the 13th century, this garden at the foot of the Gianicolo was used to grow medicinal herbs by order of Pope Nicholas III; it was transformed into the city's Botanical Gardens in 1833. Today, it's a restful place to escape from the heat of the city: Baroque steps are

flanked by waterfalls, and an array of fountains and statues interspersed with exotic plants make a stroll here a pleasure. There's also a collection of highly perfumed and tactile species dedicated to the vision-impaired.

Villa Pamphilj

Main entrance Porta San Pancrazio; daily dawn–dusk; bus: 791; map p.136 B3

Laid out on this sloping site between the Vatican and Monteverde in the mid-17th

---

Via Appia is a perfect place to spend a day, preferably a Sunday, when the road is closed to traffic. A good transportation option is the Archeobus, a minibus leaving daily from Termini every 40 minutes (9.30am–4.50pm). Tickets can be purchased online or on board, and are valid all day. www.trambusopen.com; tel: 06-6840 901.

Above: the ruins of the Ancient Roman aqueduct can be seen throughout the Parco degli Acquedotti.

the **Appian Way** is embellished by snaking stretches of ancient Roman aqueduct, made famous in the opening scene to Fellini's *La Dolce Vita*. Aside from a few benches, it has very few facilities, but the novelty value of picnicking in the shadow of such imposing ruins can't be denied.

SEE ALSO CATACOMBS, P.38

Parco Regionale dell'Appia Antica
Via Appia Antica; always open; bus: 660

The wild countryside around the ancient **Appian Way** is within surprisingly easy reach of the city. A good day to visit is Sunday, when the road is closed to traffic; rent a bike at the Centro Visite

Parco Appia Antica (Visitor's Centre; Via Appia Antica 42; tel: 06-5126 314; www.parcoappia antica.org; Sun and public holidays 9.30am–5.30pm; book ahead), or simply wander along the cobbled Appian Way, which is lined with ancient tombs. There are also a number of **catacombs** to explore in the area; ask at any tourist office or at the visitor's centre for details.

SEE ALSO CATACOMBS, P.38

Beaches

When the heat and bustle of the city get too much, Romans head to the beach. The coast is only a short train journey away, but because of this it can get incredibly crowded in the

hottest months. Sunseekers looking for a more relaxed experience need to head further afield.

Lido di Ostia
30 mins by train; metro: Piramide to Lido di Ostia.

Lido di Ostia and the surrounding beaches are the most popular around Rome, and locals start descending on them at weekends in their hundreds of thousands from late May or early June. This is to its convenience as the nearest resort to Rome, and the fact that it is packed with *stabilimenti* – amenities, and a rather chaotic nightlife.

Fregene
40km west of Rome; 1 hr by bus or train; bus: from Lepanto or train: Termini to Maccarese & bus: Fregene.

Once the glamorous retreat of the *Dolce Vita* set, this appealing resort, backed by a pine wood and luxury villas, is fashionable again.

Capocotta
10km south of Ostia; gates close *c.*7.30pm; train: Piramide to Cristoforo Colombo & bus: Mare 2.

A once-infamous nudist beach, it has totally cleaned up its act and is now run by a Rome City Council-backed consortium which offers free *stabilimenti*. Located behind several gates, this stretch of coastline is clean, well kept and of some natural beauty, since it is located within the protected Parco del Litorale Romano.

FURTHER AFIELD
For the first really clean water and large sandy beaches south of Rome you will have to go a bit further, to **Sabaudia** (buses leave from the EUR Fermi metro stop), or the ancient Roman port of **Sperlonga** (about halfway between Naples and Rome).

Below: in the summer thousands of Romans flee the city to sit on the over-crowded Lido di Ostia beach.

R

Restaurants

This is probably not the city to hunt down the top restaurants – few consider *la cucina romana* the best of Italy's regional cuisines – but Rome may well be one of Italy's most pleasurable cities in which to eat. Most restaurants plan on one seating per evening, so you will not be rushed, or pressured to leave. Often, what might seem to be slow service is merely the Roman way of stretching a meal far into the night. When in Rome, make a point of having a long, lingering meal – and have it in the open air, if the weather is good. Some excellent *enotecas* (wine bars) can be found in restaurants, *see Bars and Cafés* for more options.

Capitoline Hill and The Forum

Forum Pizzeria
4–38 Via San Giovanni in Laterano; tel: 06-7759 1158; daily noon–3pm, 7.30–midnight; €; metro: San Giovanni; map p.138 B3
A large pizzeria serving delicious, thick-crusted pizzas from a wood-fired oven.

Ristorante Mario's
9 Piazza del Grillo, off Piazza Venezia; tel: 06-6793 725; Tue–Sun noon–3pm, 7–10.30pm; €; bus: 40; map p.137 E4
Traditional Roman food (fish is their speciality) and a lovely pergola in the square outside, at affordable prices.

San Teodoro
49–51 Via dei Fienili; tel: 06-6780 933; Mon–Sat 1–3pm, 8–11.30pm; €€€€; bus: 170; map p.137 E3
Located in a tranquil piazza, this elegant restaurant offers

Price includes dinner and a half-bottle of house wine:
€ under €25
€€ €25–€40
€€€ €40–€60
€€€€ more than €60

traditional food successfully updated and centred on seasonal availability. Staples are fish carpaccios and pasta.

Vecchia Roma
18 Piazza Campitelli; tel: 06-6864 604; Thur–Tue 1–3pm, 8–11pm; €€€€; bus: 64; map p.137 D4
At Vecchia Roma you pay for the location, the service and some of the city's finest outdoor seating. It's expensive for what you get, but memorable.

The Trevi Fountain and the Quirinale

Al Presidente
95 Via in Arcione, off Via del Lavatore; tel: 06-6797 342; Tue–Sun 1–3.30pm, 8–11.30pm; €€€; bus: Piazza San Silvestro; map p.133 E2
A family-run restaurant, with a lovely outdoor area. High-quality food and a good wine list. A gem in this touristy area.

Le Tamerici
79 Vicolo Scavolino, off Via del Lavatore; tel: 06-6920 0700; Mon–Sat 12.30–3.30pm, 7.30–11.30pm, Sun 7.30–11.30; €€€; bus: 175; map p.133 E2
Innovative, seasonal cuisine from an all-female team. With

Above: Il Margutta RistorArte.

a minimalist décor providing dramatic contrast to the Baroque extravagance outside. This level of quality and service does not come cheap.

Vineria Il Chianti
81 Via del Lavatore; tel: 06-6787 550; Mon–Sat 12.30–3.30pm, 7–11.30pm; €€; bus: Piazza San Silvestro; map p.133 E2
A buzzing, rustic *locale* with young staff and a Tuscan slant. Expect to find hearty soups, quiche, wild boar fillet; pizzas in the evening. Stays open late.

Piazza di Spagna and Tridente

Dal Bolognese
1–2 Piazza del Popolo; tel: 06-

Left: relaxed dining at Il Margutta RistorArte.

feature is the outdoor seating. Booking advisable. Open late.
SEE ALSO BARS AND CAFÉS, P.34

Hostaria dell'Orso
25C Via dei Soldati, off Via del Coronari; tel: 06-6830 1192; Mon–Sat 8pm–12.30am; €€€; bus: Lungotevere Tor di Nona; map p.133 D2

Milanese superstar chef Gualtiero Marchesi is at the helm of the exclusive Hostaria dell'Orso in a *palazzo* that has been an inn since medieval times. It has an expensive take on Italian haute cuisine which can be ordered à la carte or from four different set-price menus *(menù degustazione)*.

Il Margutta RistorArte
118 Via Margutta; tel: 06-3265 0577; daily 12.30–3.30pm, 7.30–11.30pm; €€–€€€; metro: Spagna, Piazzale Flaminio; bus: Piazzale Flaminio; map p.133 E3

This is one of Rome's oldest vegetarian restaurants and offers refined contemporary Italian cuisine. At lunch there is a set-price buffet, and there's a good brunch on Sunday.

Matricianella
3–4 Via Aia, off Largo F. Borghese; tel: 06-6832 100; Mon–Sat 12.30–3pm, 7.30–11pm; €€; bus: Piazza Augusto Imperatore; map p.133 D2

Traditional Roman food in a cheerful setting. To start, try their crispy *fritto vegetale* (fried vegetables). Closed three weeks Aug.

Nino
11 Via Borgognona; tel: 06-6795 676; Mon–Sat 12.30–3pm, 7.30–11.30pm; €€–€€€; metro: Spagna; map p.133 E2

Genuine Tuscan food has been consumed here for over 70 years. Sample the leek soufflé, wild boar with polenta and pappardelle with hare sauce. At the upper end

---

Romans may love a leisurely meal, but stopping off for a slice of pizza, a few scoops of ice cream or a shot of fruit and crushed ice is an essential part of any *passeggiata*.

3611 426; Tue–Sun 1–3pm, 8:15pm–midnight; €€€€; metro and bus: Piazzale Flaminio; map p.133 D3

This smart restaurant with uniformed waiters and couches on which to sip your *aperitivo*, serves good-quality staples from the Emilia Romagna region to a loyal clientele of politicians, film producers and assorted artists and celebrities. Closed three weeks Aug.

Da Gino
4 Vicolo Rosini, off Via Prefetti; tel: 06-6873 434; Mon–Sat 1–3.30pm, 8–10.30pm; €€; bus: Piazza Colonna; map p.133 D2

Vaulted ceilings and frescoes adorn this trattoria, where affordable Roman specialities are served following the traditional weekly calendar, which means fish on Tuesday and Friday. No credit cards. Closed Aug.

'Gusto
9 Piazza Augusto Imperatore; tel: 06-3226 273; wine bar: daily 11.30am–2am, pizzeria: daily 12.30–3.30pm, 7.30–11.30pm, restaurant: daily 12.30–3.30pm, 7.30–11.30pm; €–€€€ restaurant; €€–€€€ pizzeria; bus: Piazza Augusto Imperatore; map p.133 D2

'Gusto is an empire: a pizzeria downstairs, an upmarket restaurant upstairs, a wine bar on the other side, an *osteria* next to that. The service is fast and friendly, and the general standard is high. In warm weather, an added

Below: preparing food at the gastronomic empire, 'Gusto.

Left: Osteria dell'Ingegno.

serving excellent local cuisine for nearly a century. Word has spread to the international style set, and it's not unusual to catch a Hollywood star or two slurping up the restaurant's signature pasta *all'amatriciana* (pasta in a sauce of tomato, bacon, and onion).

La Pergola dei Cavalieri Hilton
101 Via A. Cadlolo (Monte Mario); tel: 06-3509 2152; Tue–Sat 7.30–11.30pm; €€€€; bus: 907, 919, 990

Further north, German superstar chef Heinz Beck has made this a place worth making a detour for. Enviable views, attentive staff and ultra-refined food.

Osteria dell'Angelo
32 Via G. Bettolo; tel: 06-3729 470; Mon, Sat 8–11pm, Tue–Fri 12.30–2.30pm, 8–11pm; €€–€€€; metro: Ottaviano San Pietro; bus: 32; map p.132 B4

This neighbourhood trattoria is always packed to the gills. Try the *fritti* to begin with and then a flavourful version of the Roman standard *tonnarelli cacio e pepe* (pasta with pecorino and pepper). Booking advisable. No credit cards.

Siciliainbocca
26 Faà di Bruno; tel: 06-3735 8400; Mon–Sat 1–3pm, 8–11.30pm; €€; bus: 32; map p.132 B4

Come here for a cheerful ambience and good Sicilian food seasoned with the island's flavours: lemons, olives, capers and plenty of sunshine. Their classic ricotta-filled *cassata* is excellent.

Zen
243 Via degli Scipioni; tel: 06-3213 420; Tue–Fri, Sun 12–3pm, 7.45pm–midnight; €€–€€€; metro: Lepanto, bus: 30, 70; map p.132 C3

Indisputably the city's best, if priciest, sushi restaurant,

---

of this price scale, and well worth it. Closed Aug.

L'Osteria
16 Via della Frezza; tel: 06-3226 273; daily 12.30–3.30pm, 7pm–1am; €€; metro: Spagna, bus: Piazza Augusto Imperatore; map p.133 D3

Informal but chic, and further proof that anything the 'Gusto team *(see p.113)* touches turns to gold. The menu is a skilful combination of traditional and contemporary, with 400 cheeses, cured meats, deep-fried delicacies and good main courses. All served with excellent wines from a selection of 1,700 labels.

PizzaRé
14 Via di Ripetta; tel: 06-3211 468; daily 12.15–3.30pm,

7.30pm–midnight; €; bus: 628; map p.133 D2

For a simple pizza after a heavy day's walking, try PizzaRé, maker of the thick and crusty Neapolitan variety. Set-price menus, including pasta and grilled meats at lunchtime. Pizzas at reduced price on Monday evenings.

Taverna Ripetta
158 Via di Ripetta; tel: 06-6880 2979; daily 12.30–4pm, 7–11.30pm; €€; bus: 628; map p.133 D2

Romantic and atmospheric, this restaurant is perfect for lunch as well as dinner. The menu incorporates pasta, meat and fish. Try the outstanding *semifreddo* for dessert.

The Vatican and Prati

Il Matriciano
55 Via dei Gracchi; tel: 06-321 3040; Thur–Tue 12.30–2.30pm, 7.30–11.30pm; €€–€€€; metro: Ottaviano San Pietro, bus: Piazza Risorgimento; map p.132 B3

This restaurant has been

Price includes dinner and a half-bottle of house wine:
€ under €25
€€ €25–€40
€€€ €40–€60
€€€€ more than €60

Zen's strong point is extraordinary freshness and high-quality, classic Japanese cuisine. The crowd is chic and dressed to kill. Book ahead.

Piazza Navona and the Pantheon

L'Altro Mastai

53 Via Giraud, off Corso Vittorio Emanuele II; tel: 06-6830 1296; Tue–Sat 7.30–11.30pm; €€€€; bus: Chiesa Nuova; map p.133 C1

This gourmet restaurant specialising in Mediterranean haute cuisine pairs a warm, homely atmosphere with impeccable service. Chef Fabio Baldassare was trained under Heinz Beck of La Pergola (see p.114), and widely regarded as the best chef on Italian soil. Sensational dining comes at sensational prices.

Casa Bleve

48–59 Via del Teatro Valle; tel: 06-6865 970; Tue, Sat 1–3pm, 7.30–10.30pm, Wed–Fri 1–3pm, 7–10pm; €–€€; bus: San Andrea delle Valle; map p.133 D1

Set against the stunning backdrop of the Palazzo Medici Lante della Rovere, Casa Bleve's enormous semicircular counter is laden with cold meats, salads and cheeses. With an exceptional wine list, this is a high-level *enoteca* worth seeking out. Closed three weeks Aug.

Convivio Troiani

31 Via dei Soldati, off Via dei Coronari; tel: 06-6869 432; Mon–Sat 8–11pm; €€€€; bus: 30, 70; map p.133 D2

Il Convivio is one of the city's foremost gastronomic temples. Equal emphasis is placed on vegetable, fish and meat options, but they are always combined with something unexpected. Three elegant rooms and well-trained staff make for a truly gourmet experience.

Cul de Sac

73 Piazza di Pasquino; tel: 06-6880 1094; daily noon–4pm, 6pm–12.30am; €€; bus: Chiesa Nuova; map p.133 D1

One of the best-stocked wine bars in Rome. Space may be tight, but the atmosphere, prices and array of cheeses, cold meats, Middle Eastern-influenced snacks, hearty soups and salads all hit the right spot. Be prepared to queue.

Myosotis

3–5 Vicolo della Vaccarella, off Via della Scrofa; tel: 06-6865 554; Mon–Sat 7.30–11.30pm; €€; bus: Chiesa Nuova; map p.133 D2

A discreet, high-level restaurant with an exemplary wine list. A gourmet experience at an affordable price.

> Avoid the overpriced cafés on the Piazza Navona. For a glass of wine and plate of cheese, cold cuts, pâté or any combination of snacks and salads, the Cul de Sac wine bar *(see below)* on Piazza di Pasquino is a welcome alternative.

O' Pazzariello

19 Via Banco di Santo Spirito, off Lungotevere Tor di Nona; tel: 06-6819 2641; Tue–Sun 7pm–midnight, Thur–Sun 12.30–3pm; bus: 40, 64; 916; map p.132 C1

With an exhibitionist pizza-cook and *simpatico* waiting staff, this is a sure bet for a fun and affordable evening. The pizzas are thick-crusted and range from small to gigantic.

Osteria dell'Ingegno

45 Piazza di Pietra; tel: 06-6780 662; Mon–Sat noon–3pm, 7pm–midnight; €€; bus: 52, 63, 70, 80; map p.133 E1

Much frequented by politicians due to its location near Parliament, this modern *osteria* specialises in light, inventive dishes. The desserts are homemade and the wines well chosen.

Riccioli Café

13 Via delle Coppelle; tel: 06-6821 0313; €–€€€; Mon–Sat noon–1am; bus: Corso Rinascimento; map p.133 D1

Riccioli Café was the first oyster bar in the city and serves sushi and sashimi. It's one of the buzziest bars in the area at *aperitivo* hour.

La Rosetta

8 Via della Rosetta, off Via Giustiniani; tel: 06-6861 002; Mon–Sat 12.30–3pm, 7.30–11.30pm; €€€–€€€€; bus: Corso Rinascimento; map p.133 D1

One of the best seafood restaurants in Rome, where the produce is guaranteed to have been caught that morning and cooked by an experienced chef.

Below: handmade chocolates and sweets round off a meal nicely.

Da Tonino

18 Via del Governo Vecchio; no
phone; Mon–Sat 12–4pm; €;
7pm–midnight; bus: Chiesa
Nuova; map p.133 C1

As the weekend queues tes-
tify, this is one of Rome's best-
loved eateries. Stark lighting,
basic décor and excellent
local food, served in generous
portions at fair prices. No
credit cards.

Trattoria

25 Via del Pozzo delle Cornacchie,
off Corso del Rinascimento; tel:
06-6830 1427; Mon–Sat 12.30–
3pm, 7.30–11.30pm; €€–€€€;
bus: 30, 70, 492; map p.133 D1

A Pulitzer-nominated photo-
journalist, saucy Sicilian chef
and seducer Filippo LaMantia
has a fresh take on Sicilian
cuisine, utilising fresh herbs
and citrus zest. Watch the
chefs in action through a
glass wall.

Campo de' Fiori and the Ghetto

Antica Trattoria Polese

40 Piazza Sforza Cesarini; tel:
06-6861 709; Mon, Wed–Sun
noon–3pm, 7pm–midnight; €€;
bus: 40, 64; map p.133 C1

Less packed than its rowdier
neighbour Da Luigi, Polese
has outdoor seating in a small
piazza off Corso Vittorio, and
a refined Roman menu based

> Brush up on your bad language
> and visit La Parolaccia restaur-
> ant (3 Vicolo del Cinque;
> Mon–Sat) in Trastevere. Here
> food is served accompanied by
> bawdy language (the restaur-
> ant's name means swear word)
> and a brusque but entertaining
> Roman manner.

on what is available at the
market that morning.

Il Bacaro

27 Via degli Spagnoli, off Via
della Scrofa; tel: 06-6872 554;
Mon–Sat noon–2.30pm,
8pm–midnight; €€; bus: 30,70;
map p.133 D2

The Bacaro oozes charm, and
is perfect for a romantic
soirée. Its cobbled stone and
trellised outdoor area, and tiny
internal room are much sought
after, so booking is essential.

La Bottega del Vino di Anacleto Bleve

9A Via Santa Maria del Pianto, off
Via Arenula; tel: 06-6865 970;
Tue–Sat 12–3pm, aperitivo
6–8pm; €–€€; bus: H, 23, Largo
Argentina, tram: 8; map p.137 D4

A quintessentially Roman
enoteca (wine bar) whose
buffet is loaded with dozens
of delicacies such as smoked
swordfish, salmon rolls, sfor-
mati (flans) and cod carpac-
cio. Locals come here for the

good food, well-chosen wine
list and the simpatia of its
husband-and-wife owners,
Tina and Anacleto.

Da Giggetto al Portico d'Ottavia

21A Via di Portico d'Ottavia; tel:
06-6861 105; Tue–Sun 12.30-
3pm, 7.30–11.30pm; €€; bus:
Lungotevere Cenci and Largo
Argentina; map p.137 D4

It may be very popular with
tourists, but don't let that
put you off – they take their
Roman-Jewish cooking very
seriously here. Try one of
five menus, all of which usually include carciofi alla giu-
dia (deep-fried whole
artichokes), stuffed cour-
gette flowers or salted cod
fillets.

Il Gonfalone

7 Via del Gonfalone, off Lungotevere del Sangallo; tel: 06-6880
1269; daily noon–3.15pm,
7.30–11pm; €€; bus 40, 64,
map p.132 C1

This restaurant with lovely
outdoor seating is an understated gourmet experience.
The cuisine style is a nouvelle
take on Mediterranean.
There's a bar downstairs
where people drink and
dance until the small hours.

Da Luigi

23–24 Piazza Sforza Cesarini;
tel: 06-6865 946; Tue–Sun
12.30–3pm, 7.30–11.30pm; €€;
bus: 40, 64; map p.133 C1

Traditional Roman fare at this
always-packed venue on a
small square off Corso Vittorio Emanuele. There's a
pleasant breeze and a con-
vivial atmosphere on the outdoor patio. Frequented by
tourists and locals alike.

Il Pagliaccio

129A Via dei Banchi Vecchi; tel:
06-6880 9595; Mon 8–10.30pm,
Tue–Sat 1–2.30pm, 8–10.30pm;
€€€; bus: 40, 64; map p.133 C1

This smart restaurant has a
limited but creative menu
with an emphasis on beauti-

Below: Restaurant Giggetto al Portico d'Ottavia.

Above: a selection of fried foods in the Jewish Ghetto.

Above: a waiter prepares to serve at Da Giggetto al Portico d'Ottavia.

ful presentation and quality ingredients. It's expensive, but, as its regular customers agree, well worth it.

Dal Pompiere
38 Via S. Maria dei Calderoli; tel: 06-6868 377; Mon–Sat 12.30–3pm, 7.30–11.30pm; €€–€€€; bus: H, 23, tram: 8; map p.137 D4

Waistcoated waiters dance attendance on customers in the wood-panelled and frescoed rooms of this fine restaurant occupying the first floor of the Palazzo Cenci. The food is Roman-Jewish and consistently good.

Roscioli
21 Via dei Giubbonari; tel: 06-6875 287; Mon–Sat 12.30–4pm, 8pm–midnight; €; bus: 116; map p.137 D4

This family-run deli-cum-restaurant receives rave reviews for its authentic produce and inventive food combinations, such as its signature dish, tonnarelli with grouper fish, pistachios and fennel seeds. Cheerful, pleasant atmosphere.

Price includes dinner and a half-bottle of house wine:
€ under €25
€€ €25–€40
€€€ €40–€60
€€€€ more than €60

Sora Margherita
30 Piazza delle Cinque Scole, off Lungotevere dei Cenci; tel: 06-6874 216; Apr–Sept Mon–Thur 12.45–2.45pm, 8–11.30pm, Fri 8–11.30pm, Oct–Mar Tue–Thur 12.45–2.45pm, 8–11.30pm, Fri, Sat 8–11.30pm; €€; bus: 23, 63, 280, H; map p.137 D4

A small, basic trattoria in the heart of the former Jewish Ghetto, serving simple and hearty fare (much of it vegetarian). No credit cards.

Via Veneto and Villa Borghese

Cantina Cantarini
112 Piazza Sallustio; tel: 06-4743 341; Mon–Sat noon–3.30pm, 7.30–11pm; €€; bus: 63, 80; map p.134 B3

A high-quality family-run trattoria where the price is still right. Dishes are meat-based the first part of the week, fish-based Thur–Sat.

Al Ceppo
2 Via Panama; tel: 06-8419 696; Tue–Sun 12.30–3pm, 7.30–11.30pm; €€–€€€; tram: 19, bus: 63, 86

A class act with impeccable and imaginative food, a vast wine list and homemade sweets.

Girarrosto Fiorentino
46 Via Sicilia; tel: 06-4288 0660; daily 12.30–3pm, 7.30–11.30pm; €€–€€€; bus: Piazza Fiume;

map p.134 A3

An island of reliability in a sea of tacky venues. All the classic Roman dishes are on offer, along with some Florentine specialities, including wonderful T-bone steaks.

Papà Baccus
36 Via Toscana; tel: 06-4274 2808; Mon–Fri noon–2.30pm, 7.30–11.30pm, Sat 7.30–11.30pm; €€€; bus: Piazza Fiume; map p.134 A3

Renowned for its attentive service and Tuscan cuisine. Meat features heavily, but there are also fish and vegetarian options.

La Terrazza dell'Eden
49 Via Ludovisi; tel: 06-478 121; daily 7.30–10.30pm; €€€€; bus: Piazza Fiume; map p.134 A3

One of the capital's top restaurants, with a panoramic terrace that's as much of a draw as the food. The extensive wine list (650 bottles to

Visitors on a tight budget might consider Der Pallaro (15 Largo Pallaro; tel: 06-6880 1488; Tue–Sun noon–3pm, 7.30–11.30pm; €; bus: 40, 64; map p.137 C4). There is no menu, but for about €20 (house wine and water included) you are served several courses that will leave you more than satisfied. Open late. No credit cards.

choose from) is another mark in its favour.

Trastevere and the Gianicolo

Alberto Ciarla
40 Piazza San Cosimato, off Via Luciano Manara; tel: 06-5818 668; Mon–Sat 8.30–midnight; €€€€; bus: 780, tram: 8; map p.136 C3
Friendly staff, sophisticated décor and six set-price gourmet fish menus or à la carte. One of the top fish restaurants in the city, but it's not cheap. Reserve.

Antica Pesa
18 Via Garibaldi; tel: 06-5809 236; www.anticapesa.it; Mon–Sat 8–11pm; €€€; bus: 115, 870; map p.136 C3
This historic restaurant serves up all the usual Roman classics, along with some surprises. Booking advised.

Asinocotto
48 Via dei Vascellari, off Via dei Genovesi; tel: 06-5898 985; Tue–Sun 8–11pm; €€€; bus: 23, 30, 280; map p.137 D3
A blend of traditionally simple southern Italian cooking and elaborate dishes complete with surprising flavour combinations and decadent gar-

nishes. The restaurant is also a favorite of the gay and lesbian community, which makes for a uniquely alternative atmosphere all round.

La Cornucopia
18 Piazza in Piscinula; tel: 06-5800 380; Wed–Mon noon–3.30pm, 6.30–11pm; €€; bus: 23, 280; map p.137 D3
Specialising in fish dishes, this restaurant's other selling point is its lovely garden, perfect for dinner in summer.

Enoteca Ferrara
41 Piazza Trilussa; tel: 06-5833 3920; daily 8–11.30pm; €€–€€€; bus: 23, 280; map p.136 C4
Minimalist décor and creative menu (with organic ingredients), comprehensive wine selection (850 labels). Light snacks or full meals. Reservations essential at weekends.

Alle Fratte di Trastevere
49–50 Via delle Fratte di Trastevere, off Viale di Trastevere; tel: 06-5835 775; Thur–Tue 12.30–2.30pm, 7.30–11.30pm, Sun 12.30–2.30pm; €€; bus: 780, tram: 8; map p.137 C3
A family-run, authentic Trastevere trattoria serving up Roman dishes with Neapolitan touches. In summer, request one of the few outside tables.

The best falafel in Rome resides at Le Piramidi (11 Vicolo del Gallo; tel: 06-6879 061; Tue–Sun 10am–12.30am; map p.137 C4), along with spiced rice, cous-cous, kebabs and pitta sandwiches. Take lunch or dinner away and eat in bustling Campo de' Fiori or nearby in calmer Piazza Farnese.

Jaipur
56 Via San Francesco a Ripa; tel: 06-5803 992; daily noon–3pm, 7pm–midnight; €€; closed Monday for lunch; bus: H, tram: 8; map p.137 C3
If you just can't face another pizza, Jaipur is one of the city's best Indian restaurants, with a great selection of tandoori dishes. Particularly strong on vegetarian options.

Le Mani in Pasta
37 Via dei Genovesi; tel: 06-5816 017; Tue–Sat 12.30–3pm, 7.30–11.30pm; €€; bus: 23, 30, 280; map p.137 D3
Inviting restaurant serving meat and fish carpaccios; homemade pastas are cooked in myriad different ways. No menu, but the prices are reasonable. Booking advised. Closed three weeks Aug.

Panattoni
53 Viale Trastevere; tel: 06-5800 919; Tue–Sun 12.30–2.30pm, 7.30–11pm; €€; tram: 8; map p.136 C2
Not the most inspiring of interiors, but a Rome classic for its thin crusty pizzas, large antipasti buffet, low prices and its quicker-than-lightning, brusque Roman service.

Paris
7A Piazza San Calisto; tel: 06-5815 378; Tue–Sat 12.30–3pm, 7.45–11pm; €€€; bus: 780, tram: 8; map p.137 C3
Elegant, slightly dated décor and reliably excellent traditional Roman-Jewish cuisine. Small outdoor eating area. Closed three weeks Aug.

Below: Rome has a fine selection of pizzerias.

Left: popular Celio restaurant, Le Naumachie, *see p.120.*

cooking with the 'poor' ingredients that this area is famous for: *coda alla vaccinara* (oxtail in a tomato-based stew), tripe and the like. Desserts are similarly traditional.

Le Bistrot
160 Via delle Sette Chiese; tel: 06-5128 991; www.ristorante lebistrot.com; daily 7.30pm–midnight; €€–€€€; metro: Garbatella

A little way from Testaccio in villagey Garbatella, this cosy restaurant offers a variety of vegetarian dishes; the menu is split between pasta and dishes with a French slant.

Checchino dal 1887
30 Via di Monte Testaccio; tel: 06-5746 318; www.checchino-dal-1887.com; Tue–Sat 12.30–3pm, 8pm–midnight; €€€; bus: 23, 30, 95, 673; map p.137 D1

Typical Roman cuisine, excellently prepared. Known throughout the city. Booking advisable. Closed Aug.

Doc
9 Via Beniamino Franklin; tel: 06-5744 236; Mon–Sat 7.30–11.30pm; €€; bus: 23, 30, 95, 673; map p.137 C1

A refined but informal interior sets the tone for this small restaurant specialising in fish, though meat-eaters and vegetarians are well catered for.

Estrobar
20 Via P. Matteucci; tel: 06-5728 9141; daily 7.30pm–midnight; €€€; bus: 23, 271

This classy restaurant within the designer Abitart Hotel has an arty theme. Exhibitions of young artists' work provide a suitable backdrop for the sophisticated menu. There's also a tasting menu and an extensive wine list.

Da Felice
29 Via Mastro Giorgio; tel: 06-5746 800; Mon–Sat 12.30–3pm,

Dar Poeta
45–46 Vicolo del Bologna, off Via delle Scala; tel: 06-5880 516; daily 7.30–midnight; €; bus: 23, 280; map p.136 C3

Pizzas made with a blend of yeast-free flours which creates an incomparably fluffy base. Tasty toppings. No reservations.

Rivadestra
7 Via della Penitenza; tel: 06-6830 7053; www.rivadestra.com; Mon–Sat 8–11.30pm; €€–€€€; bus: 23, 115, 280; map p.136 B4

This recently opened 'concept restaurant' bases its menu round fresh, seasonal ingredients. Predominantly Roman flavours are spiced up with the odd oriental touch.

Spirito Divino
31A/B Via dei Genovesi; tel: 06-5896 689; www.spiritodivino. com; Mon–Sat 7.30–11.30pm; €€; bus: 23, 30, 280; map p.137 D3

History permeates this restaurant which stands atop the remains of a synagogue and an ancient Roman house. Classic dishes, many based on recipes used in ancient Rome. The wine list is international and has won plaudits.

Da Vittorio
14A Via di San Cosimato; tel: 06-5800 353; Mon–Sat 7.30–midnight; €; bus: 780, tram: 8; map p.137 C3

One of Trastevere's most popular pizzerias, Da Vittorio serves up delicious Neapolitan-style pizza. Great atmosphere and good value.

Aventino and Testaccio

Agustarello
100 Via G. Branca; tel: 06-5746 585; Mon–Sat 12.30–3pm, 7.30pm–midnight; €€; bus: 23, 30, 271; map p.137 C1

This restaurant specialises in

Price includes dinner and a half-bottle of house wine:
€ under €25
€€ €25–€40
€€€ €40–€60
€€€€ more than €60

Several of the clubs and restaurants built into Monte Testaccio *(see p.25)* offer a view of the amphorae shards at their lower levels. The wine cellar of Checchino dal 1887 *(see p.119)* uses the shards of ancient plates to keep the wine cool.

8–11.30pm; €€; metro: Piramide; bus: 23, 30, 280; map p.137 D1
A Testaccio institution, this bustling restaurant serves up classics of Roman cuisine such as roast lamb with rosemary potatoes. Closed three weeks Aug.

The Kitchen
3 Via dei Conciatori; tel: 06-5741 505; Mon–Sat 12.30–3pm, 7.30–11.30pm; €€; metro: Piramide, bus: 23, 30, 280
A slick, designer-style restaurant, as befits its location in trendy Ostiense, The Kitchen offers creative Italian cuisine. The kitchen is open, so diners can watch their meals being prepared.

Da Oio a Casa Mia
43 Via Galvani; tel: 06-5782 680; daily 7.30pm–midnight; €€; bus: 23, 30, 95, 673; map p.137 D1
Well-made Roman specialities (pasta classics and lots of meat- and offal-based dishes) in a friendly neighbourhood trattoria.

Pecorino
64 Via Galvani; tel: 06-5725 0539; Tue–Sun 8–11.30pm; €€€; bus: 23, 30, 95, 673; map p.137 D1
Modern and inviting restaurant that does classic *cucina romana*, with an emphasis on meat dishes.

Remo
44 Piazza S. Maria Liberatrice, off Via Giovanni Branica; tel: 06-5746 270; €; Mon–Sat 7pm–1am; bus: 23, 30, 271; map p.137 D2
One of the best pizzerias in the area, with good starters. No booking.

Tuttifrutti
3A Via Luca della Robbia, off Via Galvani; tel: 06-5757 902; Mon–Sat 8–11.30pm; €; bus: 23, 30, 280; map p.137 D1
A friendly, charming restaurant hidden down a side street. The menu changes on a daily basis but always contains Italian classics. Closed two weeks Aug.

Celio, Monti and Esquilino

Africa
26 Via Gaeta; tel: 06-4941 077; Tue–Sun 9.30am–midnight; €–€€; metro: Castro Pretorio, bus: 38, 310; map p.134 B2
An exotic interior and spicy food from Ethiopia and Eritrea set this place apart.

Eating with your hands is standard procedure, but forks are available.

Agata e Romeo
45 Via Carlo Alberto; tel: 06-4466 115; Mon–Fri 12.30–3pm, 7.30–10.30pm; €€€€; metro: Piazza Vittorio Emanuele; map p.138 B4
Despite their weekend closing and the fact that the kitchen shuts down at 10.30pm, this is still one of the city's best dining experiences. Highly creative dishes and a huge wine selection from its renowned cellar. Booking essential.

Arancia Blu
55 Via dei Latini; tel: 06-4454 105; daily 8.30pm–midnight; €€–€€€; tram: 3, 19; map p.135 D1
Loved by vegetarians and vinophiles alike, passionate owner and head chef, Fabio, turns out fabulously original dishes in portions that satisfy, regardless of the gourmet factor.

Gli Angeletti
3 Via Angelotto, off Via Leonina; tel: 06-4743 374; daily noon–3pm, 7pm–midnight; €€; metro: Cavour; map p.138 A4
Enjoying a great location, overlooking a picture-postcard *piazza*, Gli Angeletti serves up tasty dishes such as tagliolini

Below: veal with parma ham and sage leaves.

Below: the chef prepares fresh nigiri sushi at Hasekura in the Monti district.

with red onion, pancetta and balsamic vinegar.

Alle Carrette
14 Vicolo delle Carrette, off Via Cavour; tel: 06-6792 770; daily 7.30–11.30; €; metro and bus: Colosseo; map p.138 A4

Here, tucked away in a little side street close to the Forum, is what many consider the best pizzeria in the area. There's a beer tavern feel to it and some outdoor seating.

Cavour 313
313 Via Cavour; tel: 06-6785 496; June, July, Sept Mon–Sat 12.30– 2.30pm, 7.30pm–12.30am, Oct– May Mon–Sat 12.30–2.45pm, 7.30pm–12.30am, Sun 7.30– 12.30am; €–€€; metro: Cavour; map p.138 A4

This attractive *enoteca* has an impressive 500 bottles on its wine list and friendly staff who are happy to advise on which of their platters of cheeses and cold meats pairs best with your chosen vintage.

Crab
2 Via Capo d'Africa; tel: 06-7720 3636; Mon 7.45–11.30pm, Tue–Sat 1–3.30pm, 8–11:30pm; €€€; bus: 85, 87, 571; map p.138 B3

A reputable but expensive seafood restaurant with the best oysters in town, as well as every kind of crustacean and mollusc imaginable.

F.I.S.H.
16 Via dei Serpenti; tel: 06-4782 4962; Tue–Sun 7.30pm–midnight; €€€; metro: Cavour, bus: Via Nazionale and Via Cavour; map p.138 A4

A trendy fusion and sushi restaurant. The menu is fish-based and divided into four sections – oriental, oceanic, Mediterranean and sushi/sashimi. At the lower end of this price scale.

Il Guru
4 Via Cimarra; tel: 06-4744 110; Mon–Sat 12.30–2.30pm, 7.30–11pm; €€; metro: Cavour; map p.138 A4

Above: a crowded tank of crustaceans at the aptly named Crab.

One of the most welcoming Indian restaurants in town. Choose various dishes from the tandoori or curry options or one of three fixed menus – vegetarian, fish, meat.

Hang Zhou
33C Via San Martino ai Monti; tel: 06-4872 732; daily 12.30–2.30pm, 7.30–11pm; €; bus: 71, 117; map p.138 B4

One of the better Chinese restaurants in Rome, Fixed menu or à la carte. Closed three weeks Aug.

Hasekura
27 Via dei Serpenti; tel: 06-4836 48; daily noon–2.30pm, 7–10.30pm; €€€; metro: Cavour, bus: Via Nazionale and Via Cavour; map p.138 A4

A small, streamlined interior makes a classic Japanese setting for sushi, sashimi and tempura. At lunchtime you can choose from one of many degustazione menus priced at €15–35.

Isadoro
59A Via San Giovanni in Laterano; tel: 06-7008 266; daily noon– 3pm, 7–11pm; €€€; metro: San Giovanni; map p.138 B3

Fifty pasta first courses, mostly suitable for vegetarians, although on Fridays many of them are fish-oriented. You can ask to try several different varieties of pasta on one plate.

La Naumachie
7 Via Celimontana; tel: 06-7002 764; daily 1–3pm, 7pm– 12.30am; €€; metro: Colosseo; map p.138 B3

A convenient location near the Colosseum serves quality dishes from both the Roman and pan-Italian culinary canon. The grilled meats are excellent.

La Piazzetta
23A Vicolo del Buon Consiglio, off Via del Colosseo; tel: 06-6991 640; Mon–Sat noon–3.30pm, 7.30–midnight; €€; metro: and bus: Colosseo; map p.138 A4

A popular and cosy restaurant, which can get very busy. Fish and large portions of pasta, and desserts are excellent. Some seating in the medieval lane outside in summer.

La Tana dei Golosi
220 Via di San Giovanni in Laterano; tel: 06-7720 3202; Mon– Sun 11am–midnight; €€; metro: San Giovanni; map p.138 B3

A different regional Italian cuisine is featured every two months. High-quality and often organic ingredients, and a refined ambience. Fixed-price cheaper lunch menu.

Trattoria Monti
13A Via San Vito; tel: 06-4466 573; Tue–Sat 12.45–2.45pm, 7.45–11pm; €€; metro: Cavour; map p.133 B1

The owners of this narrow, elegant trattoria are from the Marches region and the menu reflects this: home-made vegetable lasagne, chicken or rabbit in *potacchio* (with tomato, onion, garlic and rosemary), roast turkey with balsamic vinegar. Closed three weeks Aug.

Price includes dinner and a half-bottle of house wine:
€ under €25
€€ €25–€40
€€€ €40–€60
€€€€ more than €60

Shopping

Rome has plenty to offer the dedicated shopper, from haute couture, chic boutiques and designer homeware to leatherware stores, bustling street markets and small, traditional and specialist shops. In a city that refuses to leave behind the values of solid craftmanship so intrinsic to the 'Made in Italy' mark, a savvy shopper will delight in the objects on offer. This chapter gives a general introduction, with listings of one-stop stores and our pick of shops and markets that are unique to the city. Note that shops for books, fashion, shoes, accessories, food and wine are covered respectively under *Literature*, *Fashion* and *Food and Drink*.

Shopping Districts

Those into serious shopping head to the Piazza di Spagna area and explore the high-fashion temples on **Via Condotti**, **Via Bocca di Leone** and **Via Borgognona**. For a more leisurely shop-a-thon, weave your way through the backstreets, starting from **Piazza del Popolo**. Be sure not to overlook the hip **Via del Babuino**. **Via del Corso**, the road stretching from Piazza del Popolo to Piazza Venezia, is far more budget-oriented. Here you'll find everything from the national and international fashion and retail stores, high- and lower-end labels, and all the books, music and trinkets you're after.

The areas around **Piazza Navona**, the **Pantheon** and the **Campo de' Fiori** are teeming with boutiques, houseware shops and fabulous shoes and accessories, not to mention some delicious food shops and pampering perfumeries.

More off the beaten track, the hilly side streets of **Monti** are peppered with art galleries, bric-a-brac shops and funky boutiques, while across the Tiber, **Trastevere** is bursting with knick-knack shops, artisans' workshops and jewellery stores. It is also the site of **Porta Portese**, the massive Sunday market.

The **Vatican-Prati** neighbourhood to the north is home to shopping street **Via Cola di Rienzo**, a popular strip lined with youthful retail chains, speciality food and drink shops and COIN, Rome's best department store.

In and around **Piazza Vittorio**, Rome's modest Chinatown near the station, ethnic clothing and accessories abound. The major **Via Nazionale** is the place to go for bags and shoes.

In the more upscale area around **Piazza Fiume** and the beginning of Via Salaria, you'll find some pretty retailers of clothing, shoes and accessories plus the Rinascente department store.
SEE ALSO FASHION, P.52–7; FOOD AND DRINK, P.64–5

Department Stores

A Roman rarity, one-stop shopping is found at these

Above: shopping on the Via Condotti.

department stores, which range from elegant to downright discount.
COIN
173 Via Cola di Rienzo; tel: 06-3600 4298; Mon–Sat 9.30am–8pm, Sun 10am–8pm; metro: Lepanto, bus: 23, 81; map p.132 C3
A dependable one-stop shop, with well-made and imaginative linen and household items, comfy underwear and pyjamas, and a fantastic handbag and beauty supplies department.
MAS
1 Via dello Statuto; tel: 06-4468 078; Mon–Sat 9am–1pm, 4–8pm; metro: Vittorio Emanuele,

LGARI

Left: find luxury jewellery and luggage at the Spanish Steps.

4132; www.intimissimi.com; Mon–Sat 9am–8.30pm, Sun 11am–8.30pm; bus: 116, 117; map p.133 E2

Mid-range sets are fun and sexy for the ladies, and cosy and cotton for men.

La Perla
78 Via dei Condotti; tel: 06-6994 1934; www.laperla.com; Mon 3–7pm, Tue–Sat 10am–7pm; metro: Spagna; map p.133 E2

World-renowned and wildly sexy, La Perla delicates are a pleasure to purchase and to wear.

Tezenis
83–85 Via Nazionale; tel: 06-4893 0117; www.tezenis.com; Mon–Sat 9.45am–9.45pm, Sun 11am–7.45pm; bus: Via Nazionale; map p.134 1A

Great prices for fresh cotton underwear for men and women. Season collections get racy, but the shop is renowned for comfy, cheap undies.

Yamamay
288 Via Cola di Rienzo; tel: 06-6813 5834; www.yamamay.com; Mon–Sat 10am–8pm; metro: Ottaviano-San Pietro; map p.132 B3

Frilly, fun and nicely priced underwear, pyjamas and swimwear.

Opening hours in Rome are a law unto themselves. What visitors find most surprising is the tendency for many shops to close for at least two hours at lunchtime and all of Monday morning. However, shopping hours in Italy are changing. In highly commercial areas such as the Tridente, Via del Corso, the Trevi Fountain and Via Nazionale, most shops now operate a so-called *orario continuato* (continuous opening hours), which means they stay open for lunch and may be open on Monday morning.

Socks and Intimate Apparel

Calzedonia
101 Via Ottaviano; tel: 06-3973 7159; Mon 3.30–8pm, Tue–Sat 9am–8pm, Sun 10am–2pm, 4–8pm; metro: Ottaviano-San Pietro; map p.132 B3

The city is dotted with branches of this quintessential sock and stocking emporium. Peruse bikini sets in the summer.
(Also at: 64 Via Frattina; tel: 06-6992 5490; map p.133 E2 and various locations)

Intimissimi
167 Via del Corso; tel: 06-6992

Gifts and Souvenirs

Marmi Line
113 and 141–145 Via dei Coronari; tel: 06-6893 795; Mon–Sat 10am–8pm; bus: 40, 46; map p.133 C1

Busts, vases, bowls and all manner of antiquity-inspired pieces come in all sizes and colours at this marble emporium. Contemporary designs in red and Numidian marble are also available.
(Also at: 11/12 Piazza San Pantaleo; tel: 06-680 2466; map p.133 D1; 90–90A Via della Lungaretta;

bus: 16, 714; map p.138 B4

A sprawling, chaotic, bargain wonderland of a shop. You'll have to sift with an expert eye, but gems in clothing and basics for the home are hiding there.

La Rinascente
20 Largo Chigi, off Via del Tritone; tel: 06-6797 691; Mon–Sat 10am–10pm, Sun 10am–8pm; bus: Piazza San Silestro; map p.133 E2

A grand and beautiful building offering a vast range of clothing and homewares.

Below: silk ties can be found in Rome's department stores.

Left: retro homewares.

Stationery

Cartoleria Pantheon
15 Via della Rotonda; tel: 06-6875 313; Mon–Sat 10.30am–8pm, Sun 1–8pm; bus: 30,40; map p.133 D1
Stock up on delicate, hand-painted Florentine stationery, quill pens, sealing wax and stamps, to inspire romantic letter-writing.

Fabriano
173 Via del Babuino; tel: 06-3260 0361; www.cartierefabriano.it; Mon–Sat 10am–7.30pm; metro: Spagna; map p.133 D3
Since 1782, Fabriano has been making professional-quality paper and beautiful paper products for artists and writers. Buy sketchpads and hand-pressed stationery.

Perfume and Cosmetics

Antica Herborista Romana
15 Via di Torre Argentina; tel: 06-6879 493; Mon–Fri 8.40am–7.30pm, Sat 9am–7.30pm; bus: Largo Argentina; map p.133 D1
Antique wooden bookshelves and miniature drawers house the creams, teas, tinctures, and all-natural beauty and health products for sale at this rustic apothecary.

Beauty Point
12 Piazza di Spagna; tel: 06-6920 0947; Mon–Sat 10am–8pm; metro: Spagna; map p.133 E3
The city's most popular stop for all things cosmetic at great prices. Look for promotions posted on the front entrance, and look out for sale tags on selected merchandise, from body cream and sponges to mascara and perfume.

Olfattorio – Bar à Parfums
34 Via Ripetta; tel: 06-3612 325; Tue–Sat 11am–7.30pm; bus: 81, 117, 119; map p.133 D2
Pure perfume essences line

06-5814 860; Mon–Sat 10am–8pm; map p.136 C3)

Too Much
29 Via Santa Maria dell'Anima; tel: 06-6830 1187; www.toomuch.it; daily noon–midnight; bus: 30, 40, 70; map: 133 D1
A kitschy novelty shop selling everything from funny T-shirts and Jesus and Pope figurines to oddly shaped pasta, Lomo cameras and inflatable boyfriends.

House and Home

Art'è Pantheon
32 Piazza Rondanini, off Via delle Coppelle; tel: 06-6833 907; daily 10am–7.30pm; bus: 30, 40, 70; map p.133 D1
A serious collection of sleek Italian names in utensils and kitchen accessories.

Fratelli Bassetti Tessuti
73 Corso Vittorio Emanuele II; tel: 06-6892 325; Mon 3.30–7.30, Tue–Sat 9am–1pm, 3.30–7.30pm; bus: 30, 40, 70; map p.133 D1
Seamstresses and would-be artisans alike marvel at the

floor-to-ceiling fabric selection in over five cavernous rooms. The professional staff and quality of goods feed the creative urge for everything from new curtains to that dream dress.

Modigliani
24 Via Condotti; tel: 06-6785 653; Mon 3.30–7.30pm, Tue–Sat 10.30am–7.30; metro: Spagna; map p.133 E2
The warm, earthy tones and artful curvature of Modigliani ceramic is famous worldwide. The entire collection of table service and houseware is available at this elegant *palazzo*-turned shop.

Trevi Gallery
15 Via delle Murratte; tel: 06-6920 0725; daily 9.30am–8pm; metro: Barberini; map p.133 E1
This is the place for glittering Murano glass chandeliers and lamps, vases, figurines, and jewellery in classic and contemporary designs from the renowned island in Venice. Worldwide shipping is available.

As a general rule, it's next to impossible to return merchandise for a refund. While sales clerks are notoriously unrelenting, by law, unused items may be exchanged on site.

the wall behind this olfactory paradise. As you sample each fragrance, expert noses guide you to your favourite scent. Exclusive lines of French and English perfumes are available for purchase.

Pro Fumum Durante

87–89 Viale Angelico; tel: 06-3725 791; www.profumum.com; Mon 2.30–7.30pm, Tue–Fri 10am–1.30pm, 2.30–7.30pm; metro: Ottaviano San Pietro; map p.132 B4

Gorgeous packaging and Mediterranean-inspired fragrances are the essence of this Roman perfume and bath products boutique. Scents like linen, tomato vines and orange flower are Italy in a bottle. (Also at: 10 Via di Ripetta; tel: 06-3200 306; map p.133 D2; 4 Piazza Mazzini; tel: 06-3200 306; map p.132 C4)

Sabon

241 Via Cola di Rienzo; tel: 06-3208 653; www.sabon.it; Mon–Sat 10am–8pm, Sun 3.30–8pm; metro: Lepanto; bus: 23, 81; map p.132 B3

This Israeli import sells sliceable soap in luscious scents, and body scrubs with Dead Sea salt, almond oil and natural perfume essences. The men's line comes packaged in a retro cigar box style.

Sephora

Termini Station, lower level; tel: 06-4782 3445; www.sephora.com; daily 8am–10pm; metro and bus: Termini; map p.134 B2

The world-famous beauty emporium is located on the lower level of Termini Station. Shop for your favourite brands, or try the great-value Sephora cosmetics, tools and beauty kits.

Markets

The fair weather and tendency to alfresco living has led to the cropping up of all kinds of markets, from the anything-goes flea market to tents filled with used and antique items, regional food products and handmade clothing and accessories.
SEE ALSO FOOD AND DRINK, P.64

Porta Portese

Via Portuense starting at Porta Portese, Trastevere; no phone; Sun 5.30am–2pm; bus: 23, 280, tram: 3, 8; map p.137 C2

The city's best-known and always crowded everything market. If you can handle the crowds and the pickpockets, there are odds and ends of all sizes and shapes, a vast quantity of fake designer bags, Middle Eastern imports and great used clothes for the discerning and persistent shopper.

Borghetto Flaminio

32 Piazza della Marina, off Via Flaminio; tel: 06-58 80 517; Sun 10am–5pm; bus: 88, 490, tram: 2, 19; map p.133 D4

A plentiful cluster of stands and tents is affectionately referred to as the 'garage sale', and as the name would imply, this the place to sift through plenty of trash-or-treasure kinds of items, including some great antiques.

Piazza Navona Christmas Market

Piazza Navona; no phone; 1 Dec–6 Jan 10am–midnight; bus: Corso Rinascimento; map p.133 D1

Tourist-driven as it may be, there's something deliciously nostalgic about the Christmas Market at Piazza Navona. Peruse candy stands, old-fashioned toys and stuffed animals, as well as handmade marionettes. The retro carousel is a big draw, along with the metre-long liquorice chords.

Mercato Piazza Risorgimento

Piazza del Risorgimento; no phone; dates vary, 10am–10pm; bus: Piazza del Risorgimento; map p.132 B3

Every few months a tent goes up on this sprawling *piazza*, near the entrance to the Vatican Museums. Inside, artisans sell jewellery, knitwear, handbags and crafts, all handmade and quite reasonably priced. A number of stands are dedicated to regional produce like honey, pasta sauces, olive oil and cheese.

Below: browse bric-a-brac at Rome's markets.

Below: the ultimate Italian accessory: sunglasses.

125

Sports

Romans love everything about sport – the fashion, the fan clubs, and the excitement of a social gathering. Football (soccer) is the national favourite, though basketball and rugby aren't far behind. Where personal fitness is concerned, gym-going has yet to take the city by storm – and tends to be no more strenuous than the occasional bench press. Any further physical activity is dictated by trends. Salsa and tango, yoga and pilates, kung fu and t'ai chi, have all swept the city, and are still available within large gym facilities. For information on attractive spots for a brisk walk or run, *see Parks and Gardens*.

Spectator Sport

You can find information on sporting events in just about every Italian publication, though *Corriere dello Sport* and *Gazzetta dello Sport* are dedicated solely to sporting events and news. The best way to keep updated is to follow a team and its respective websites.

Football

Rome constantly has football on the brain, and with two home-town teams, someone's always playing.
Stadio Olimpico
Viale dello Stadio Olimpico; tel: 06-3237 333; bus: 32, 280, tram: 2
From September to May, **SS Lazio** (www.sslazio.it) and **AS Roma** (www.asromacalcio.it) play at Rome's Olympic Stadium. Come game day, look out for team scarves (blue and white for Lazio; Red and orange for Roma) and wild fans hanging from car windows. A trip to the Stadio Olimpico is a fabulously authentic way to spend an afternoon or evening, though not for the faint of heart. Be prepared for down-

Above: Italy's Sergio Parisse is tackled in the 2007 Rugby World Cup.

right rowdiness, screaming, and pyrotechnics. Due to increased stadium violence, a photo ID is now required for stadium entry. Check details when you purchase your tickets.

For fixtures, ticket information and official team paraphernalia, head to the official fan-club stores.
Original Fans Lazio
34 Via Farini; tel: 06-4826 688; Mon–Sat 9am–7pm; bus: 40 express, 64, 70, 492; map p.134 B1

AS Roma Store
360 Piazza Colonna; tel: 06-6786 514; Mon–Sat 10am–7.30pm, Sun 11am–7.30pm; bus: Piazza San Silvestro; map p.133 E2

Rugby

Italy's participation in the Six Nations (www.rbs6nations.com) has fostered a growing interest in the game. Home games are played at Stadio Flaminio (Viale Tiziano; tel: 06-3685 7309). See www.federrugby.it for details of upcoming games.

Major Events

The city attracts an international crowd for several sporting events throughout the year.

The Rome **City Marathon** is by far the year's biggest sporting event. For one day in mid-March, the city is entirely blocked to traffic, as thousands complete the 42km run. For those keen to participate but not ready for the big one, check out the 5km fun run-walk that starts after the official marathon start. Details at www.maraton adiroma.it.

Left: AS Roma and SS Lazio in action at the Stadio Olimpico.

The Concorso Ippico Internazionale (**International Horse Show**) takes place in May at Piazza di Siena in the gardens of the Villa Borghese. The prestigious event welcomes national champions in showjumping, as well as performance by Italy's special mounted police force, the Carabinieri a Cavallo. (www.piazzadisiena.com) Also in May is the **Italian Tennis Open** (www.internazionalibnld italia.it), held at the Foro Italico. Between paparazzi flashes and cocktail parties there are some great matches scheduled between the world's best players. SEE ALSO FESTIVALS, P.58

Gyms

The trend for gym (*palestra*) culture has brought on a cropping-up of little gyms throughout the city. The big, shiny gym experience is limited to a select few. Most offer day entry passes, which can run as high as €30 a day.

Roman Sport Center
33 Viale del Galoppatoio, Villa Borghese; tel: 06-3201 667; www.romansportcenter.com; Mon–Sat 8am–10pm, Sun 9am–3pm; bus: Piazzale Brasile; map p.133 E4
This mega gym was the first of its kind to grace the city, and is known by locals as 'la Roman'. It boasts two Olympic sized swimming pools, a plethora of courses, and a beauty parlour.

Farnese Fitness
35 Vicolo delle Grotte, off Via del Giubbonari; tel: 06-6876 931; www.farnesefitness.com; Mon, Wed 8am–10pm, Tue, Thur 8am–9pm, Fri 9am–9pm, Sat

11am–7pm, Sun 10.30am–1.30pm; bus: 30, 40, 64; map p.137 C4
The 16th-century building offers a uniquely Italian vacation-style workout.

Dabliu
A brand new chain with fancy Technogym machines and qualified training staff, located at various locations around the city, including: **Parioli** (22 Viale Romania; tel: 06-8552 433; bus: 910), **Prati** (43 Viale Giulio Cesare; tel: 06-3211 0158; metro: Lepanto, bus: 30, 70; map p.132 C3), and **Piazza Barberini** (30 S. Nicola da Tolentino; tel: 06-4201 2515; metro and bus: Piazza Barberini; map p.134 A2; www.dabliu.it)

Virgin Active
75 Via Dario Niccodemi, Talenti, North Rome; tel: 80-0914 555; www.virginactive.it; Mon–Fri 10am–8pm, Sat, Sun 9am–6pm; bus: 342
A bit far afield, but those craving the familiar mega-brand franchising, and a massive facility, including a pool and numerous aerobics rooms, will feel right at home here.

With the seashore so close, outdoor pool facilities in Rome are rarer than overcooked spaghetti. Those that do exist are mostly located within luxury hotel settings, so be prepared to pay up for a quick dip. The Hotel Hilton Cavalieri (*see p.73*) is the most luxurious of pay by the day pool outings, at c.€45. Hotel Parco dei Principi (*see p.76*) costs €60 for the day, but the Villa Borghese setting is just about worth it. Grab the shuttle to Spanish hotel chain Sol Meliá, which is just outside the centre, but charges a wallet-friendlier €15 a day pool rate.

Below: the city marathon starts on the Via dei Fori.

Transport

R ome is easy to get to, but less easy to get around. Planes and trains deliver tourists to the city from all over the world with speed, efficiency and regularity. On arrival, however, brace yourself for a chaotic transport system – the bus network is hard to get to grips with, the metro coverage inadequate and driving a nightmare. The good news is that most places of interest in the city centre are within walking distance. A good map and comfortable walking shoes will be your best investment. This chapter gives you the lowdown on how to get around Rome, no matter your chosen mode of transport.

Arriving in Rome

Scheduled flights from around the world land at the main airport in Fiumicino (**Leonardo da Vinci Airport**; tel: 06-6595 1; www.adr.it), about 30km southwest of Rome.

There are frequent train services to **Trastevere Station** and **Stazione Termini** (6.37am–11.37pm; 35 minutes; €11). For suburban rail stations take a train bound for Orte (5.48am–11.27pm; €5). By law, a **taxi** to the centre should cost no more than €40.

Below: attempting to direct the traffic at the Piazza Venezia.

Charters and low-cost airlines **easyJet** and **Ryanair** fly in to **Ciampino** (tel: 06-794 941), about 15km south-east of the city.

To reach the centre, take the **Terravision coach** (tel: 06-7949 4572; www.terravision.eu; 40 min; €8) to Stazione Termini. There is a coach for every scheduled Ryanair and easy-Jet flight. **Schiaffini buses** (tel: 06-474 4534; www.schiaffini.com; 10.30am, 1pm, 3pm, 5pm, 7pm, 12.15am and 12.45am; €5) go to Termini. **Taxis** to the centre should be no more than €30.

Motorists arriving in Rome will first hit the **Grande Raccordo Anulare** (GRA), the ring road. When leaving the GRA, follow white signs for the road you want. The city-centre sign is a white point in a black circle on a white background.

Getting around by Train

Stazione Termini (tel: 06-892 021; www.ferroviedellostato.it) is the main railway terminal, the meeting point of the two metro lines and the main stop for many city buses. Reservations are required for the **Eurostar**, the fastest, most luxurious

trains, and optional for the **InterCity**. Slower regional trains (*diretto*, *espresso*, *regionale* or *interregionale*) stop at many stations. There are ticket machines in Stazione Termini, or you can book online or by phone. Pick up your tickets at machines at the station or on the train (choose 'ticketless' when booking). Tickets must be stamped on the day you travel at one of the machines at the head of each platform (except for Eurostar).

City Transport

Public transport, run by ATAC (tel: 800-431 784; www.atac.roma. it), is quite efficient and inexpensive, but overcrowded at peak hours. **Tickets** are available from bars, tobacconists and newspaper kiosks, and from metro vending machines. Once validated in the metro turnstile or machine at the back of the bus, single-

European (EU) driving licences are valid in Italy. Travellers from other countries normally require an international driving licence.

Left: Rome's metro has seen better days.

lowing radio taxi services – tel: 06-3570, 06-8822 or 06-4994.

Prices for licensed taxis are fixed and start at €2.33.

Driving

Generally, a car is of little use within the city. Parking is hard to find, one-way systems are complex, and much of the city centre is closed during business hours, and parts of it in the evening. The **Italian Automobile Association** (ACI) provides a breakdown service (freephone: 803-116).

Bicycles and Mopeds

On car-free Sundays (about once a month) you will see mopeds darting along the Via dei Fori Imperiali. Traffic is also restricted along the Appian Way on a Sunday; you can rent a bike from the visitors' centre (42 Via Appia Antica; tel: 06-512 6314; www.parcoappiaantica. org; Sun 9.30am–5.30pm; €3/hr).

Bicycle rental companies in the city include: Bici & Baci, 5 Via del Viminale, tel: 06-482 8443 (8am–7pm), www.bicebaci. com; Happy Rent, 3 Via Farini, tel: 06-481 8185; Scooters for Rent, 84 Via della Purificazione, tel: 06-4202 0675 (9am–7pm); www.happyrent.com.

In much of the city centre the best way to get around is on foot. Some parts of the centre are for pedestrians only, such as the second half of Via del Corso, roughly from the Piazza San Silvestro to Piazza del Popolo and Piazza Navona. Cross the road with confidence, staring down nearby drivers. If you wait timidly at a pedestrian crossing for the traffic to stop, you will spend the whole day there.

station to the **city centre** and then **St Peter's**; watch out for pickpockets. Electric minibuses serve the *centro storico*: the 116 passes through or alongside **Campo de' Fiori**, **Piazza Navona**, the **Pantheon** and **Piazza Barberini**. Bus 81 runs from the **Colosseum** to **Piazza del Risorgimento** near the **Vatican Museums**. The No. 8 tram links **Largo Argentina** in the centre to **Trastevere** in the west. From **Piazza di Spagna** to **Stazione Termini**, take metro line A. For the **Colosseum**, do the same and change at Termini to line B.

The city is served by two **metro** lines (A and B), intersecting at Stazione Termini. The metro operates from 5.30am to 11.30pm and until 12.30am on Saturday night.

use tickets (*bit*; €1) are good for unlimited bus or tram rides and/or one metro ride for 75 minutes. One-day tickets (*big*; €4), and weekly tickets (*carta settimanale*; €16) are also available.

Buses, Trams and Metros

Bus and **tram** services run from 5.30am to midnight, with an all-night service on the 22 bus line (N22).

Board buses at either the front or rear doors and stamp your ticket. Ring the bell to request the next stop and exit through the centre doors.

Buses 40 and 64 are the quickest way to get from the

Taxis

Licensed taxis are white and always have a meter. There are ranks outside Termini Station, outside both airports, and in many parts of the *centro storico*. You can hail a taxi on the street as long as it has a light on; or call one of the fol-

Below: car-free days are a great opportunity to hire a bike.

Atlas

The following streetplan of Rome
makes it easy to find the attractions
listed in our A–Z section.
A selective index to streets and sights
will help you find other locations
throughout the city.

Map Legend

Autostrada		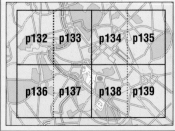 Metro station	
Dual carriageway		Bus station	
Main roads		Tourist information	
Minor roads		★ Sight of interest	
Footpath		Cathedral / church	
Railway		☾ Mosque	
Pedestrian area		✡ Synagogue	
Notable building		🛉 Statue / Monument	
Park		✉ Post Office	
Hotel		Hospital	
Urban area		❋ Viewpoint	
Non urban area		∿ Vatican boundary	
Cemetery			
Market			

p132	p133	p134	p135
p136	p137	p138	p139

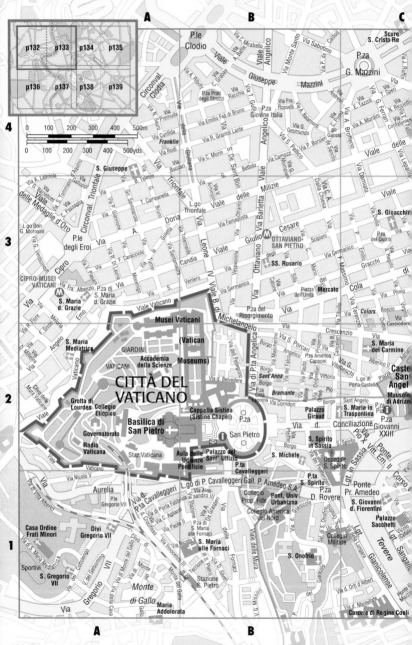

D · E

Accademia d. Romania
P.le Jose di S. Martin
P.za Cervantes
Galleria Nazionale d'Arte Moderna
Viale del Giardino Zoologico

Lgt. G. Nicotera
Via G. Filangieri
P.za della Marina
Ministero Difesa Marina
Valle Giulia
VILLA STROHLFERN
P.za Paolina Borghese
VILLA Museo Canonica

Lgt. d. Armi
Via G. P. S.
Via A. Azuni
Via Flaminia
Via di Santo Eugenio
Viale Madama
P.le Firdusi
Tempio d. Esculapio

Via C. Menotti
Via G. Giannone
Via G. Maticotti
Ponte P. Nenni
Via Flaminia
Via Fortuny
Viale Esculapio
Museo Carlo Bilotti
GIARDINO D. LAGO
VILLA BORGHESE

tiri di Belfiore
P.za Cinque Giornate
Villa Ruffo
Via degli Orti Giustiniani
P.za del Fiocco
Viale Fiorello
Via Pietro Canonica
P.za di Siena

Settembrini
Cesare
Ponte P. Nenni
Staz. Flaminio
Via Washington
Via Flaminia
Victor Hugo
La Guardia
P.za Canestre
Viale S. Paolo di Brasile

-ilizie
Via Tomacelli
Via C. Beccaria
P.le Flaminio
Viale
Monte
Viale dell'Obelisco
Viale delle Magnolie
Tempio d. Diana

Via L. di Savoia
Via Ferdinando di Savoia
M **FLAMINIO**
P.le Napoleone I
Pincio
GALOPPATOIO

Farnese
Scipioni
Via A. Brunetti
Via M. Cristina
P.za del Popolo
S. Maria d. Popolo
Viale dell'Obelisco
Torto

S. Vincenzo d. Paoli
Magno Orsini
Via L. di Savoia
S. Maria in Montesanto
De Russie
Casina Valadier

Gracchi
P.za della Libertà
P.za della Penna
Via della Penna
Via Oca
S. Maria dei Mirac.
Viale del Belvedere
VILLA MEDICI
Muro

Via dei
P.za Margherita
Valadier
Via del Vantaggio
Valadier
Casa di Goethe
Viale Trinità dei Monti
Villa Medici

P.za Rienzo
Ponte Margherita
Viale G. Visconti
Emilio O. Visconti
Via di Ripetta
S. Giacomo
Via S. Giacomo
Hotel Art
Via d. Mino
SPAGNA M

PRATI
Via Cicerone
G. G. Belli
Via del Corso
Accademia di Belle Arti
P.za Ferro di Cavallo
Via dei Greci
Via del Babuino
Porta Pinciana

Teatro Adriano
M. Dionigi
Via V. Colonna
Via d. Frezza
S. Cecilia
Via Vittoria
SS. Trinità dei Monti
S. Isidoro

Chiesa Valdese
Via della Palestrina
Via V. Colonna
Ponte Cavour
Mausoleo di Augusto
L.go Lombardi
Via d. Croce
Via d. Carrozze
Casa di Keats-Shelley
P.za Trinità
Hassler
Gregoriana

-scenzio
Via Tacito
Via F. Cossa
Ara Pacis
S. Rocco
S. Carlo al Corso
Portrait Suites
Spagna dei Monti
Modigliani

P.za
Via Cavour
Porta Ripetta
Imperatore
Inn at the Spanish Steps
Mighanelli
Via Gregoriana
Casa Howard
Suisse
Sistina

Ex Palazzo di Giustizia
Via Tomacelli
Via dell'Arancio
Palazzo Ruspoli
Palazzo Spagna
Propaganda Fide
Casa Howard

Casa Madre d. Mutilati
Adriana
Lgt.
Via del Clementino
Palazzo Borghese
L.go F. Borghese
Palazzo Bernini
Via Frattina
S. Andrea d. Fratte

Castello
Ponte Umberto I
P.za Nicosia
Due Torri
Fontanella Borghese
Palazzo Fiano
Via del Gambero
S. Silvestro

-gt.
Tor di Nona
Via M. Brianzo
Museo Napoleonico
S. Antonio d. Portoghesi
S. Lorenzo in Lucina
S. Claudio
Palazzo Poli
Fontana di Trevi

S. Salvatore
S. Simeone
Via dell'Orso
S. Agostino
Palazzo Montecitorio
Palazzo Chigi
S. Maria in Via
GIARDINO DEL QUIRINALE

-lais
coronari
S. di Lauro
S. Agostino
Campo Marzio
Camera d. Deputati
P.za Colonna
Galleria Alberto Sordi
Via d. Muratte
Via della Dataria

Palazzo Taverna
Raphael
Cinque Lune
Via delle Coppelle
U. d. Vicario P. di Montecitorio
Museo Naz. d. Paste Alimentari
Palazzo del Quirinale

-azzo erna
S. Maria della Pace
S. Maria d. Anima
Via Giustiniani
P.za di Pietra
Palazzo della Borsa
Via dell'Umiltà
Scuderie del Quirinale

ri Campo
S. Agnese in Agone (Navona)
S. Luigi d. Francesi
Pantheon
S. Macuto
S. Ignazio
S. Marcello
P.za del Quirinale

Chiesa Nuova
Teatro della Pace 33
S. Eustachio
P.za d. Rotonda
Collegio Romano
Palazzo Odescalchi
SS. Apostoli
VILLA COLONNA

nuele II
Palazzo del Gov. Vecchio
Palazzo Madama (Senato)
S. Ivo
S. Maria Minerva
Palazzo Doria Pamphilj
Palazzo Colonna
S. Silvestro

S. Maria d. Monserrato
Palazzo Braschi
Archivio di Stato
Grand Hotel de le Minerve
Galleria Doria Pamphilj
P.za dei SS. Apostoli

-eligio
Chiesa Nuova
Palazzo Massimo
Navona
Palazzo Valle
P.za Minerva
Palazzo Altieri
Palazzo Bonaparte
IV Novembre

S. Maria d. Monserrato
Pal. della Cancelleria
Museo Barracco
S. Andrea della Valle
Palazzo Vidoni
Palazzo Grazioli
S. Marco
Prefettura
L.go Magnanapoli

S. Maria d. Monserrato
Mercato
Campo de' Fiori
Palazzo Vidoni
Area Sacra dell'Argentina
V. Emanuele II
Chiesa del Gesù
Palazzo Venezia
Col. Traiana
Foro di Traiano

Teatro di Pompeo
Teatro Argentina
Barrett
N. d. Plebiscito
Venezia

D · E

133

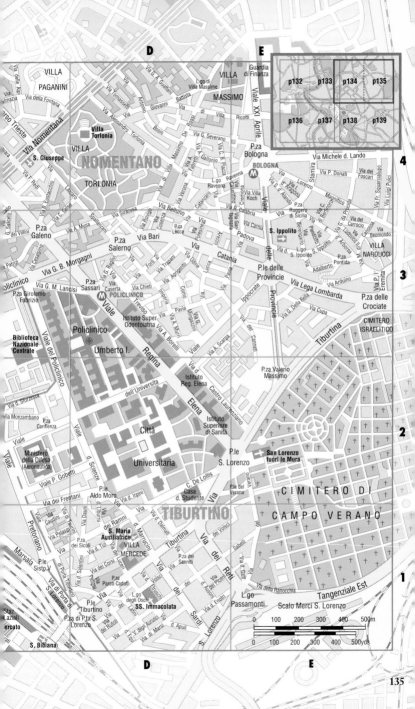

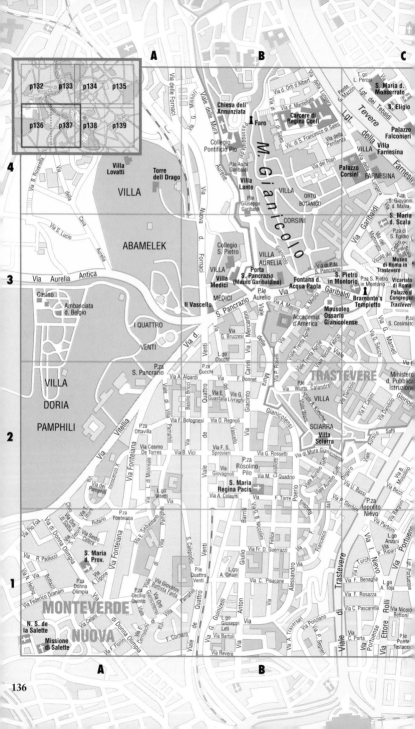

Via delle Fornaci

Via G. Missori

Via delle Mura

Via B. Roverella

Via delle Fornaci

Via Nuova

Via S. Lucio

Cava

Aurelia

Chiesa dell'Annunziata

Via d. Orti d'Albert

Via d. Mantellate

Via d. Orti d'Albert

Vic. d. S. Francesco di Sales

Via della Penitenza

Lgt. dei Tebaldi

Lgt. della

Tevere

L.go L. Perosi

Ponte G. Mazzini

S. Maria d. Monserrato

S. Eligio

Palazzo Falconieri

VILLA Villa Farnesina

FARNESINA

P.za S. Giovanni d. Malva

S. Maria d. Scala

P.za di S. Egidio

Museo di Roma in Trastevere

Vicolo del Cedro

Vicariato di Roma

Palazzo d. Congregaz Trastevere

Faro

Carcere di Regina Coeli

Collegio Pontificio Pio

P.le Anita Garibaldi

Aurelia

Villa Lante

P.le Giuseppe Garibaldi

Via del Riari

Palazzo Corsini

Palazzo Falconieri

M. Gianicolo

CORSINI

ORTO BOTANICO

VILLA CORSINI

Via di P.ta S. Pancrazio

Villa Lovatti

Torre dell Drago

VILLA ABAMELEK

VILLA

Collegio S. Pietro

Via Fornaci

VILLA MEDICI

Porta S. Pancrazio (Museo Garibaldino)

VILLA AURELIA

Fontana d. Acqua Paola

Via di P.ta S. Pancrazio

S. Pietro in Montorio

P.za S. Pietro in Montorio

Bramante's Tempietto

Via Aurelia Antica

Via Aurelia

Casino

Ambasciata d. Belgio

I QUATTRO VENTI

Il Vascello

MEDICI

S. Pancrazio

P.le Aurelio

Via A. Masina

Via G. Medici

Via Garibaldi

Via di P.ta S. Pancrazio

Accademia d'America

Mausoleo Ossario Gianicolense

P.za S. Cosimato

Via N. Fabrizi

Via G. Sacchi

VILLA DORIA PAMPHILI

Via Vitellia

Via Innocenzo X

Via di Villa Pamphili

Via d. Venti

P.za S. Pancrazio

L.go Cocchi

Via A. Algardi

Via F. Bonnet

L.go Cucchi

Via Carini

Via delle Mura

Via L. Mercantini

Via P. Roselli

Viale Trenta Aprile

Viale delle Mura Aurelie

Via Nicola Fabrizi

TRASTEVERE

Viale Glorioso

Ministero d. Pubblica Istruzione

Via Dandolo

Via F. Cavallotti

Via di Villa

Basilio Bricci

Via E. Guastalla Livraghi

Via F. Bolognesi

Via O. Regnoli

Via Giacinto Carini

P.le Wurts Calandrelli

VILLA SCIARRA

Via di Kircher

Via Calandrelli

Viale delle Mura Aurelie

Villa Sciarra

SCIARRA

Via Aurelio Saffi

Saffi

P.za Ottavilla

Via Cosmo De Torres

Via B. Vici

Via F. S. Sprovieri

Via G. Rossetti

Viale Aurelio Saffi

Via Dandolo

Via F. Cristofori

Via B. Musolino

P.za Rosolino Pilo

Via M. Quadrio

Via Giovagnoli

Via di Mura Gianicolensi

Viale Aurelio Saffi

Via L. Cadorna

P.za Ippolito Nievo

Via U. Bassi

Via P. Sterbini

Via B. Musolino

S. Maria Regina Pacis

Via A. Colautti

Via F. Torre

Poerio

Via G. B. B. Nicolini

Cavalotti

Via P. Bassi

VILLA DORIA PAMPHILI

Via dei Pamphili

Via di Donna Olimpia

Via di Monreale

Via di Monreale

L.go Vitetti

P.za Fonteiana

S. Maria d. Prov.

P.za Donna Olimpia

Via Fonteiana

Viale di Villa Pamphili

S. Calepodio

Venti

Giulio

Via Fr. D. Guerrazzi

Felice

Francesco

Alessandro

Anton

Via di Trastevere

Via A. Traversari

Via I. Ripari

P.za Bagnoni

Via Parboni

Via Anziani

Via di Trastevere

Via R. Paolucci

Chio. Pio

Via d. Orti di Cesare

Via Vittore

Via Sesto Celere

Via E. Sebastiani

Via Calandrelli

Via Rutario

S. Maria d. Prov.

Via A. Ugone

P.za Cecilio Quinto

Via Giovanni Battista Falda

Viale dei Quattro Venti

P.le Quattro Venti

P.le A. Orlani

L.go Giuseppe Leti

Via G. Guintelli

Via C. Pisacane

Ponziano

Via P. Sperari

Via F. Benaglia

Via F. Rosazza

Via C. Pascarella

Via di Trastevere

Via F. Turchi

L.go A. Toja

Via Nicolo Bettoni

Via C. Porta

Via P. Sperari

Ettore

Rolli

Viale

di Trastevere

P.le Pontel Testaccio

MONTEVERDE

NUOVA

N. S. de la Salette

Missione di Salette

Via Federico Ozanam

Via di Donna Olimpia

Via A. Helfin

Via Bottani

Via R. Paolucci

Via Celani

Via di Donna Olimpia

Via Semiselli

Via A. Fiorini

Via F. Cornaro

Via V. Bartoli

Via Revera

p132　p133　p134　p135

p136　p137　p138　p139

Pal. della Cancelleria
Museo Barracco
P.za S. Andrea della Valle
Palazzo Altieri
Palazzo Vidoni
Prefettura
L.go Magnanapoli
Villa Aldobrandini
Via Panisperna

Campo de' Fiori
Palazzo d. Valle
Via del Sudario
V. Emanuele II
V.d. Plebiscito
P.za S. Marco
Col. Traiana
Foro di Traiano
SS. Domenicani e Sisto
Via Baccina

Mercato
Teatro di Pompeo
S. Andrea d. Valle
Teatro Argentina Barret
Area Sacra dell'Argentina
Chiesa del Gesù
Via d. Botteghe Oscure
Palazzo Venezia
Fori Imperiali
Inn at the Roman Forum

Palazzo Farnese
Teatro di Pompeo
S. Carlo ai Catinari
Palazzo Mattei
Crypta Balbi-Museo Naz. Romano
Monumento a Vittorio Emanuele II (Vittoriano)
Foro di Augusto
L.go Corrado Ricci

Residenza Farnese
Palazzo Spada
Palazzo d. Monte di Pietà
P.za Cairoli
P.za dei Mattei
S. Maria in Aracoeli
SS. Luca e Martina
Basilica Aemilia

Ponte Sisto
Palazzo Cenci
Via del Portico d'Ottavia
P.za Capizucchi
Pal. dei Conservatori
Musei Capitolini
Palazzo Senatorio
Arco di Settimio Severo
Basilica Giulia
Via Frangipane

Ministero di Grazia e Giustizia
Lgt. dei Vallati
Lgt. dei Cenci
Teatro di Marcello
P.za di Campitelli
M. Capitolino
Atrio d. Vestali
Tempio di Venere e Roma
Imperiali

Santa Maria S. Maria in Trastevere
Ponte Garibaldi
Fatebenefratelli
Isola Tiberina
S. Nicola in Carcere
Hotel 47
Uffici d. Comune
Via d. Consolazione
S. Teodoro
Foro Romano
Arco di Tito
Arco di Costantino

Calisto
Ospedale d. S. Gallicano
Lgt. d. Anguillara
Antico Borgo Trastevere
S. Bartolomeo all'Isola
Ponte Rotto
Arco di Giano
S. Giorgio in Velabro
M. Palatino
S. Gregorio

Via L. Manara
Trastevere
Arco del Lauro
Lungaretta
Piscinula
Ponte Palatino
Tempio di Fortuna Virile
Casa di Livia
Domus Flavia

S. Crisogono
Residenza Arco de Tolomei
Tempio di Vesta
S. Anastasia
Domus d. Augustana
Stadio di Domiziano
Antiquarium

Via Grande
S. Cecilia
Monopoli
Via di State
P.za Bocca d. Verità
S. Maria in Cosmedin
Uffici Comunali
Terme Severare

Palazzo d. Esami
S. Francesco a Ripa
S. Vincenzo de Paoli
Circo Massimo
S. Gregorio Magno

San Francesco
P.ta Portese
Monumento a G. Mazzini
P.le Ugo La Malta
Torre d. Molette
Largoud Caduti di Nassiriya
P.ta Magno
Obelisco di Axum

Via M. Carcani
S. Sabina
S. Alessio
P.za S. Prisca
CIRCO MASSIMO
F.A.O.

S. Maria d. Priorato di Malta
P.za Cavalieri di Malta
Sant'Anselmo
S. Pio
M. Aventino
Tempio Diana
PARCO DI PORTA CAPENA

S. Anselmo
P.za dell'Emporio
P.za Albania
S. Balbina

Testaccio
S. Maria Liberatrice
Mercato
PARCO DELLA RESISTENZA DELL'8 SETT.
S. Saba

MARCO al Mattatoio
MONTE TESTACCIO
CIM. ACATTOLICO
Museo di Via Ostiense
P.ta S. Paolo
Piramide di Caio Cestio
P.za Ostiense
PIRAMIDE

0 100 200 300 400 500m
0 100 200 300 400 500yds

D   E

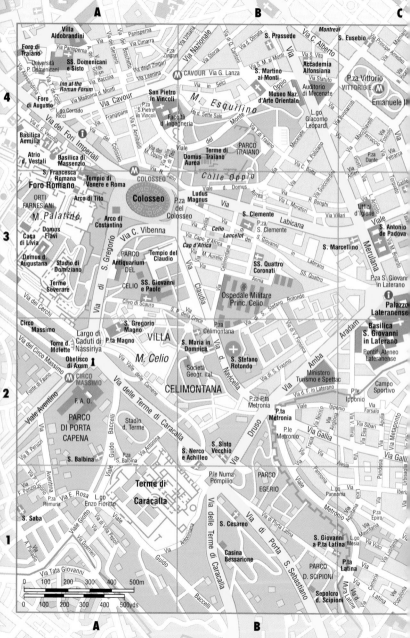

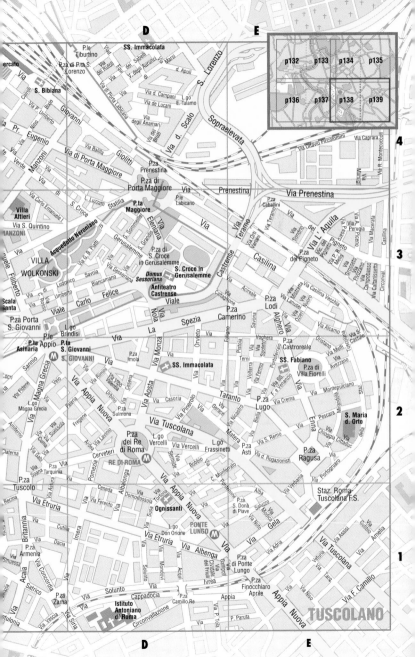

Selective Index for Street Atlas

PLACES OF INTEREST

Index

Insight Smart Guide: Rome

Text by: Natasha Foges, Annie Shapiro, Fiona Benson, Marc Zakian, Jon Eldan and Cathy Muscat
Edited by: Joanna Potts
Proofread and indexed by: Neil Titman
Photography by: Alamy 19B, 24B, 24T, 26, 37B&T, 40B, 52T, 56T, 93R, 97B, 108B&T, 109, 111T; Art Archive 80T; Axiom 2T, 5BR, 9B, 79L, 94T, 125; Bridgeman Art Library 92, 94B, 97T, 99L; Contrasto 61, 66B&T, 67, 96, 100T, 102B, 103B; Corbis 10, 38B, 50, 58T, 60T, 79M, 93L, 99R, 110, 111B, 117T; 4 Corners 2T, 5, 7, 88B, 113, 114, 116, 117B, 118, 119, 120T, 121, 128B; Eyevine 59B; Getty 5ML, 16, 21B, 40T, 51T, 62B&T, 126B, 126T; Hemis 2B, 3B, 4, 12, 13T, 15B, 15T, 30T, 128T; Britta Jaschinski/APA 2B, 3B,4B, 5BL, 5MR, 5TL, 7B, 9T, 11B&T, 13B, 17B&T, 18, 19T, 20, 21T, 22, 23B, 24, 27B, 27T, 32B&T, 33B, 34B, 35T, 36T, 41B, 51B, 52B, 53B, 54B, 54T, 55, 64, 70, 78B, 82, 82B, 83B, 87L&R, 88T, 89, 95, 98, 104B, 104T, 105B, 112B&T,

122B, 112T, 129; Mockford/Bonetti/APA 4B8, 5TR, 8, 84; PA PHOTOS 75B, 127; Photolibrary 78T; Photoshot 6, 23T, 38T, 39B; Pictures Colour Library 8, 9, 14, 56B, 123B; Rex Features 60B; A. Santerelli/APA 57B&T, 79R; Stockfood 63B, 65TL, 65TR, 115, 120B

Picture Manager: Steven Lawrence
Maps: Neal Jordon-Caws
Series Editor: Jason Mitchell
First Edition 2008

© 2008 Apa Publications GmbH & Co. Verlag KG Singapore Branch, Singapore.
Printed in Singapore by Insight Print Services (Pte) Ltd
Worldwide distribution enquiries:
Apa Publications GmbH & Co. Verlag KG (Singapore Branch) 38 Joo Koon Road, Singapore 628990; tel: (65) 6865 1600; fax: (65) 6861 6438
Distributed in the UK and Ireland by:
GeoCenter International Ltd
Meridian House, Churchill Way West, Basingstoke, Hampshire RG21 6YR;

tel: (44 1256) 817 987; fax: (44 1256) 817 988
Distributed in the United States by:
Langenscheidt Publishers, Inc.
36–36 33rd Street 4th Floor, Long Island City, New York 11106; tel: (1 718) 784 0055; fax: (1 718) 784 0640l
Contacting the Editors
We would appreciate it if readers would alert us to errors or outdated information by writing to:
Apa Publications, PO Box 7910, London SE1 1WE, UK; fax: (44 20) 7403 0290;
e-mail: insight@apaguide.co.uk